Erratum

This printing of *Worthy As You Are* contains an error on page 19. The following underlined sentence was omitted:

A Fourfold Process of Healing and Establishing Well-Being

As we seek to heal and establish greater well-being in our lives, we make four primary efforts:

1. We explore what we think and believe, consciously and subconsciously, and challenge our thoughts and beliefs that are not fact-oriented and accurate and that hinder our well-being. This is weeding the inner garden.

2. We affirm in their place fact-oriented and accurate thoughts that foster our well-being. This is planting new beliefs.

3. We work to stop or decrease the actions in our lives that hinder our well-being.

4. <u>We strive to increase the amount we act in our lives in support of our well-being.</u> This includes engaging in actions to help us healthfully process emotions and sensations, like mindfulness, meditation, and relaxation exercises, as well as connecting with our inner guidance.

Praise for *Worthy As You Are*

"*Worthy As You Are* is a beautiful follow-up to Durgadas Allon Duriel's masterful *The Little Work*. Within this book you'll find practical tools to tend to your inner garden, cultivate compassion, and heal. Weaving Cognitive Behavioral Therapy with affirmations and life stories, you'll learn how to shift your thinking to an empowered, healthy place. This is a must-have book for anyone who wants to change from the inside out and stand in their true power. No matter where you are right now, you can transform —and this book will show you how." —**Theresa Reed, author of *Tarot: No Questions Asked***

"*Worthy As You Are* is one of the best psychology books of our era. Like a compassionate friend, Durgadas reveals his wisdom on the most common topics as well as less-discussed ones such as chronic conditions, gender, and spiritual bypassing. Readers will learn the most current methods to help them heal and thrive." —**Astrea Taylor, author of *Intuitive Witchcraft* and *Air Magic***

"We all want to know that we are deserving of love and every wonderful thing. But we don't always know how to get there. Luckily, Durgadas Allon Duriel has given us a masterful roadmap. This book is not just a pep talk: it's a scientific system for getting from where you are to where you want to be. If you're serious about changing your inner monologue to one that magnetizes blessings, heals you on all levels, and transforms your life in the most positive possible way, don't just read this book. Read it carefully. Follow its instructions. And do your best to live its wisdom every day. You'll be amazed." —**Tess Whitehurst, author of *The Self-Love Superpower***

"Psychology and spirituality don't have to be two separate paths but can instead act as twin serpents winding up the caduceus of self, offering a truly integrated approach to self-inquiry. In *Worthy As You Are*, Durgadas embodies, exemplifies, and expands on this, effortlessly incorporating tried and true methods of CBT therapy with spirituality, to truly make a difference in the lives of readers who engage with this sort of inner gardening. Written with compassion, reverence, and honesty, this book is a gift to anyone who wants to transform themselves and their world from the inside out." —**Gabriela Herstik, author of** *Inner Witch, Bewitching the Elements,* **and** *Sacred Sex*

worthy
as you are

About the Author

Durgadas Allon Duriel (San Francisco, CA) is a licensed clinical social worker and a certified holistic health practitioner working in private practice. He is also an astrologer, yogi, and magic worker, having practiced magic since childhood and eventually discovering modern Paganism and Wicca in high school and later initiating into a Hermetic order in 2005. He trained there intensively for two and a half years, focusing on astrology, Kabbalah, yoga, tarot, and ritual, which he continues to study and practice. He holds a master's degree in social welfare from UCLA.

To Write to the Author

If you wish to contact the author or would like more information about this book, please write to the author in care of Llewellyn Worldwide Ltd. and we will forward your request. Both the author and the publisher appreciate hearing from you and learning of your enjoyment of this book and how it has helped you. Llewellyn Worldwide Ltd. cannot guarantee that every letter written to the author can be answered, but all will be forwarded. Please write to:

Durgadas Allon Duriel
⁒ Llewellyn Worldwide
2143 Wooddale Drive
Woodbury, MN 55125-2989
Please enclose a self-addressed stamped envelope for reply,
or $1.00 to cover costs. If outside the U.S.A., enclose
an international postal reply coupon.

Many of Llewellyn's authors have websites with additional information and resources. For more information, please visit our website at http://www.llewellyn.com.

worthy
as you are

DURGADAS
ALLON DURIEL

WEED OUT
UNHEALTHY BELIEFS AND
NOURISH YOUR
AUTHENTIC SELF

Llewellyn Publications
Woodbury, Minnesota

FIRST EDITION
First Printing, 2022

Book design by Christine Ha
Cover design by Cassie Willett
Figures (pages 51 & 52) by Mary Ann Zapalac

Llewellyn Publications is a registered trademark of Llewellyn Worldwide Ltd.

Library of Congress Cataloging-in-Publication Data (Pending)
ISBN: 978-0-7387-7241-7

Llewellyn Worldwide Ltd. does not participate in, endorse, or have any authority or responsibility concerning private business transactions between our authors and the public.
   All mail addressed to the author is forwarded but the publisher cannot, unless specifically instructed by the author, give out an address or phone number.
   Any internet references contained in this work are current at publication time, but the publisher cannot guarantee that a specific location will continue to be maintained. Please refer to the publisher's website for links to authors' websites and other sources.

Llewellyn Publications
A Division of Llewellyn Worldwide Ltd.
2143 Wooddale Drive
Woodbury, MN 55125-2989
www.llewellyn.com

Printed in the United States of America

Also by Durgadas Allon Duriel
The Little Work: Magic to Transform Your Everyday Life

For everyone who was ever told they were less than for being themselves.

Acknowledgments

Thanks to the healers, teachers, mystics, and friends I have known in my life, who have all contributed to this book to some degree, large or small. Specifically, thanks to my editors Elysia Gallo and Lauryn Heineman, whose input was invaluable in polishing this work. To my first spiritual teacher and three degree mentors in my spiritual training, who helped me discover the power I had. To my second spiritual teacher, who taught me how to open my heart and kneel within it. Finally, to the wonderful city of San Francisco, where this book was written and I found my home, and whose spirit contributed much to it.

Disclaimer

The material in this book is not intended as a substitute for psychotherapy from a licensed professional, nor is it intended as psychiatric, psychological, or medical advice for the treatment of any individual person or health condition. Readers are advised to consult with their personal healthcare professionals regarding any mental or physical health conditions they have. The publisher and author assume no liability for any actions that may occur from the reader's use of the content contained herein.

Contents

Introduction

"It's not okay to be you. You are not good enough as you are."

These messages exist in one form or another in so much of the world today that we may not even register them most of the time, but they are there, whether intentionally or not. We might see an airbrushed and edited photo of a model that makes us feel self-conscious about our bodies or a parade of luxury that we can't afford in a film. Perhaps there's a gross lack of representation of a group we're a part of in popular media or an advertisement for a new product that promises to revolutionize our lives, which are painted as less than to some degree without it. If we change ourselves in the ways we're being guided to though, buy the novel item, or make ourselves more like what we see that is presented as valuable, maybe we'll arrive at okay or good enough. If not? Too bad for us.

Many if not most of us received messages about not being okay as ourselves or good enough as we are from family members too, who themselves likely received messages like these from others in a cycle sometimes going back centuries. It is also common to hear some version of this messaging from our peers while growing up, and to implicitly and sometimes

1

explicitly be exposed to it in school and other community settings. Even if no one has ever said words like these to us outright, most of us have experienced and internalized these sentiments in some fashion because of popular media and advertising, as in the examples shared above. I think people often don't even realize that this messaging is part of what they're saying or implying, as it is such a subtle, constant element in our world.

The impact of these sentiments on our lives, that we are not okay as ourselves or good enough as we are, is profound, particularly the more we feel targeted by them, which can vary from group to group, family to family, and so on. I believe these kinds of sentiments and the ramifications of them are among the root causes of much of the low self-esteem and insecurity we see in the world today.

As adults, many of us who grew up conditioned by these messages want to find a greater sense of well-being and peace in our lives but don't know how. Having been constantly influenced to seek what is valuable outside of ourselves, that's where most of us look. We do things like participate in fitness fads and trends, buy fancy gadgets, climb the corporate ladder, and jump through all sorts of hoops in pursuit of happiness, and where do we end up? We might have some pleasurable and rewarding experiences, feel proud of ourselves at times, and certainly feel more comfortable if we went from financially insecure to financially stable, but often, we don't stray that far from where we started in terms of our inner lives. We still experience a mix of good days and bad days with our mindset being largely at the mercy of the rollercoaster of life. Even with "success," we may feel caught in the web of our past, trapped in thoughts that feel destructive and unsupportive, or unable to see a path to feeling sustainably better from where we are. We might still feel an ocean away from "okay" or "good enough."

What if there was another way, though, and that began with recognizing that what we have been told throughout our lives, sometimes from thousands of different sources, is untrue: that it is okay to be ourselves, as we are, right now? Not only is it okay, but it is sacred, and we are always good enough. We may not all be equally talented or capable when it comes to competition and completing tasks in the human world, but as divine beings in human form who are perfectly imperfect, we are always okay and good enough, and nothing can change that. In working on ourselves in a manner that helps us own and experience this, we can make sustainable steps toward the wellness, peace, and contentment we seek. The greatest source of the emotional healing and well-being we desire is already within us. We just need to find it.

That was what I needed to learn many years ago when I found myself at the doors of an intensive spiritual training program. Back then, I felt like my life was doomed. I had grown up being persistently bullied in elementary and middle school, to the point of dehumanization in the latter, and I'd spent most years since then experiencing a terrible, suffocating depression at some point. I had also been ill in some manner for almost all my life, which continues to this day, and that weighed on me mightily, in addition to long-standing family problems that were rough too. I will elaborate on these issues in the sections of the book where they are relevant, but suffice it to say that I was a mess in many ways. A silver lining I found in feeling so broken, though, was that it humbled me enough to seek help and heed the guidance I was offered.

For the next two and a half years, I challenged myself to do whatever my teacher and mentors in my spiritual training advised and to glean what value I could from what they taught. As I did that, my life changed for the better at a dramatic pace. I learned two primary things that I will share and elaborate on in this book: that I could change my life by changing my thinking and that I could connect with the divine in a palpable way. I experienced both of those things profoundly during my spiritual training and watched as my life began to blossom in light of them. I was in holistic health school at the same time, and that integrated a focus on self-care and wellness with the work I was doing that greatly benefitted me. I also read the *Tao Te Ching*, which I would go on to read from daily for about five years, and it instilled in me the importance of having compassion for myself and others. Compassion became the core of my approach to life and is central in this book. I was amazed as I went from being a mess to someone who could weather the adversity in my life and thrive much of the time, and who could set a variety of intentions and realize them. My everyday thoughts went from feeling poisonous to nourishing, which stunned me then and still makes me smile to think about now. This isn't to suggest that I don't have tough days and occasionally get caught up in trauma cycles, but my life is so much better, to a degree that it often surprises people who knew me before my spiritual training.

After I left the spiritual training program, I studied for many years with a spiritual teacher from India who emphasizes love, compassion, and service and who continues to be an inspiration in my life. My experiences with her deepened my understanding and appreciation of those things. I also learned that many of the techniques I was taught for working with my mind in my spiritual training are paralleled in a popular, research-supported brand of psychotherapy: cognitive behavioral therapy (CBT). I thrilled at the prospect of being able to do work that yielded such powerful results in my life as my day job and subsequently went to graduate school to become a social worker. Since graduating in 2013, I have worked within a cognitive behavioral framework in each of my jobs, whether as a psychiatric case manager or a psychotherapist.

Our Work Together

The notions that we can change our lives by changing our thinking and that our thoughts affect our experience of life and shape our reality are hardly new. We can see analogous concepts to these in the teachings of the Buddha and the sages of Hinduism, as well as the writings of Shakespeare. What the pioneers of cognitive therapy, including Dr. Alfred Ellis and Dr. Aaron T. Beck, did with them that is new is systematize them into clinical interventions that can be practically applied in everyday life. It's not too difficult to intellectually recognize that how we conceive of life influences how we experience it. We can even casually observe this when we look around the world and see cultural concepts that differ. For example, some cultures embrace sexuality with unapologetic relish while others shy away from it. Some highly value work and achievement while others prioritize family life more. In all of this, we see a theme: cultures can imprint beliefs upon us that shape how we perceive life. Recognizing that thought influences perception isn't enough, though, if we want to use that knowledge to make holistic, healthy changes. This is where CBT skills come in.

In this book, I present a refined, simplified version of the CBT model featuring the techniques I have seen be most effective with my clients and in my personal life. As we develop as therapists, we tend to naturally recognize what works well and what doesn't in our practice, and what feels superfluous or essential. We grow as we accumulate new information, experience, and insight, and this shapes our approach. The results of my version of that process are what I present here. The system in this book also integrates key elements I have learned from my other studies and experiences, like the centering of compassion and tools that help promote well-being, including affirmations and mindfulness practice. I share a step-by-step method I designed for healthfully processing difficult emotions too. CBT techniques help us dismantle the beliefs within us that don't support our well-being—like that we are not okay as ourselves—and cultivate supportive self-talk that aids us in feeling better. They help us deal with the difficulties that linger with us from the past and embrace the opportunities before us in the present. In proper CBT, that is usually where the mental work ends, but it is not where our work concludes here.

As I shared earlier, I first learned these kinds of techniques in a spiritual training program, and because of that, I witnessed the power that comes when they are wedded to spiritual practice. I believe that the dramatic results I experienced happened not only because I was on top of my mind with cognitive tools, but also because of the intimacy with the divine that my spiritual practices fostered in me. The spiritual experiences I had inspired me, motivated me, nourished me, guided me, and supercharged me to deepen with this work.

Consequently, the divine is also at the core of our work together: connecting with it, working with it, and experiencing it as part of our everyday lives. Though I do believe an atheist can probably find value from most of the practices in this book, it is intended for a spiritual audience. What you individually believe about the divine can vary substantially from me, which we will explore more later, but the integration of spirituality with personal development and healing, in my experience, is immensely helpful. We will touch upon it many times in this book.

I also want to emphasize that the work we do here is not about adding new layers of belief to ourselves or climbing some inner mountain to prove our worthiness. We will use CBT techniques to challenge the negative conditioning we have received that stands in the way of our authenticity, and then in partnership with the divine, we will work to release that conditioning and connect with our deeper selves. The thoughts we cultivate in that objective affirm our growing awareness of what is already within us more than they create something new. In doing this, we can experience a profound degree of freedom and healing and also come to touch our natural well-being. That is the sense of ease within ourselves that most of us had as children as we lived in alignment with the flow of the divine. From there, you can use the freedom and healing you experience to whatever ends you desire, and none of this is to suggest that there isn't value in working to hone qualities within ourselves or taking substantial action in the world. The problem comes when we look for our worth and peace in what we can do and achieve. When people complete the work we will undertake here, they are generally far more able to enjoy whatever else they decide to do with their lives because of not looking for their self-worth in that, celebrating it for what it is instead.

The tools in this book can also aid us in transforming our lives in a profound manner and realizing our intentions for ourselves because they help us step out of our own way. When a goal is attainable for us, which means that we could feasibly achieve it from where we are given our ability, capacity, privilege, and access to opportunities, what usually keeps most of us from accomplishing it is forces within us: the beliefs and mental and behavioral patterns we have that hinder us in achieving it, alongside our innate resistance to change. In my experience, these beliefs and patterns often come from environmental influences and our reaction to them. Practicing the techniques in this book can foster our ability to navigate through these obstacles and claim our power to create positive change in our lives, and we feel better and better about ourselves as we do so. Not because of making dramatic shifts that win us self-worth trophies, but through appreciating how miraculous, wonderful, and divine we already are.

This book is for anyone who feels ready to start that journey and who is willing to devote some time most days each week to personal and spiritual development. At first, that can be as little as five minutes a day, growing incrementally as the process unfolds, expands, and deepens. Our work here occurs in three primary segments, which compose the three parts of this book. In the first part, we explore the framework and root techniques of the overall approach. This is where we sift through the mechanics of how CBT works, as well as learn a practice for connecting with the divine. We will also review ways to prepare ourselves for the work ahead. In part 2, we move through a series of what I call "affirmative talks." These are explorations of some challenges and difficulties many of us face within a variety of life domains, followed by affirmative statements to help us undo unhealthy conditioning in those areas and feel better. Part 3 looks at difficult emotions and experiences that are natural parts of life and ways to approach them that are informed by the spiritually integrated system in this book. While many spiritual models pathologize or minimize difficult emotions and experiences, I have found tremendous value, empowerment, and freedom in accepting them and meeting them head-on. In that part, I will share some ways to do that.

The Inner Garden

During our work on the mind, I feature a metaphor of it as an inner garden, which I also use as the structure for how I frame the material in those sections. Many people have conceived of the mind this way before, and some of the reasons why I favor this metaphor will become apparent as it shows up in the book. For now, though, I want to share that I use this metaphor in part because of how CBT is sometimes perceived and even practiced. It can come across as being a rigid, almost robotic type of modality in which the human mind is likened to a computer. If we change the inputs (i.e., thoughts), for example, we get different outputs (i.e., emotions and perceptions). The whole process can seem sterile and like it doesn't grasp the complexity, depth, and texture of the human experience. Many people are turned off by CBT because of this.

In contrast to that, the inner garden is organic. Our thoughts and beliefs make up the plants within our respective inner gardens, and they grow in a natural way. Some are lustrous and wonderful, while others are harmful weeds. In our efforts together, we undertake the work of planting supportive thoughts and nurturing them and weeding the thoughts and beliefs that are unhealthy or unhelpful for us, and we allow the processes of life to unfold within us. As we care for our inner gardens consistently, as we would a physical garden, they begin to change, resulting in an improvement in our mindset and mood. Recall for a moment the most amazing garden you've ever seen or imagine a magnificent one. How would it feel if your mind were like that?

Another reason I use this metaphor is that a garden, at its best, is a demonstration of humanity working with nature in alignment with an intention. It reflects the harmony possible between human creativity and ingenuity and the natural world. Similarly, inner gardening is about cultivating harmony with what we authentically are, our inner nature, through the way we think. It is an organic process of marrying intention with self-discovery, one of deep caring and enrichment. As we will repeatedly see in this book, the way we think of things affects how we perceive them. Consider how different the process of working on ourselves could be by thinking of it as inner gardening as opposed to programming our minds like a computer.

In terms of how to read this book, I recommend that you first read it all the way through, completing the exercises along the way. Various sections are meant to be reread, and in those sections, I include suggestions for how to do that. Most of all, I want to emphasize that this is a journey of compassion, self-love, authenticity, and spiritual connectedness, and those are the true great powers at the heart of our work together. I know some of this may seem very simplistic, and it is. Let it be. Healing does not need to be complicated. There is nothing here to achieve, and there is nothing to prove. We are holy and worthy exactly as we are. Let me show you what helped me realize that within myself so that it may help you do the same.

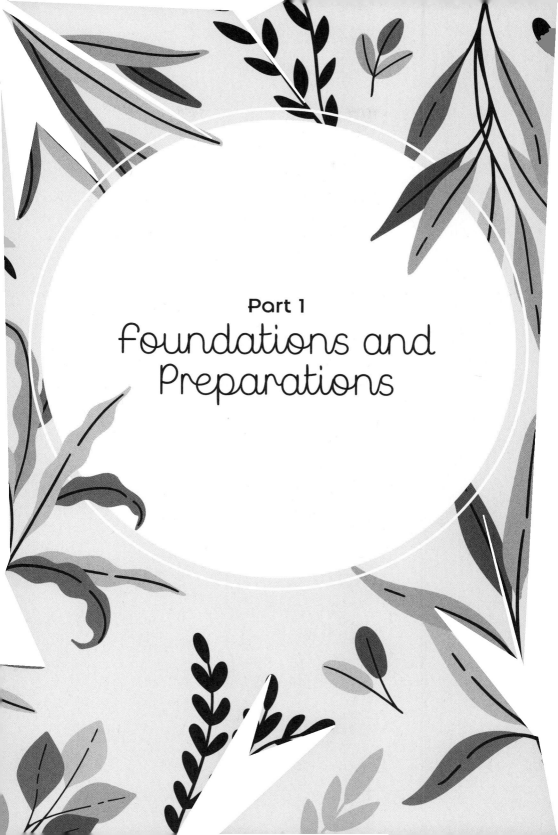

Part 1

Foundations and Preparations

In this part of the book, we will review the foundational material of our work together. Chapter 1 focuses on the theories and basic techniques of the system we'll use. As a therapist, I have found that some people find motivation in understanding the nuts and bolts of how the healing and wellness approach they are working with functions. They prefer to know why we do what we're doing. Others could not care less, and there is a spectrum of interest in between those extremes. If you are one of the latter types of people, feel free to skim the portions of the first and third chapters that are heavy on theory, though I encourage you to perform all the exercises and pay close attention to the techniques. These techniques will equip you to practice this system independently beyond what is shared here.

In chapter 2, I focus on the divine: ways to connect with it and manners in which it is relevant for the work we will undertake together. As I wrote in the introduction, I believe spirituality supercharged my healing journey, and I can't emphasize enough how much daily spiritual practice was part of that. In this chapter, I include instructions for performing a daily meditation that has profoundly benefitted me and others, and I review some of the amazing powers I have witnessed in our relationship with the divine that are helpful to know about when working on ourselves. Spirituality is the greater backdrop upon which this entire approach is founded, and we will explore that in this chapter as well.

Chapter 3 mostly includes preparational material that I think is helpful to be aware of as we embark upon this journey. There are some difficulties that surface for most people when performing work like this, and in my experience, it is best to know about that and prepare for them. This chapter features techniques for dealing with those difficulties as well as an exploration of what this process generally entails. We will also review the kinds of resistance to the process that tend to come up and techniques for navigating them.

Chapter 1
The Basis and Basics of Our Work Together

When we are young children, our inner gardens are wide open with rich, fertile soil. As we grow up, other people give us seeds to plant there, in the form of thoughts and beliefs, and lacking the advantage of adult discernment, we can't help but accept them. The seeds germinate and the plants grow, and by the time we are able act on our own behalf within this garden, it is mostly full. If we don't take the time to recognize that this process has happened within us and claim ownership of our role as gardeners, we will largely continue as we have.

Some of the seeds we are given are passed directly to us. Others come from the implicit messages of our environment and the behavioral modeling of the prominent figures in our lives. From early childhood, an architecture of reality forms within us, composed of the plants that grow within our inner gardens. This reality is predominantly thought-dependent, which is to say that it depends on thought to exist. Thought-dependent elements of reality cease to be without our continual affirmation that they are real. When many people affirm that something that is thought-dependent is real, it becomes part of a group reality they co-create, called a consensus reality. A large-scale example of the phenomenon of consensus reality is the nations of the world. They exist because of a shared agreement that they do. The second that agreement disappears, so will they, like the nations of old that are consigned to history.

Thought-dependent reality contrasts with inherent reality, which is the reality that abides without our mental participation. The human body, for instance, and the geological structures of the earth exist whether we believe they do or not. As long as we believe a thought-dependent element of reality is real, it feels as real to us as things in inherent reality do, and alongside that comes whatever pleasure or pain we associate with it.

The plants in our inner gardens usually keep growing as we age unless they are uprooted. This uprooting can happen in many ways. Generally, it occurs when we gain new information, wisdom, or insight that contradicts a thought-dependent element of our reality, or we have an experience that does. For example, if I was taught that women can't be mathematicians and I meet a woman who is one, that will shift my thought-dependent reality. We can also actively challenge a thought or belief about reality that we hold, which we will focus on in this book.

Much of what we perceive and feel extends from what we think and believe, the reality created within our minds. As I touched upon some in the introduction, this is a central tenet of CBT. If I know what a stop sign is, for example, I know what to do when I see one. But if I don't? It's just an object in my environment with no set meaning. On an emotional level, if I believe the person cutting me off on the freeway is a rude, reckless driver, I will probably feel angry, frustrated, or scared as that happens. If I believe this person is in a hurry to reach a loved one at a hospital, I might feel concern for them instead. If I believe it is important for me to be better than other people at things, like that relates to my worth as a person, I am likely to feel envious or threatened when someone achieves something or beats me in a contest, even a friend. Without this belief, I may only feel excitement and pride for a friend who achieves something. There is a model of this that is popular in CBT called "ABC" that was created by Dr. Albert

Ellis, where an activating event (A) is filtered through our beliefs about it (B), resulting in a consequence (C) in terms of how we feel or act.

Our actions can affect how we feel too, which is also a central tenet of CBT. If I treat myself well and engage in healthy actions, for example, that will likely make me feel good or improve my mood some. If I act in ways that are harmful to me, I will probably feel bad or worse than I do now. In CBT, we actively recognize that our thoughts, actions, and emotions are intertwined, with our thoughts and actions generally being responsible for our emotions. Other factors can influence what we feel too, like the weather, our environment, mental and physical illness, dealing with burdensome circumstances, art that's emotionally evocative, and so on. Often, though, our emotions follow our thoughts and beliefs, conscious and subconscious, and our actions.

Our thought-dependent reality beliefs can seem so real, and our habits of thought can be so persistent and entrenched, that we feel we have no power to change them. The way we think, feel, and perceive seems like it is simply "how things are." I believed that when I embarked upon my spiritual training program, and then my teacher and mentors taught me specific ways to think differently and to shift the beliefs in my subconscious mind. As those beliefs changed, my perception of reality did too, and so did many of the emotional reactions that followed from how I perceived reality and thought of the events and circumstances in my life. Pairing that with the spiritual experiences I had in my training, I began healing from traumatic experiences in childhood and adolescence and their effect on my mindset. I didn't even know that some of those experiences were still active within me and reflected in my outlook, though one might think my annual bouts of depression may have clued me in to the possibility of that. I thought with age and wisdom, I'd set aside the beliefs that grew from that trauma. Meanwhile, what really happened was that those beliefs were hiding behind a facade of unconscious denial. What I needed to do was examine, dismantle, and replace them and practice techniques to help me connect with my spirit, body, and emotions. By virtue of doing that in my spiritual training program and while studying holistic health, the clouds started to part within a life that had often been painful and terrifying. As the sunlight hit my inner garden for the first time in years, I began to believe in my power to heal. That was when I realized something I had been deeply skeptical of before: that I could be okay again, and as I believed that, it started to become true.

I discovered one of the most powerful insights that has guided my life since then: many of the issues that plagued me were derived from thoughts and beliefs, and because of that, they were malleable. What thought created, thought can change. Not only was there a way because there was a will, but much of the suffering within me was like a mirage, albeit one that left potent, real scarring. It could be dispelled. Consider for a moment all the meaning we project onto the environment around us and how in the absence of our thoughts, that would cease to be. None of that was real for you at one point, and the thought-dependent elements of your reality that feel harmful to you needn't remain as real for you as they are now. There is immense power here and, with that power, hope for healing and greater well-being.

I mentioned the subconscious mind before because it plays a central role in how we perceive reality. For simplicity's sake, I define the subconscious mind as being the part of us that thinks and acts within our lives outside of our conscious awareness. We know that the subconscious mind exists because, for example, we don't have to remind ourselves to breathe and when we go to drive a car, we don't have to first think about how to do it. There are many beliefs we hold and things we know about life, ourselves, and the world that spring into action automatically in our minds, enabling us to function at higher levels. This is mostly beneficial, but there can be times when we believe something subconsciously that works against our well-being or that of others, and it's important that we shift that as best we can. For instance, after working in several toxic work environments, someone might subconsciously believe that all future employers will disappoint or betray them. This belief will shape how they perceive those employers, even if they never consciously think anything along these lines.

We can even hold a belief in our conscious mind that differs from what we believe subconsciously. When this happens, my experience is that the subconscious belief will usually win out in terms of influencing our perceptions and emotions. For example, if traumatic experiences growing up inclined me to believe that cisgender heterosexual men are dangerous, I may not consciously believe that yet still feel afraid when I see a stranger whom I perceive as a cisgender heterosexual man. In that moment, my subconscious belief that cisgender heterosexual men are dangerous holds more power than my conscious belief, which may be something like "Some cisgender heterosexual men are dangerous, but most are harmless."

When we have beliefs from trauma or childhood experiences, they can be wholly subconscious and only become apparent by analyzing the emotional reactions and behavioral patterns we have. We can discover these beliefs by introspecting into those reactions and patterns and observing the bigger picture that they suggest, connecting the dots between them and our past to see if there are any underlying themes. These beliefs usually extend from the experiences we've had or influences we were exposed to in a linear manner (i.e., if we ask ourselves "Why might this reaction and pattern be here?" we can generally trace it to our experiences and influences). This process often reveals core beliefs about ourselves and the world, like "I'm not good enough" or "I can't trust people." An example of this could be a person who keeps finding small problems with everyone they date, which causes them to break things off. Upon reflection, they might recognize that this is a trend and, after considering their past, appreciate that "My father dying when I was young resulted in a belief that all men will leave me, so I don't give potential partners a fair chance."

Issues like these usually become apparent as we make a habit of exploring the beliefs that seem like they inspire our emotions and behavioral patterns. This makes the subconscious conscious, which can help us shift those beliefs and patterns, as we can actively work on unhelpful or unhealthy beliefs once we are aware of them. As in the earlier example about toxic work environments, the fault-finding dater may never have considered that their father dying left them with a belief that men will leave them. Meanwhile, that belief has actively governed a significant part of their life at the subconscious level. Before recognizing this, they likely believed they gave the men they dated a fair shot. With an awareness of the deeper mechanics of this unhealthy pattern, they can work to shift it. Also, I think it is important to recognize that some of the unhealthy beliefs and patterns we have from childhood and trauma likely served as a form of defense for us, being what we needed back then to protect ourselves. Today, though, they are in the way of our well-being, so it is important to work to release them.

Subconscious beliefs are most responsible for what we feel and perceive, which we can see in our reflexive emotional reactions and the myriad things we understand every day without having to stop and think about them. They govern much of how we experience life and ourselves. To make deep healing changes, we must reach the subconscious level. In my experience, subconscious beliefs can be shifted through recognizing the beliefs that are already in our subconscious mind (and conscious mind), dismantling the ones that are problematic, and then affirming new thoughts that support our well-being that we don't struggle to believe. Usually, dismantling thoughts involves recognizing the ways in which they are distorted, biased, or otherwise faulty or harmful to us. In terms of new thoughts, when we struggle to believe them, our doubt in them can actually reinforce the old beliefs we're trying to change, making those beliefs feel truer. We'll explore this and a process for designing new thoughts like these, which are called affirmations, later in this chapter.

As we actively affirm new thoughts while challenging and dismantling old beliefs, these new thoughts become what we believe about the topic in question, first consciously and eventually subconsciously. In the beginning, this process may feel fruitless, but it is like watering the soil that we planted a seed in. With time and care, the seed germinates and the plant takes root, eventually pushing through to the surface. We can recognize this in action because as our subconscious beliefs change, our perceptions and emotional reactions follow suit in a process that feels like magic. It is as if the fabric of our reality has shifted to align with our new beliefs, and in terms of our thought-dependent reality, it has. When we experience this, we have an opportunity to appreciate that there is a tremendous amount of healing and freedom available to us if we make the decision to garden within our minds.

Exercise

Journal about the concept of thought-dependent reality and where you can see it at play in your life. Are there ways in which you have seen your conceptions of your identity or the world change based on beliefs or ideas you were exposed to while growing up? What takeaways come up for you in contemplating that process of change?

A Fourfold Process of Healing and Establishing Well-Being

As we seek to heal and establish greater well-being in our lives, we make four primary efforts:

1. We explore what we think and believe, consciously and subconsciously, and challenge our thoughts and beliefs that are not fact-oriented and accurate and that hinder our well-being. This is weeding the inner garden.
2. We affirm in their place fact-oriented and accurate thoughts that foster our well-being. This is planting new beliefs.
3. We work to stop or decrease the actions in our lives that hinder our well-being.
4. This includes engaging in actions to help us healthfully process emotions and sensations, like mindfulness, meditation, and relaxation exercises, as well as connecting with our inner guidance.

These steps are a simplified presentation of the work generally performed in CBT. This book mainly focuses on the first two, with some attention to point four as we discuss relaxation and meditation in chapter 2 and mindfulness in chapter 3. Points three and four are also explored in the section on behavior in this chapter. In much of this book, we will actively challenge beliefs that many of us hold that work against our well-being while affirming ones that support it. As a therapist, I often say to my clients that CBT is like physical therapy for the mind, and like physical therapy, it requires consistent practice of its techniques. We were conditioned into unhealthy mental habits, and while we can shift them, we must persistently and attentively apply the skills we learn to do that.

The worksheet at the end of this chapter provides detailed instructions for how to challenge a thought and belief, but fundamentally, we question whether or not they are true and supportive of our well-being. This involves considering if they are fact-oriented, accurate, wise, and compassionate. When I say a thought and belief are fact-oriented, I mean they are grounded in a reflection of the facts. This means they are built from an objective presentation of a circumstance in question. "The sky was overcast," for example, is a fact-oriented statement, as is "It was raining and I felt sad that morning," assuming that is how I felt. "Overcast days make everyone feel sad," on the other hand, is not a fact-oriented statement because though it is true that some people tend to feel sad on overcast days, there are plenty of people who enjoy them. Along these lines, it is important when looking at our thoughts to recognize the difference between facts, opinions, and assumptions. "Red is a color," for instance, is a fact, but "Red is the best color" is an opinion, and "Red is everyone's favorite color" is both an opinion and an assumption. Mistaking opinions and assumptions for facts can foster highly distorted thinking, which is often present in some forms of mental illness and relationship problems.

When I say a thought and belief are accurate, I mean they present facts in a manner that is dedicated to the greatest rendering of truth available to us. As anyone who's studied statistics knows, we can skew facts inaccurately to support a false narrative, which is why both words are included in this process. For example, someone might say, "This young man was caught stealing food from the grocery store. Kids these days have no respect!"

If the reason that person stole the food is because they needed to feed their family and couldn't see another way to in that moment though, that paints a highly different picture of the situation. Even though the quoted statement is fact-oriented, it is not accurate because without acknowledging the person's motivation, the situation can easily be misconstrued, as it was in the example. Another instance of an inaccurate representation of facts is a company that advertises that they are "consistently superior to the competition" because they score higher on consumer reporting most years. If those scores are only higher by a small amount though, this statement is misleading. It is technically fact-oriented in that the company outperforms the others, but it implies a greater difference in quality than is accurate. Many people experiencing depression fall into thinking that is not fact-oriented or accurate because of the depression, often including distorted thoughts like "I can't do anything right" and "I'm unlovable." If we examine their lives, we can usually see plenty of examples of these thoughts not being true, which is a standard technique in CBT for helping them mitigate or release these thoughts. To that end, making a habit of challenging negative, distorted thoughts is often a critical part of treatment for depression. Many find a significant improvement in their mood from consistently questioning and dismantling these thoughts.

We'll explore compassion and wisdom in depth later in this chapter, but generally, thoughts and beliefs are compassionate and wise if they are empathetic and reflect a holistic understanding of life, ourselves, and other people. Beyond these considerations, challenging a thought and belief can also include examining how they influence how we feel, think, and act. We can further reflect upon where we picked up thoughts and beliefs or what inspired them, assuming that feels helpful. This information enables us to see how thoughts and beliefs shape our perceptions and emotional reactions and understand why they must be changed or released for us to feel better when that is so. After we dismantle or shift a thought or belief, we can replace it with a supportive thought that we affirm, which is appropriately called an affirmation.

Exercise

Over the course of a day, write down strong statements you notice yourself making, internally or externally, or that you overhear others voicing. Consider whether or not the statements are fact-oriented and accurate, and to what degrees. Ask yourself questions like these: Where is the line between opinion, assumption, and fact here? Does it seem like this statement involves a selective sifting of the facts to support a particular position? If so, what would be a more accurate statement about this situation?

Affirmations and Affirmative Talks

Affirmation is the use of thought to influence one's reality. There are many ways to affirm, and really, any time we think, we practice affirmation. We either sustain the reality we currently perceive, develop it further, challenge it, or create something new, and we have affirmed throughout our thinking lives whether we realized it or not. Every thought-dependent element of our reality was affirmed into being.

When we practice affirmation formally, there are usually two approaches. The most common one is to design a small, specific statement (or statements) that affirms something we want to experience as being true in our reality (e.g., "I am strong," "I am always safe," "My life overflows with abundance"). We then recite that affirmation at least a few times a day, silently or aloud, until our perception of reality reflects it, which means that it has gone from being a thought to a subconscious belief. The other approach is to engage with more extensive material that affirms the sought shift in our reality, like reading a self-help book about the topic in question, listening to a spiritual presentation, or giving ourselves a pep talk. This book will mainly focus on the latter type of affirmative work, particularly in part 2's affirmative talks, though the process I generally use for creating small, individual affirmations is shared and explored below. I also include individual affirmations in part 3 to help with digesting that material.

When I work with people on individual affirmations, I usually start with ones that are not too far from where they are emotionally with a subject, with the intention of incrementally moving along a trajectory. This is different from how affirmations are traditionally practiced, where affirmations are generally bold, highly positive statements like those shared earlier. I do this because it is often difficult for people to believe something that feels vastly better than how they currently do about an issue, and as I mentioned before, when we doubt what we affirm, that tends to reinforce the beliefs involved in our doubt rather than erode them. If someone winces when they affirm "I love myself exactly as I am," for example, they are likely to feel a greater conviction that they don't love themselves as they are. So we don't begin there, though we do aim for it. Instead, we may start with an affirmation like "I have some lovable qualities," provided that feels at least somewhat true, and move in the direction of unconditional self-love over time. Once an affirmation like "I have some lovable qualities" feels true to the degree of second nature, we move on to one like "Everyone deserves love" (which includes us, by implication). Eventually, we reach the original affirmation, and having taken small steps to it and built a structure of beliefs around it, we tend to believe it more assuredly and find it easier to sustain our belief in it.

It's crucial when affirming to bring ourselves into an emotional state where we feel the truth or potential truth of each affirmation we're working with and stay in that state as we affirm them. We also want to recite affirmations with the presence of mind and centeredness we'd have when offering words of comfort to a loved one. This helps the affirmations have a greater impact on us, resonating throughout our being, which makes them more likely to be accepted as true by our subconscious mind.

Many people have had bad experiences with affirmations when they tried to work with traditional ones that felt too far from where they were with a topic, with the process of affirming feeling unproductive or counterproductive. I get that and have been there myself. If that is your experience with affirmations, I encourage you to give this incremental approach a try. I used to think affirmations were silly, but now I swear by them. I have seen affirmations erode negative thinking patterns in myself and others, sometimes in a matter of weeks. For example, affirming to myself that

"It is okay to need help," which I consciously believed but subconsciously didn't, dramatically assisted with my healing journey. So much internal pressure was bound up in the belief that "It is not okay to need help," and the best tool I found to aid me in releasing that belief and pressure was affirming that "It is okay to need help" each day. That was something I really needed to hear, and when we realize we need to hear something and digest it, one of the most effective ways I know of ensuring that happens is to turn it into an affirmation that we recite often.

Affirmations also needn't be part of a grand trajectory from where we are. Even little shifts in how we think can be potent. Just moving from "I am powerless" to "I feel powerless," for example, holds mountains of possibility. The former indicates a terribly depressing and static sense of self, while the latter may only imply a passing moment of feeling weak. Change one word and it's like living in a different reality. Our subconscious mind hears what we literally say, not what we mean (when that is different), so it's important to be careful with our words. For instance, we may intellectually recognize that we aren't powerless. By telling ourselves we are, though, our emotional state will mirror that specific statement, as will our perception of reality, either right away or over time as we persist with that thought.

Sometimes people can feel like far-reaching affirmations are true as they affirm them, but then they stumble in the face of challenging life events because their subconscious minds are oriented otherwise. Other times the far-reaching affirmations take root quickly for them and hold. You will figure out what approach works best for you as you practice. Just know that the most important thing is that you feel like an affirmation is true or could be as you affirm it.

Having said that, the resistance we feel as we affirm an ill-fitting affirmation can provide us with powerful information. It can help us see the depth of our feelings about a topic and the pain and trauma we have wrapped up in it (e.g., if we wince when we say, "I love myself," that tells us a lot about how we feel about ourselves). This then helps us gain clarity around where to focus our healing work and where it might make sense to engage in a more holistic assortment of practices. In the case of wincing while affirming self-love, we might decide to complete some workbooks about self-love or engage in inner child meditations to foster it. Reciting affirmations in front of a mirror can aid with gathering this information, as our emotions may show on our face and in our eyes. While this might sound hokey, I've found mirror work to be both challenging and profound. My recommendation in light of these benefits of resistance is to test out a far-reaching affirmation when you affirm about a subject and observe how it feels. If it feels fine, work with it and see how that goes. If it feels like overstraining, utilize the more incremental approach and use this information to help guide your healing work.

Affirmations are traditionally written as if the changes we seek have already occurred. This is because many people who practice affirmation believe that our thoughts affect what manifests in our reality, with manifestations matching the content of our thoughts, which we will explore more in the next chapter. For example, if we affirm "I am ready for a new job," that might make us ready for one, but it could also leave us waiting for one for years since being ready for a new job doesn't mean one is coming. Meanwhile, affirming "A wonderful new job is available to me whenever I seek one" calls one to us. I find this approach is more relevant when intending to manifest a change in external reality versus when we desire psychological healing. Sometimes, an affirmation like "I am healed and whole" is too much for us. That may feel like affirming something that will never happen, but "I am willing to begin the healing process" is usually right on and extremely helpful. This is a recommendation I learned from the work of Louise Hay: the first step, especially when we don't see a path to a sought change, is to just be willing. Then we can work our way up to the far-reaching affirmation over time, which is the other reason this approach is okay: incremental affirmations are designed to change, so as we affirm them, we know we are on a journey. We create a reality where most affirmations are a stop along the way, not the destination, so they don't anchor us where we are. This helps us move forward with the affirmation process, and it sidesteps the issue of needing to affirm as if a change has already happened. I wouldn't worry about this issue unless you feel like an affirmation isn't doing what it's supposed to. It is better that you believe a supportive thought that moves in the direction of what you seek than don't believe one that affirms that it has already manifested.

Another important point about the practice of affirmation is to use language that doesn't inadvertently reinforce any unwanted conditions within us. For example, if we are building self-love but affirm "I release self-hatred," that activates our history of hating ourselves in our minds and whatever we associate with that: our thoughts of self-hatred, experiences that made us feel worthy of hatred, and so on. Instead, we would affirm something like, "I am open to self-love," which conjures none of those things, or at least not to the same degree. In some instances, including an unwanted condition is helpful though. For example, an affirmation like "I've survived every depressive episode in my life. I can make it through this one too" can be extraordinarily powerful. We just wouldn't affirm that indefinitely, as it anchors depression in the fore of our minds. We'd use it until we were out of that depressed state enough to affirm one closer to our ultimate affirmative goal in this area of life.

A Process for Designing and Performing Individual Affirmations

1. Identify a belief you want to shift (e.g., "I can't do anything right").
2. Identify the theme(s) of this belief (e.g., capability).
3. Identify the spectrum of possibilities along this theme (e.g., "I am totally incapable" to "I can do anything possible for me that I set my mind to").
4. Affirm the far-reaching affirmation. Note what emotions and thoughts come up, and then use your feelings to identify your place along this spectrum (e.g., "I feel like I can't do anything right, but I know I've done some things well in my life").
5. Design an affirmation that is a step above where you currently are psychologically with this subject that you don't struggle to

believe (e.g., "I have done some things well and I can build my effectiveness and confidence over time"). A helpful question to ask ourselves in formulating this affirmation can be "What would I need to believe to move closer to the change I seek?"

6. Recite this affirmation five times or more. Do this daily until it feels true. Then, create a new affirmation that is closer to where you want to go with this issue (e.g., "My effectiveness and confidence grow a little bit each day as I work on them"). Repeat this process until you reach a point within this trajectory of affirmations where you feel complete enough with this topic.

One powerful practice with affirmations is to listen to a recording of them in a state of deep relaxation or while falling asleep, which some believe gives the affirmations easier access to the subconscious mind. In this scenario, the focus is on being totally receptive to the affirmations yet also quiet and peaceful.

Some of the affirmations in this book's affirmative talks are far-reaching. This is because the talks follow an incremental trajectory of well-being within each topic, and I have found that to be effective too: starting where we are and then listening to an inspiring talk that walks us to where we hope to be. The key with this, and affirmations in general, is honoring where we are now and being open and willing to change.

Exercises

Create two to three affirmations for yourself using the process shared in this chapter. They can relate to any issue you want. Recite these daily for the next few weeks and journal each week about the impact doing this has on you. I generally recommend that people maintain a daily regimen of affirmations, which changes depending on what they're working on (though I usually suggest involving at least one about self-love and self-acceptance). If completing this exercise feels positive to you, continue with daily affirmations, adding in new ones when you believe you would benefit from doing so and removing others when you feel complete with them.

Begin keeping a gratitude journal, in which you write down three things each day that you feel grateful for or appreciate, big or small (this can include things you're grateful to yourself for). This can be as simple as making a list like "I am grateful for food and shelter" and "I appreciate how thoughtful my partner was toward me today." As you write your items down, focus on the feeling of gratitude, and you needn't come up with new things every day. At the end of each month, review the entries you made for that month. The point of this is to create a habit of focusing on gratitude, which many people find improves their general mood. Doing this fosters a tendency to notice what we appreciate in our circumstances and opportunities too, which can help us make the most of them. It is also natural to deepen in our enjoyment of things that we consciously know we are grateful for. Having said that, you needn't do this on days when feeling grateful would be a struggle (or on those days you can write something like "I feel grateful that I needn't force myself to list things I feel grateful for on days when I don't feel up to that"). If we practice gratitude in small doses when it feels all right doing so, the practice will flower on its own in our inner gardens.

Compassionate Thinking

We've discussed thoughts being fact-oriented and accurate. Now we will consider in greater depth what it means for them to be compassionate and wise. I believe that the most powerful healing practice available to us for our psychological well-being is compassionate thinking, particularly when utilized alongside meditation to connect with the divine. I define compassion as being the synthesis of love and wisdom, of empathy and awareness. It is the marriage of an open mind and open heart. Compassion sees the big picture, the small ones, and all pictures in between, with profound insight. Thinking compassionately is about being as understanding as we can be, and that is the core of what compassionate thoughts are: thoughts that reflect a holistic understanding of something, acknowledging mind, body, spirit, and circumstance, where applicable. Understanding helps us forgive where possible and move forward. It also aids us in finding the freedom within our minds to be and accept who we are and to offer that acceptance to others. For those of us who are spiritual, compassionate thinking includes applying our spiritual beliefs directly to our everyday thoughts and experiences, making sure that perspective is integrated into our lives as best we can.

At the start of inner gardening, unconditional self-love and self-acceptance are far away from where many of us are, too far for that to be where we begin aside from holding them as an intention. Compassionate thinking is in reach for most of us, though, even if we must start small with it. It's a practice that helps us learn to love and accept ourselves over time, and it erodes and neutralizes the beliefs within us that stand against self-love and self-acceptance.

To help with formulating compassionate thoughts, I frequently give clients prompts to complete, like "It is normal to ...," "It is understandable that ...," and "It is healthy to ..." For example, "It is normal to need time for yourself," "It is understandable that I would feel exhausted and be short-tempered after not getting enough rest," and "It is healthy to plan self-care activities so I can be better rested."

When discussing compassion and forgiveness, I think it's useful to differentiate between the two, as people sometimes put unhealthy pressure on themselves and others to forgive, with forgive meaning "I'm over it." For many of us, focusing on that objective can do more harm than good because it's not within our power to just decide to be totally over something, while being compassionate is. When we have trauma, compassion is the treating of the wound with understanding, which helps us heal when we feel ready to go there. It is an active process of applying empathy and awareness of context that aids us in accepting the reality of the human experience and, in most cases, making peace with things at the intellectual level. It's what helps us look at a situation and say, "I recognize how that person was probably doing the best they could with the understanding, awareness, and capacity they had, against the backdrop of their circumstances." This aids us in getting on with our lives. I find it usually works best to start with compassion for ourselves when we feel harmed by others before trying to extend compassion to them, which should not be rushed or forced and may take considerable time to get to, if ever in extreme situations. Importantly, this process is not about making it okay that something happened (or condoning a behavior), but rather experiencing the relief that many feel through understanding how and why it likely did. When we tell people we've forgiven them because we've done this work yet still feel stung by the wound, we are being compassionate with them, but we haven't truly found forgiveness.

Forgiveness is a subconscious healing process. Like an immune response, it has its own timetable and that will be whatever it is. Forgiveness can't be forced, and it is not our work. We can bar forgiveness from happening by salting past wounds or otherwise keeping them fresh, and we pave the way for it with compassionate thinking, but forgiveness itself happens in the subconscious mind. We know forgiveness has occurred when a wound has healed. It doesn't smart anymore or it barely does. For example, I had a turbulent relationship with my mother for many years, which I will revisit a few times in this book. Healing from that began with working to empathize with her. Understanding her life as best I could helped me make peace with how she was while she was alive, such that I could enjoy her final years with her, and one day, a few years before she died, I found she was forgiven. After applying the ointment of compassion enough times, the wound healed.

Sometimes this happens, and other times it doesn't, and that is part of why it's so important to accept that compassion, not forgiveness, is our work. Trying to force ourselves to feel forgiveness when we aren't ready is one of the biggest obstacles we can create to actually forgiving. When we are able and it feels safe enough, we treat the wound with compassion, as many times as we need to. If it heals, wonderful. If not, that's okay too. We create the conditions for forgiveness as best we can and then leave that process be.

Although I include wisdom in my definition of compassion, I separate the word out in compassionate thinking practice because for many of us, the words "wisdom" and "compassion" conjure different enough responses that it is valuable to focus on them both. For instance, in therapy, I often ask clients, "What does your wisdom say about this?" and then,

"Knowing yourself, what compassionate words would you offer yourself?" I usually get highly disparate, helpful answers to these questions.

When I say that a thought is wise, what that generally means to me is two things. First, that it resonates with our inner knowing, which is to say that it feels true in the depths within that we can touch. Second, that it reflects what conventional wisdom and common sense say about a topic. If we take a step back from our individual perspective and apply what we know is true of the average human experience, what do we find? These are sentiments like "Nobody's perfect," "People can change their minds about what they want as they age," "It is normal to need help sometimes," and "Two people can love each other and still not be able to make a relationship work." They're the notions that become clichés. I have found that even though most of us know and accept that these types of statements are true, many people don't often apply them, at least regarding themselves. This can cause them to suffer considerably. In essence, a wise thought is one that recognizes and honors the reality of the human experience. Many of the statements I make in the affirmative talks about the respective domains of life involve my understanding of this concept.

There is a psychological phenomenon called the "fundamental attribution error" that I think it's important to be aware of when learning how to practice compassionate thinking. The fundamental attribution error, simply put, is the tendency to overemphasize a person's involvement or personality in an issue while underemphasizing situational factors and greater context. For example, a "problem child" may be looked at as fundamentally flawed, without regard for their troubled family life, the effects of poverty on them, the bigotry in their society that harmed them, the prevalence of violence in their neighborhood, and so on. Meanwhile, these factors could be far greater contributors to their behavioral problems than the child themself.

Many of us who have depression or low self-esteem hold ourselves accountable for our lives in this way. We see ourselves as defective and therefore hopeless cases who have made a mess of the opportunities presented to us (or so it seems when we feel depressed). We each have our contexts, though, full of elements that influenced us as we grew up, and we all deserve to be seen in light of them. None of us are wholly responsible for who we are today, and sometimes, we are the least deserving of blame when we examine the bigger picture of why we are where we are.

Remember: no one plants the majority of what is in their inner garden. That was put there by others and environmental influences. All of this is important to acknowledge as part of healing, and appreciating it alone can be tremendously healing if we accept it as true and allow some of the emotional weight of self-blame to fall off our shoulders. When we acknowledge our context while empathizing with how we feel, we are being compassionate with ourselves. When we do this while centered in our connection with the divine, it can profoundly transform our lives.

This doesn't mean we absolve ourselves of all responsibility for our actions, but it does mean that we carry a fair burden, which is often far lighter than what we carry now and easier to set down one day. As we recognize the contexts that shaped our behavior and thinking (and that of others), we become more able to accept our humanness and we pave the way for forgiveness. By accepting ourselves and loosening the past's grip on us with compassionate thoughts, our lives open and our well-being can flow with fewer restrictions.

When I bring up the subject of compassionate thinking with clients, they often remark that it is new to them in the sense that they have never tried to have compassion be the primary lens through which they view life and themselves. Because of that, I have seen what happens in many people's lives when they take this practice on, even to a small degree. The results are almost always compelling. Within a short period of time, many people begin to notice improvements in their mood and their everyday experience of life. This was true for me too. When I first learned of compassionate thinking, I was skeptical and a bit taken aback by it. I was so used to being critical of myself and others, to an extent that it was almost like an unconscious default. As I started bringing the perspective of compassion into my thought process, that began to change, and as I understood myself and others better, I felt emotionally healthier and became a better participant in my relationships. I also became far less judgmental because I was less prone to making assumptions, which decreased the everyday mental load I carried and helped me be more fair-minded when navigating adversity. Practicing compassionate thinking was like pouring spring water into my mind that incrementally purified what was there.

Compassionate thinking enables us to learn from our regrets and move forward from them, and it aids us in witnessing and understanding the cycle of violence. As many have said before, hurt people hurt people, and people can't teach others what they don't know themselves. I believe the vast majority of the violence in this world is the result of a trauma cycle perpetuating itself and people within it not knowing how to break it. So many of us have lost touch with our divine nature, and we act accordingly. Fortunately, we have the power to end this cycle within ourselves, which helps us end it in general. We can choose compassion instead, to whatever degree we are able to, and start to leave the harm behind.

Exercises

Think about the last few times you criticized yourself or others or overheard someone criticizing others. Apply what we've explored in this section about compassionate thinking to those criticisms. How might they shift?

The following thoughts are likely not fact-oriented, accurate, wise, and compassionate in most situations. Imagine a hypothetical one in which they are not and analyze why (sample answers provided below).

* I have no power to improve my life.
* I'll never be a good romantic partner.

After analyzing the thoughts, write what is probably a more fact-oriented, accurate, wise, and compassionate thought in that imagined scenario. Consider how thinking this new thought might affect the person in question's mental and emotional state as contrasted with the effects of the initial thought.

The thought "I have no power to improve my life" is so extreme that there's a good chance it's neither fact-oriented nor accurate. This person may not have the power to improve their life that they want to have, but they likely have some power to make positive change there. This relates to one thing wisdom might suggest about this thought: it seems more indicative of a feeling than the truth, and it is fruitful to explore the power this person has. Compassion calls us to look at the instances where this person did make improvements in their life, large and small, as well as their potential to grow and act. Not to mention the reasons why they feel powerless to improve their life. A more fact-oriented, accurate, wise, and compassionate thought for this situation would probably be something like, "I feel like I have no power to improve my life, which is a symptom of depression or stems from the adversity I've faced, but I imagine I can make some improvements."

The thought "I'll never be a good romantic partner" may be rooted in past romantic failures, so it could be fact-oriented to a degree, but it predicts the future, and that means it is likely inaccurate or at least could be. What if this person decides to study relationship skills and work on themselves? They might be amazing in their next relationship! Also, it is possible that this person isn't giving themselves the credit they're due for how they behaved in their past relationships, even if those relationships didn't pan out. Wisdom reminds us that we have the capacity to learn and grow from where we are, and making mistakes in the past doesn't mean we're doomed for the rest of our lives in most cases. Particularly if we're proactive with our development. Wisdom and compassion highlight that there are two people at minimum in a relationship, and the situation may be more complicated than the person sees. Are they assuming a higher level of blame for their past relationship outcomes than they deserve? A more fact-oriented, accurate, wise, and compassionate thought for this situation would probably be something like "I have made mistakes in my past relationships and they haven't worked out, but if I learn relationship and communication skills, it is possible that my next one could."

The Illusory Truth Effect and Confirmation Bias

Two other powerful psychological phenomena are at play in the healing work we're embarking upon that I think are helpful to learn about beforehand. These are the illusory truth effect and confirmation bias, and learning about them aids us in understanding another level of why inner gardening is important and how affirmations work. The illusory truth effect, in a nutshell, is the phenomenon wherein the more we are exposed to information or an idea, the likelier we are to believe that it is true or could be. Technically, the illusory truth effect is about our tendency to believe false information, but the psychological processes involved in it also hold for true information. It is a subconscious, automatic effect. For example, let's say someone tells me that a local government representative is lying about his finances to defraud the city. As I hear this accusation over and over, particularly from multiple sources, I will start to believe there could be some truth to it or that there is, especially if I don't question the truthfulness of this accusation. The illusory truth effect is part of how we end up believing the far-fetched claims of advertisements, to where they guide our desires. We tend to believe that information or an idea we're repeatedly exposed to is true or could be, particularly if it goes unchallenged.

Confirmation bias is the tendency to filter, process, and recall information in a manner that reinforces what we already believe. Like the illusory truth effect, it is a subconscious and automatic process. Our minds highlight or prioritize what we perceive that validates what we believe, and they downplay, disregard, or don't even register what doesn't. Politics is an excellent venue for witnessing confirmation bias in action, as it is often easy to observe members of different groups cherry-picking the positive aspects of themselves while overemphasizing the negative ones of their opponents. This isn't usually because they're skewing the others as a political tactic, though some people may do that. It's because confirmation bias has fortified their perspective so much that they can barely see outside of it.

On an individual level, confirmation bias is frequently at work in depression, perpetuating and deepening the depressed state. Many people with depression hold a belief like "Nothing ever works out for me," and because their subconscious mind has come to agree with that, it filters reality accordingly. A plethora of things could've worked out for them in their lives, and there may be a myriad of wonderful opportunities around them now that they could do well with, but none of that feels real to them. Instead, they feel stuck where they are, unable to make positive changes. As their minds continue filtering reality in accord with this belief, they feel increasingly hopeless. Confirmation bias becomes like an agent of self-fulfilling prophecy.

The main antidote to having the illusory truth effect and confirmation bias negatively hijack our lives and moods is to commit to being critical thinkers. Fortunately, this automatically happens as we make a habit in our inner gardening process of questioning whether our thoughts and beliefs are true or not. That's the heart of what critical thinking is: Why might this notion not be true? Where did it come from? Was that source reputable? What in this is opinion and what is fact? What assumptions are present here? Is this too much of a stretch in terms of interpretation? What all these questions have in common is a commitment to seeking truth, and when we ask them of our thoughts and beliefs consistently, we inevitably begin to ask them of other information we encounter too.

The psychological processes behind the illusory truth effect and confirmation bias are huge assets in affirmative work. The more we affirm our new thoughts, the truer they start to feel, assuming we don't experience substantial doubt when we affirm them. As our subconscious mind digests these thoughts and comes to believe them, confirmation bias kicks in and begins filtering reality accordingly. Our work becomes far less difficult as we automatically find evidence around us in support of our growing well-being. This assumes there isn't a contrary critical force that we're immersed in, though, like an antagonistic relationship or a hostile work environment. When there is, we usually must be more proactive in our efforts and perhaps also act to make change in the physical world.

Acting for Well-Being

Earlier in this chapter, I mentioned that the latter two steps of the fourfold healing process in this system are to stop or diminish engaging in behaviors that harm us and to participate in ones that support our well-being. In my experience, it's good to have some intentionality around this. First, consider the typical behaviors in your life: Do any strike you as healthy?

Unhealthy? I think it can be helpful not only to reflect on that, but to keep a journal for a week or two and make note of what we tend to do and how those actions affect us.

Once we have this awareness, we can consider if we have any habits or frequent behaviors that seem unhealthy that we could possibly reduce or stop. If there are some, we then make a realistic plan for doing that. I say realistic because for most of us, "I'm going to stop doing all these harmful behaviors immediately" is not feasible. Generally, these behaviors are with us for a reason. Some are probably defensive and some, though harmful, may help us cope with difficulties, which can make them hard to stop. Also, the inertia of our behaviors, and whatever thoughts and beliefs we have that contribute to those behaviors, will usually take time to process through. If we use them to help us cope, it may be helpful to identify healthier coping strategies to try to replace them with. We might also decide to keep around some of them that aren't too bad (like overeating comfort food once in a while).

It is often wise with behavioral change to smart small, taking a gentler, persistent approach of baby steps, assuming we follow through with them. This is because bold behavioral change tends to cause a high level of resistance to arise within many if not most people, which we will explore in depth in chapter 3. The path of least resistance generally leads to the most effective and sustainable changes. We can also use tools like checklists of action items to help us stay aware and on track in reducing harmful behaviors. Whatever approach we take, it's critical to be compassionate with ourselves throughout this process and not fall into undue guilt and perfectionism. We just do our best and mind the goal of reducing our harmful behaviors.

On the side of acting in support of our well-being, this is where we engage in what's called "behavioral activation" in CBT, which is a practice of planning out activities to foster well-being. In my work, I use the term "self-care" as the label for these types of activities, with self-care being any action we take on behalf of our well-being. One of the points of focusing on self-care is to appreciate that all of us, like everything that lives, need care to thrive. Many of us would never dream of treating our dog or cat with as little care as we give to ourselves, and thinking about what a dog or cat needs in terms of care can provide us with insight into our own self-care needs. For example, we all need healthy food, water, rest, exercise, socialization, affection, stimulation, and recreation, relative to our individual constitutions and preferences. When we don't prioritize self-care, and many of us grew up in homes where we were told implicitly or explicitly that doing so is selfish, we tend not to get enough nourishment and nurturing. That can lead to a sense of dissatisfaction and discomfort with where we are in our lives, among many other problems that result from being depleted. This is another thing that's good to keep in mind while we analyze our behaviors: How much time is spent in true self-care? For many of us, it's nowhere near enough.

I think it's useful to regularly remind ourselves, particularly if this is an area we struggle with, that self-care is a need, not a want. If we have some beliefs about not deserving to prioritize our care, it's important to work through them. Sometimes these beliefs may be subtle. In my family, for example, I don't recall the subject of self-care ever being discussed, and I think that is true of many families during the time when I was growing up. I don't think self-care was even part of the broader cultural conversation then. The message I remember receiving, which was more implicit than explicit, was that it was good to keep busy and that it was bad to "be lazy." Self-care has nothing to do with being lazy, though. It's about honoring our natural need for rest, fun, and pleasure, and we all deserve to prioritize it. Given our circumstances, we may not be able to provide ourselves with as much self-care as we need, and when that is the case, we just do the best we can.

In terms of strategizing how to engage in self-care, what I usually do in therapy is break it down into three categories and then help clients identify activities from each category that they can include in the following week, which we then repeat in subsequent sessions. The first category is life hygiene. These are the things we must do to keep up with our lives. For example, we need to take the garbage out, clean the bathroom, open our mail, shower regularly, and so on. Some people have an easy time with life hygiene, while others struggle with all or parts of it. For people who struggle with it in general, creating a plan around it that doesn't feel too overwhelming can be helpful, like doing the dishes on Saturday and Wednesday and opening the mail at least twice a week. We can also start small with this and build as we establish new habits.

The second category is self-nurturing. These are actions we take with the primary intention of feeling cared for and nourished. They can be occasional events, like taking a relaxing bath or getting a massage, but also everyday activities, like having a contemplative cup of tea in the morning and slowing down when we don't need to be in a hurry.

The third category is pleasurable activities. These are things like entertainment, eating out at restaurants, playing games, and socializing with friends. I separate these from self-nurturing because some of them may tire us out. For instance, if we're introverted, we may feel exhausted after socializing with friends, but overall, it benefits our mood to do so.

It's important to make time to enjoy ourselves. When we don't plan this out, what many people default to is watching TV at night or scrolling through social media. While that may be enjoyable to a degree, there might be other activities that they would feel more satisfied doing instead that they could readily do with a little planning.

One of the classic symptoms of depression is a deficit forming in these three areas, and one of the most effective and common CBT interventions for depression involves planning out activities within them via behavioral activation.[1] Though many people have challenges with this at first, as they go through the motions of these activities and begin with small steps, they usually find greater enjoyment and nourishment in time and start to experience an elevation in their mood. For our purposes, the most salient point to appreciate is that a lot of what helps us feel well in life is acting

1. David Ekers, Lisa Webster, Annemieke Van Straten, Pim Cuijpers, David Richards, and Simon Gilbody, "Behavioural Activation for Depression; An Update of Meta-Analysis of Effectiveness and Sub Group Analysis," *PLoS One* 9, no. 6 (June 2014): e100100, doi:10.1371/journal.pone.0100100.

on behalf of our well-being. It is important to do our best to make sure we experience enough pleasure and take advantage of the opportunities in our lives for enrichment that feel meaningful to us.

There are myriad ways to act on behalf of our well-being. What satisfies this objective for you may be highly different from what does it for me, but there are some things that can do it. We each have the freedom to find out what that they are for ourselves. A powerful habit to cultivate in service of self-care is to regularly ask ourselves, particularly when we feel bad, "In this moment, what do I need?" If we aren't used to tuning in to ourselves like this, it may take some practice for the answers to this question to show up readily. It is my experience, though, that most of the time, part of us knows what we need, and if we get quiet and ask, that clarity will come, whether the self-care need is rest, pleasure, play, alone time, support, food, and so on. Also, when it comes to self-nurturing and pleasurable activities, I think it's beneficial to recognize that what we feel up for doing can vary based on our mood. If I feel exhausted or overwhelmed, for example, that might be a good time to binge watch TV shows rather than schedule an exercise class. Even the thought of that class could make me feel more exhausted and overwhelmed! When I feel better, though, that class might sound fun, while binging TV shows might sound like it would bring me down or leave me feeling restless. In self-care, like all things, it is important to honor and start where we are as we move in the direction of greater well-being.

Exercise

Journal about the following questions: What of your behaviors might you want to diminish or stop? How often do you engage in behaviors in the three categories of self-care? If you don't engage in them regularly, try planning one pleasurable or nourishing activity each day for the next two weeks and then see how this affects you.

Over the next week, at least once a day, close your eyes, connect with your body, take a deep breath, and ask yourself, "In this moment, what do I need?"

A Worksheet for Challenging Unsupportive Thoughts

When I work with clients in therapy, I use this worksheet to guide the sessions devoted to practicing challenging thoughts. I made it several years ago and have refined it over time. It integrates popular questions from CBT alongside ones based on my own insights. This worksheet features cognitive distortions, which are common forms of distorted thinking that are often found in people who have depression and anxiety, though in my experience, they are far more widespread than that. These cognitive distortions were identified and researched by Dr. Aaron Beck and Dr. David Burns, pioneers in the cognitive therapy movement. When we know what these distortions are, we can spot them in our thinking, which can facilitate us shifting our thinking in a healthier direction. Fundamentally, though, they each highlight a way a thought or manner of thinking is not fact-oriented, accurate, or both.

Though I share many questions below and think they are all valuable to answer, when I present this approach to clients, I emphasize four main ones to have at the ready throughout the day: Why might this thought not be true? What is the effect of believing or thinking this thought? Where did this thought likely come from (i.e., What is the story of this thought?)? And what would be a healthier thought to believe or think instead (one that is fact-oriented, accurate, wise, and compassionate)? These questions form a simplified manner of conducting this process that gets at its essence and is less of an imposition on the day than completing this entire worksheet. I also provide them with a link to this worksheet, though, and recommend that they use it when they want to explore a thought more deeply or struggle with challenging one. I recommend completing this worksheet when you recognize that a thought is likely causing significant difficulties for you. I suggest that you complete it two or three times over the next couple of weeks to get the hang of it.

1. Situation: Where were you? What was happening?
2. What thoughts went through your mind? What images?

3. Which is the thought to challenge? Pick only one.

4. What effect does believing or thinking this thought have on you? (i.e., How does it influence how you feel? Think? Act? How might it affect what you perceive—your sense of self, the world, and others? The choices you make?)

5. What assumptions are in this thought? Are there clear flaws in the logic and/or reasoning of this thought? (e.g., "I will never fall in love again." I don't know the future, so I can't justifiably make this statement in most cases.)

6. What cognitive distortions are present in this thought? How accurate is it?

   a. All-or-nothing/black-and-white thinking—no gray area; oversimplifying an issue. (e.g., "If I make one mistake, I'm a total failure," "Once a cheater, always a cheater.")

   b. Overgeneralizing—not enough information to draw the conclusion. (e.g., "Everyone in this town is unfriendly" after meeting only a few people.)

   c. Mental filtering—only filtering in the negative, seeing something skewed. (e.g., Your spouse tells you several things they appreciate about you and one negative thing, and afterward, you dwell on the negative so much it's like the positive statements didn't occur.)

   d. Disqualifying the positive—writing off positive things because they "don't count." (e.g., "It doesn't matter that I've been promoted twice in the last two years and my relationships are going well. I'm a loser.")

   e. Jumping to conclusions—acting like we can read minds or know the future; reading too much into something. (e.g., "I can tell she's not over that incident. I just know it.")

   f. Catastrophizing—seeing a catastrophe with insufficient cause or assuming one will occur. (e.g., "I have an itch on my arm. It must be a terrible disease!")

g. Emotional reasoning—assuming something is true because it feels true, rather than via the facts. (e.g., "I just know I'll never be good at this job. I can feel it.")

h. Labeling/mislabeling—giving yourself or others a global character label unfairly and fixating on it, like "I'm a creep"; giving an undue label with insufficient justification, like "I'm a horrible wife."

i. Personalization—believing things are about oneself without sufficient cause. Also, feeling responsible for circumstances in which we have little power or involvement. Examples of this include believing that other people's actions have more to do with us than they likely do. (e.g., "Did you see how the cashier looked at me? I can't imagine what I did to her," or feeling like we are to blame if our college student children get into trouble in school.)

j. Blaming—seeing others as to blame for things far beyond what is realistic, often in a way that minimizes our own agency in situations. (e.g., "My life would be great if it weren't for all the bureaucracy in this country.")

7. What fact-based evidence supports this thought being true?

8. What fact-based evidence challenges this thought being true?

9. Are there any life events or experiences you can think of that incline you to have this thought? If you've thought it over time, can you remember when you began thinking it and what experiences reinforced it?

10. What does your wisdom say about this thought?

11. What might you tell a close friend in the same situation?

12. Knowing yourself, what compassionate things would you say to yourself about this issue? Try thoughts like "It is normal to …," "It is understandable that …," and "It is healthy to …"

13. In summary, why might this thought not be true? Try to write only one to three sentences.

14. What is a more fact-oriented, accurate, wise, and compassion-ate thought?
15. How do you feel differently when you believe this new thought as contrasted with the first one?
16. Are there any resolutions you want to make or actions you want to take as a result of this process?

Chapter 2
Centering Spirit in the Process

At the center of our inner gardens, within our hearts, there is a divine spring. Mystics throughout history have discovered this spring and remarked on our essential, divine nature and the way it interconnects us with each other and all things. Here, I call this divine essence "Spirit," but I think it's important to acknowledge that mysticism, which is the lens through which I approach Spirit in this book, is about experiencing what lies beyond mental constructs. The words and ideas we impose on the divine are inherently limited, unable to fully convey or contain what they symbolize.

If you have other language you would prefer to use for the divine, or ways of conceptualizing it, that is totally okay. Simply modify the passages about Spirit to resonate with your belief system to the degree that they can. One of the most important steps with this work if we already hold spiritual beliefs is finding a manner of harmonizing it with them, which includes framing it in a way where that will occur, where possible. That will make it vastly more powerful, and it shouldn't feel dissonant, which could render it ineffective. I will also talk later about divine intelligence, which I believe is always available to us, providing insight and guidance beyond what we can see from the limited perspective of our human minds. There are myriad ways to conceptualize that too, and I suggest going with whatever feels most natural and comfortable to you.

The spring of Spirit never runs dry. It is there for us in every moment of our lives and beyond. It flows with waters that are unconditionally loving, loving in a manner that defies our intellectual understanding but for which I have found no better word. The love we feel at the human level, as magnificent as it is, is a pale shadow of this love. It is deeper than the bonds and notions of personality, somehow indescribably intimate and ecstatic yet also universal, gentle, and serene. I know this not only because others have told me so and mystics have spoken of it throughout history, but because I have experienced this love during spiritual practice.

I also use the word "love" when talking about Spirit, and the word "Spirit" itself, because they give us a foothold for spiritually connecting. That connection can help us heal as well as open to our divine nature. For example, I have found benefit in affirming that "Spirit always loves and supports us" even though, technically, we are Spirit too and the love of Spirit is not a subject acting upon an object but a truth of being. It is hard to develop a nurturing relationship with a total abstraction, though, and the conceit of subject and object, of Spirit loving us, gives us a starting point we can launch and build from. Then we realize through progressive stages of direct experience in practices like meditation that we have never been other than Spirit, save for within our minds.

There is a parallel approach to this in some sects of Hinduism, where mystics have taught that the worship of deity with a form is meant to be a ladder that takes us to the formless. Some have also said that the ultimate divinity is able to assume different forms to suit the constitutions of individual seekers, like wearing costumes. We begin where we are, as social creatures who can relate to words like "love" and the concept of a personified higher power. As we progress in our practice, symbols fall away. This is not to suggest that the formed version of the divine is unreal, at least not any more so than you or I are as individual personalities.

This type of incremental approach allows for benefit to come from relating to Spirit and its love at each step of our deepening journey of consciousness, as the terms "love" and "Spirit" gain new layers of meaning. If the path is pursued to its end, they will be set aside, alongside all words as we enter the perfection of inner stillness and what lies beyond that. If not, we've come to intimately know a divinely powerful ally that will unconditionally love, accept, and support us for the rest of our lives.

Some people ask if there is a difference between Spirit and the soul. I conceive of this in a simple way. Spirit is the essence, whereas the soul, which is made of Spirit or an extension of it, is the distinct part of us that moves from lifetime to lifetime and the container of our "higher self." This can be conceptualized with the famous metaphors of each soul being a drop in the great ocean, or each being a cell in the body of God. Also, "higher" here doesn't mean better or holier, and it isn't suggestive of any kind of morality. It simply means higher up the spectrum of consciousness, which spans from the undifferentiated radiance of pure Spirit to the apparent total separateness of gross matter. There is nothing in the manifested world that isn't as divine as the highest point of Spirit. It's all in how we look at things.

In practice, I think differentiating between the soul and Spirit can become like splitting hairs. The primary point for our work here is to assume the notion that we have a spiritual nature that we can perceive, which can bring us to an experience of unconditional love and peace. We have the power with how we use our minds to tune ourselves to a direct perception of Spirit.

Some people also ask if Spirit is the same as God. I think that depends on what you believe "God" is. I don't use that word here because I know it can be loaded and triggering for many people, while I hope the word "Spirit" is general and flexible enough to mesh with or not infringe upon what many do believe. In my personal practice, I tend to alternate between Spirit, the divine, and Goddess or Divine Mother depending on what I'm doing. If the word "God" works better for you, by all means, use it. If you are part of a religion that believes humans are fundamentally separate from an all-powerful deity or deities, that can still work with this approach if you believe, for instance, that "God always loves and supports me," or something comparable.

What does all of this mean, though, in essence? It means that we are not alone on the path, and divine support is with us in each moment of life. Divine intelligence is always available too, guiding us to the attainable healing and well-being we seek. Countless people in recovery will swear up and down that connecting with a higher power has enabled them to do what they couldn't do for themselves otherwise. That has also been my experience. The tension that leaves our lives as we learn to connect with and trust in a higher power is borderline indescribable. This doesn't necessarily mean we'll always feel the presence of Spirit or receive guidance clearly. Dark nights of the soul occur, and if we don't keep up with our inner gardening, weeds can return that obscure our view of the spring of Spirit. When we prioritize connecting with Spirit, though, those experiences happen less frequently and for shorter stretches of time, and how to act in our lives becomes clearer and clearer. Building this relationship can start simply, with making a habit of meditating each day.

Exercise
Journal about how your personal spiritual beliefs connect or contrast with the material shared in this section. Do they overlap? Are there areas of dissonance? How would you express these concepts to yourself in a manner that resonates with you?

Connecting with Spirit through Meditation

As we explore connecting with Spirit, I want to emphasize that we are never disconnected from it in a spiritual sense. That would be impossible, as it is the foundation of what we are. We can be disconnected from Spirit in terms of our awareness of it, though, and that is what connecting with Spirit is about: feeling its presence consciously. The practices that most helped me develop a strong awareness of Spirit were meditation, ritual, and affirmation. Many of you who are new to this concept may begin to feel Spirit through reading the affirmative material in this book aloud.

That said, some people seem more innately predisposed to sensing spiritual things than others, so results will likely vary here, but I believe everyone has the ability to feel the presence of Spirit. It just might come more easily or vividly to some or in different forms. We can also usually grow in our awareness of Spirit from where we are, even if we are already sensitive. I was sensitive and spiritually inclined as a child, for example, to where my sensitivity was sometimes difficult for me, particularly without spiritual training. With devoted, daily spiritual practice, though, my connection with Spirit felt like it grew exponentially, and in a manner that felt safe and strengthening. It was like the difference between hearing the sound of a radio from the open window of a nearby home and being in the same room as it and able to tune the dial.

One meditation practice I know that can facilitate connecting with Spirit is to meditate on unconditional love in the heart. The association of love with the heart is ancient and found in many parts of the world. Ancient Greek philosophers connected the heart with our most powerful emotions, including love. The heart is also referenced and worked with in many spiritual traditions. There are systems originating in India that feature an energy center called a chakra located near the physical heart in the middle of the chest, which is meditated upon, usually alongside other chakras. In the Hindu Chandogya Upanishad, it is said that "the Self resides within the lotus of the heart. Knowing this, devoted to the Self, the sage enters daily that holy sanctuary. Absorbed in the Self, the sage is freed from identity with the body and lives in blissful consciousness."[2] This affirms that the heart is the veritable seat of the soul. The *shanzhong* acupuncture point from traditional Chinese medicine is in the center of the chest and used to open it, and the *shen dao,* or spirit path point, is found along the spine, level with the heart. Some believe this point has a profound degree of spiritual significance.

In Kabbalah, one correspondence of the heart region is with Tiphareth, which can be translated to mean beauty, integration, and balance. Tiphareth

---

2. Editors of *Hinduism Today* Magazine, *What Is Hinduism?: Modern Adventures Into a Profound Global Faith* (Kapaa, HI: Himalayan Academy, 2007), 81.

is among the ten sefirot, or emanations, in the divine process of continual creation of the world and is the point on the Tree of Life that represents the merging of heaven and earth in some traditions. It relates to the sun, a bestower of light and life, and is where the higher and lower selves unite. Some Pagan traditions work with the Three Cauldrons (sometimes spelled "caldrons"), which are believed to be part of a Celtic system of energy centers that includes the Cauldron of Motion, located at the center of the chest. They are referenced in an Irish poem called "The Cauldron of Poesy" that appears in a manuscript from the sixteenth century yet is suspected to date back to the eighth century. Of the Cauldron of Motion, the poem states,

> *The caldron of motion sings*
> *with insights of grace,*
> *with currents of poetic knowledge,*
> *with strata of poetic lore,*
> *it brings enlightenment,*
> *composition of learning,*
> *a stream of honour.*[3]

Heart meditation gives us an opportunity to experience this magnificent spiritual center directly.

A Heart Meditation Practice

To practice this meditation, first, sit in a meditation posture. Two postures for beginners are shared here. If possible, take a meditation class to ensure your posture if correct. Sitting in an incorrect posture can cause injury, particularly if done regularly.

---

3. P. L. Henry, "The Caldron of Poesy," *Studia Celtica* 14–15 (1979/1980): 126.

Burmese Posture

The pictured posture is known as the "Burmese posture." For this posture, sit on a cushion that places your hips higher than your knees. I recommend buying a meditation cushion for this, called a *zafu*, and if you use one, sit on its front third. Straighten your back while focusing on feeling at ease within your body. Cross your legs in front and position the heel of your front foot above the ankle of your back foot. Place your palms face down on your thighs or knees, deferring to whichever placement is more comfortable for you, or with your right hand resting on your left palm with your thumbs touching, in the navel area (pictured). Alternate the leg you place in front each time you sit.

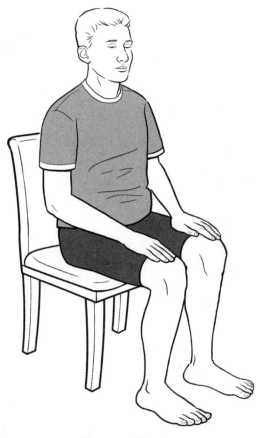

Chair Meditation

Meditating in a chair is also an option. To do this, put items like books or small blocks under its back legs to create an angle that elevates your hips above your knees or purchase a cushion designed for postural support in a chair. Straighten your back while focusing on feeling at ease within your body. Place your feet approximately hip width apart on the floor, with your palms face down on your thighs or knees, or with your right hand resting on your left palm with your thumbs touching, in the navel area.

Once you have assumed a meditation posture, close your eyes and breathe naturally or in a relaxing fashion. Breathing to facilitate relaxation can be as simple as taking deep, slow belly breaths on a count of four for the inhale, hold for four, exhale for four, hold for four, and then repeating that (if a four count feels like it strains you, try a three or two count). Then spend a few moments focusing on relaxing. Let the tension of the day fall away from you, and release your thoughts as best you can, perhaps imagining them floating away like clouds in the sky. As you do this, reflect on the fact that the oxygen we depend on for survival comes from plants and plant-like organisms. Each breath we take affirms our interrelationship with nature, our place within the greater whole. If relaxation is a struggle for you, practice progressive muscle relaxation before this.

Progressive muscle relaxation is a process of tensing and releasing muscles in a sequence to deeply relax the body. In the way I teach this technique, we imagine warm, golden light filling and relaxing our body parts in ascending order (toes of the left foot, left foot, left ankle, left calf, left thigh, right toes, right foot, right ankle, right calf, right thigh, pelvis, etc.). If an area doesn't relax from this alone, we imagine our next inhalation entering that area as we tense the muscles there. Then we hold this tension alongside our breath and release it as we exhale while imagining this area relaxing.

When we begin practicing progressive muscle relaxation, tensing and releasing each muscle group can be helpful to facilitate experiencing deep relaxation. Eventually, doing this teaches us how to enter a relaxed state at will. Once we've learned how to do that, we can usually transition from progressive muscle relaxation to a "body scan," which is where we simply bring our awareness to the different parts of our body and ask that they relax, and then they do. There are many free guided progressive muscle relaxation recordings available online and apps that can aid with learning how to do it.

After relaxing, bring your awareness to the center of your chest and visualize warm, golden light within your heart, like a small sun that shines with divine, unconditional love. Imagine it radiating out into your entire being, brighter than all the stars in creation and with a force that could create a universe. If you struggle to feel love, think of the last time you felt love for anything and then imagine that feeling entering your heart and filling you. You can also affirm the word "love" silently to yourself as you practice to help you stay present with the intention of the meditation, or other loving affirmations. For example, "I am Spirit and Spirit is love," "Unconditional love fills me in each moment," and "Love is the essence of my being." Some people are not able to visualize. If visualization isn't an option for you, focus on the feeling of the meditation rather than the image, attending to the warmth and sensation of love, as well as the concept of this sacred presence.

When you get distracted during meditation, bring your awareness back to the warm, golden light or presence, and pay close attention to how you feel, trying to gently focus on that with your entire being. The goal is to have no tension in our minds and bodies as we meditate, particularly because of our efforts to focus. This can be challenging at first, but with practice we figure out how to do it. When the time is up, wiggle your fingers and toes to ground yourself in your body and open your eyes.

Some Additional Points about Meditation

Meditating on the heart and unconditional love can bring up insecurities and old wounds related to self-worth and feeling unloved. Be kind to yourself as best you can while practicing this meditation, and if it feels like too much for you, prioritize practicing affirmations about self-love instead (we'll explore some later). Try it again when you feel more comfortable with the thought of it or drawn to it. With persistent practice, the uncomfortable feelings usually pass and the meditation starts to feel blissful and eventually ecstatic at times. That said, if heart meditation feels unsafe or extremely uncomfortable to you, I suggest that you stop performing it and seek instruction from a teacher if you want to meditate more.

Many people think they will be unable to meditate, and that was true of me when I started. Back then, I felt like my mind raced a mile a minute, and the notion of sitting still, much less quieting my mind and focusing on one thing, seemed impossible and absurd. What I discovered though was that by starting small, with just five minutes a day, I could manage it, particularly when pairing that with progressive muscle relaxation, even though I was often highly distracted for much of the practice at first. In time,

I began to experience the benefits of meditation, and those benefits compelled me to keep practicing. I started to have a different relationship with my thoughts, for example, and became more able to concentrate and guide them because I was now in the habit of sitting each day and shifting my focus to something other than them, something I chose. The ability to guide my thoughts has helped me navigate difficult thoughts as well as practice affirmations and compassionate thinking, and the increased ability to concentrate has benefitted me in many areas of my life.

Meditation has also enabled me to be less impulsive because every time an impulse arises in meditation and we don't follow it, choosing to stay with the practice instead, we become more able to do that in general, like strengthening a muscle. It helps us become able to set aside the emotional weight of everyday stressors too because each time we meditate, we do this in order to focus on the meditation's subject, even though becoming adept at it usually takes practice. Meditation became like a psychic bath for me at times as well, nourishing and rejuvenating, especially once I started experiencing how blissful it can be. It also made me more aware of my mental patterns since they were directly before me, playing out in my mind as distractions while I meditated, which helped me determine what to focus on in my healing work. Best of all, though, meditation aided me in perceiving Spirit far more strongly, experiencing stillness within, and realizing that my emotional state didn't need to always be at the mercy of my circumstances.

Meditating on unconditional love helps us experience that we can connect with the feeling of love for no reason other than that we want to. Each time we do this, we reinforce within our minds that we can, and eventually, the feeling of Spirit tends to dawn within us. Returning to our perception of Spirit day after day in meditation then forms a lightning rod for experiences of divine love. After that, it is simply a matter of deepening and maintaining this connection.

As we feel Spirit within ourselves, we become able to feel it in other things, and it is everywhere. One of my favorite places to connect with Spirit is in nature, and I also believe spending time in nature while learning how to meditate greatly strengthened my ability to feel the presence of Spirit. It was like the orchards and gardens I worked in each week as part of my spiritual training program were teaching me how to feel our shared divine presence. I highly recommend making a habit of going outdoors among plants, quieting your mind, resting your awareness upon them, and then feeling what comes up. In my experience, the plant kingdom is not only alive but communicating with us, in a language that helps us come home within ourselves.

Tuning in to Spirit increasingly fills us with a sense of love and serenity. The more we feel its presence, the more able we become to live in alignment with it. We gain a sense of what thoughts and actions take us from the perception of it or draw us toward perceiving it. This is something tuning in to plants can also help us experience, as plants live in alignment with Spirit and radiate that in each moment. When we practice living in alignment with Spirit, we discover that it is available to us even amid pain. As I alluded to in the introduction, I have multiple chronic physical and mental health conditions, some of which can be debilitating, and I grew up regularly experiencing abuse, so I say this from experience. I have found some peace even during great pain because of learning and applying this kind of information.

Before connecting deeply with Spirit, I intellectually believed I was worthy of compassion and love, and that I, like all things, was divine, but that was mostly a reasoned position. It wasn't how I usually felt, which I became acutely aware of as the subconscious self-loathing I lugged around from my childhood and adolescence surfaced during my spiritual training. As I experienced the presence of Spirit within myself during my spiritual practices to greater and greater degrees, that began to change. When we touch the holiness within, which reflects what we inherently are, it starts to become clear that even though we can deviate from this holiness in our minds, that is like believing a fictitious movie is real. It is not the truth. As my intimacy with Spirit grew, I appreciated that, yes, I deserve love and am worthy, and I needn't do anything to earn that because I am inherently and irrevocably divine, and so are you.

This is one of the main reasons connecting and aligning with Spirit is centered in this book. We can cultivate thoughts of compassion and self-love that help us release negative conditioning and feel better about ourselves, but there is nothing like knowing, to the depths of our being that we can reach, that we are holy. It may take time for our minds to catch up with our awareness of that, sometimes many years if the trauma we've experienced is severe, but even in that, there is a recognition that that is what's happening. We have crossed a threshold, and we exist in a different world when our divinity becomes an aspect of our lived experience. I know firsthand that heart meditation can facilitate that.

Exercise

Begin a daily heart meditation practice, starting with five minutes a day and adding a minute per week (but only increasing the time if you meditate regularly and feel ready and inspired to). I recommend capping your daily meditation practice at an hour a day unless you are working with a teacher or feel strongly guided to do more.

Note: if you try meditation and it isn't a fit for you, I encourage you to explore other ways of fostering an everyday connection with Spirit. For example, you could begin a practice of singing spiritual songs, performing devotional rituals, or touching your heart once an hour or so while imagining warm, golden light within. I believe there is a path to Spirit available to everyone, and if seated meditation isn't part of yours, another inroad can be found.

The Amazing Powers of Spirit

There are many other aspects of our relationship with Spirit that we haven't explored, far more than can be covered in a book and perhaps even experienced in a lifetime. One that merits addressing is our power to manifest healing and other things by virtue of how we think. Our thoughts and feelings are composed of energy, the energy of Spirit, and this energy is part of the universe's process of creating and becoming. Because of how the universe works, what we offer with our minds, consciously and subconsciously, influences what appears in our experience. It shapes our reality and creates within it, which can happen internally and externally. This is popularly referred to as the Law of Attraction in New Thought and is seen as a facet of magic in some traditions (magic can be defined and conceptualized in additional or fundamentally different ways too).

On the psychological level, we can see this in action in the way that how we think forms and sustains the thought-dependent realities of the world. Though that process isn't about drawing things to us or creating by some kind of ethereal force, it does acknowledge that the popular saying "You create your reality" has ample truth to it, even when taken secularly. It is also my experience that what we focus on with our minds becomes a bigger part of our psychological makeup and therefore a greater part of our respective thought-dependent realities. The plants we water in our inner gardens grow the most vigorously, whether they are nourishing herbs or weeds.

Metaphysically speaking, when we think about things, particularly with strong or focused emotion, we emit psychic energy that influences what manifests in our reality, with those things often appearing in some fashion. This can be literal, like thinking of a kitten and being offered one the next day, or more broadly related, where events match the tone of our thoughts and emotions, like a gray day that seems doomed from start to finish. There are various theories regarding how this works and how powerful we are, with a basis for it appearing in some form in many ancient religions, but everyone I know who has seriously practiced magic involving focused thought or tried to work with the Law of Attraction has seen this process in action. Whether it's visualizing a pink car and encountering one a few days later or intending for healing and then seeing a flyer for a workshop that becomes the ideal next step on our healing journey, there is something to this.

Some skeptics believe that manifestation can be written off as the psychological process of tending to see things in our environment once we prime ourselves to notice them. For instance, when we decide to change jobs, our subconscious minds perk up in a way where we're more likely to register "help wanted" signs in our neighborhood. In this case, if those signs were already there, it could be argued that we simply became more selectively aware of our surroundings. While that may be true of some situations, magic practitioners will affirm that there is far more to the process of manifesting than this. I'll share one example, but really, the best way to see if there is anything to manifestation is to practice it by sincerely studying manifestational magic or New Thought teachings, applying time-tested techniques, and seeing what happens as you become proficient in them.

When I decided to move to San Francisco, I faced a few challenges and opted to actively involve magic in the process because of that. First, I was going to have to break the lease on my apartment in the suburbs or find someone to take it over, which would've been costly if I didn't locate a new tenant before moving. I was worried about that and also the possibility of spending far more money on rent in the city. As I designed the spell for the new apartment, I put a few potentially difficult stipulations into it: I wanted my rent to remain about the same or be less, I wanted to find someone to take my apartment so I didn't have to pay double rent, I wanted the process to be smooth, and I wanted whoever took over my apartment to be a good fit for it. I also wanted to be a fifteen-minute walk or less from my favorite grocery store.

At that time, rents in San Francisco were exorbitant and it was the off season for renting in the suburbs, which meant there was a strong chance I would struggle to rent my apartment for two to three months or longer. I kept the faith, though, and diligently added energy to the spell each morning. Within a couple of weeks, a friend introduced me to someone at a bar he'd met that day who was moving out of a rent-controlled one-bedroom apartment that met all my criteria and was in a neighborhood that was on my list. I signed the lease for it the same day that a young couple who were denied every other apartment they applied to signed the lease for my old apartment, and I ended up paying lower rent (with utilities included!).

Many people were shocked by this because San Francisco had an extremely competitive rental market then that made it difficult to procure a unit, not to mention one that was more affordable than an apartment in the suburbs. Having practiced magic for decades at that point though, I knew that these things could happen. If moving to San Francisco aligned with the highest good, which is a condition I always put in my magic (that I only want to manifest what's good for me and others), and my stipulations were attainable, a way to move there would appear, and it did. I trusted in the divine to respond with what was best for me, and if that wasn't moving to San Francisco, with these provisos or at all, I would've accepted that too (and I would've determined this by the spell not panning out and performing a tarot reading about it).

Many of us who believe in the highest good believe that we are all involved in a process of spiritual evolution across lifetimes. Sometimes not having a desire fulfilled is what's in our highest good, which means that what we wanted didn't align with the trajectory of our spiritual evolution at that time. The experience of not getting it, of disappointment, frustration, and the like, can also be important for us to go through in our spiritual development. If divination suggests that it was better for me that a spell not succeed, I do my best to accept its failure, let the intention go for now, and try to learn and grow from the experience (and for significant spells, I usually do divination beforehand to see if they are beneficial for me to even attempt). There are hundreds of stories of manifestation like the one about this apartment in my life, to varying degrees of magnitude, as there usually are in the lives of diligent practitioners of manifestational magic and New Thought techniques. We practice magic because it works.

What does this mean for inner gardening? We want to think in ways that support our well-being, not just because that will help us feel better, but also because that will bring conditions, circumstances, and things into our lives that feel good to us and foster our wellness journey. We will inevitably have a host of thoughts each day, and through being intentional with our thinking, we can harness it to get our innate magic on our side in realizing our hopes and dreams. This will make us likelier to notice opportunities around us to aid in their manifestation, and it will draw things to us that do the same, as well as incline us to feel more confident in our ability to make the most of what comes to us. We don't even need to cast spells or perform affirmations to do this. Though I do work formal magic, I see ample evidence of my thought content manifesting apart from that simply because I keep my inner garden well cultivated and prioritize aligning with Spirit.

This doesn't mean we need to only think positive, supportive thoughts all the time, and we will explore in part 3 how harmful trying to force ourselves to do that can be. But within the bounds of what feels like it honors where we are, it's important to strive to have the overall tone of our thoughts resonate with what we're trying to create and sustain in our lives. This is particularly critical to remember with thoughts we think often or that have a substantial amount of emotional intensity. This is because when it comes to manifestation, my experience is that the greatest results emerge from either the collective momentum of frequent medium-energy thoughts that resonate with each other or the sheer power of intense ones that overshadow our everyday thinking. Ideally, we want to harness the power of both, which we do in our work here by practicing compassionate thinking (the former) and affirmations (the latter). A side benefit of compassionate thinking is that it supports the manifestation of our healthy intentions, particularly as we deepen in the practice, and there is no need to focus on positive thinking if we are cultivating a compassionate mindset. Compassionate thinking organically guides our thoughts to a supportive place most of the time.

Some people fear the power of their thoughts when they learn about this phenomenon. The good news is that most of the time, we think in ways that perpetuate where we currently are in our lives, as status quo thinking reinforces the status quo. Unless we start thinking radically differently, what we manifest will tend to align with what's already there. Additionally, it is my experience that there is almost always a gap of time between when we emanate something and when it manifests in some form in our reality. Though the length of this gap can vary significantly, there is usually an opportunity to offer a counter emanation to something we are worried about manifesting. Many of us do this unconsciously by giving our attention to a host of other thoughts and things each day, which can dissipate, redirect, or dilute the energy behind the initial emanation to the point of stopping the manifestation. When our minds are cluttered with myriad thoughts about many subjects, as most of ours are, each thought tends to have less individual power to manifest. Unless a thought is part of a broader collection of thoughts that resonate with each other, it will probably not have much of a manifestational effect. It's when we learn to concentrate and align mental and emotional energy with an intention, which meditation and affirmation practice teach us how to do, that the creative power of our thoughts becomes increasingly evident.

Some people who have intrusive thoughts from mental illness fear that those thoughts will manifest negative outcomes in their lives, and as someone who has intrusive thoughts, I understand this concern. In these cases, the more we tell ourselves that these thoughts are a symptom of a disorder and not the truth (no matter how true they feel), the less of an issue this becomes (and again, if our status quo is one of having intrusive thoughts, our current reality already reflects the impact of that and won't boldly change simply from learning about this phenomenon). Along these lines, I think it's important to clarify, though, that I do not believe this process is nearly as black and white or extreme as some spiritual teachers make it out to be: for instance, when it sounds like we're doomed if we think a negative thought, we can materialize treasures from thin air, and all illnesses derive from our mental patterns. I also do not believe that everything that appears in our experience is the direct result of our thinking and that if we always think positively, only good-feeling things will manifest for us. This is one of the most controversial issues within these types of ideas because of the danger that can come when they are taken to extremes.

Layers of Complexity within Creation

When teachers make grandiose claims that everything that manifests in our experience is a consequence of what we think, including illnesses, that can turn into victim blaming and disregarding science. Those beliefs lead some people to refuse medical treatments that are frequently effective for the illnesses they have and die because they believed they could heal themselves with thought alone. While I wouldn't say that's always impossible, even in theory that requires a level of concentration and single-mindedness that most of us don't have without years of training and practice. These beliefs also cause some people to ignore the suffering of the world and systems of oppression because they believe they have no responsibility for anyone's life but their own. People sometimes turn away from others who are ill, impoverished, or otherwise in need because of these beliefs, thinking it is harmful to be around anything they perceive as "negative." It's as if that will infect their minds with negativity that then manifests negative conditions in their lives. These beliefs can incline people to think that their actions only affect themselves or that others who are harmed inadvertently by their actions manifested that, so they're off the hook of social responsibility. In their extreme form, these beliefs lead some people to blame themselves for manifesting their own oppression. Then they work to shift their mindset, but the oppression doesn't disappear because they didn't manifest it to begin with.

I think the big picture of creation is far more complicated than this, with many factors that can be involved in what manifests in our experience, though our offering is one of them. In the case of illness, I have experienced that what we think can powerfully influence the way our bodies feel and the process of illness, at least in some instances. I also believe mental patterns may contribute to illness sometimes, perhaps even to the point of being among the causes, but not always. There are several health conditions in my life that I suspect came into being like this because it is as if there is a target on one region of my body connected with emotional trauma. The conditions have appeared as I try to heal from it, one after the other, with no apparent interconnection besides the "coincidence" of where they are located. This has gone on like clockwork for over sixteen years, to where it is hard for me to believe the emotional trauma has nothing to do with this, and I believe this trauma is centered in my subconscious mind as much as my body. We know that trauma can be a major cause of, or factor in, mental illness and that early childhood trauma is linked to an increased risk for a variety of health problems, including heart disease, diabetes, and even cancer.[4] We also know that chronic stress is thought to contribute to many health conditions, mental and physical. In light of this, is it so far-fetched to think that the psychological impact of the trauma I went through is partially responsible for the health conditions I've experienced in the area of my body most related to it? And that others might have experienced something similar?

I think myriad other factors can be involved in the generation of illness, though, some of which are part of inherent reality, like pollution, diet, physical activity level, genetics, and the fact that diseases are part of the natural world. For example, I have had obsessive-compulsive disorder (OCD) since early childhood. This is before I experienced the bullying that gave me post-traumatic stress disorder and is possibly at the root of my major depressive episodes and more generalized experiences of anxiety. Having OCD was simply part of me. It's just how I was.

Additional factors beyond these that could contribute to illness (or other things that manifest in our experience) relate to the way we cocreate reality with our fellow humans. We contribute to greater manifestation processes that we have a limited ability to influence yet are subjected to by virtue of being involved with them, like how a cell is affected by what happens in the body it's a part of. Societies, cultures, and communities are all examples of this, where group manifestations happen en masse, and differing degrees of privilege and power within groups can be doled out according to how they operate. I also believe in karma, often described in a simplified form as being the law of cause and effect across our lifetimes, which is a factor in what manifests in our lives, if not the most significant one. Karma is more complicated than most Westerners have learned about and is outside the scope of this book to explore in depth. It is something we can work through on the spiritual path, which is a central focus

---

4. Dawn M. Holman, Katie A. Ports, Natasha D. Buchanan, Nikki A. Hawkins, Melissa T. Merrick, Marilyn Metzler, and Katrina F. Trivers, "The Association Between Adverse Childhood Experiences and Risk of Cancer in Adulthood: A Systematic Review of the Literature," *Pediatrics* 138, supplement 1 (November 2016): S81–S91, doi:10.1542/peds.2015-4268L.

in traditional yoga, and some might even describe the bulk of the path as being about that, but how karma unfolds is beyond the comprehension of the rational mind. This does mean, though, that there will always be a portion in the overall picture of what manifests in our lives that stems from the past, including before we were born.

Many people also believe in grace, which can be conceptualized as "divine intervention," where regardless of what we're emanating, the divine can intercede positively in our lives (even if that doesn't feel positive to us in the moment). Relatedly, many believe that events manifest in our lives as part of a greater evolutionary process of our souls and beyond, as I mentioned earlier, or that there is a higher order and purpose in what occurs (e.g., "everything happens for a reason"). For people who believe things like this, what appears at times may not only contrast with what they were offering with their minds, but it is important for them to experience that in a grander sense as part of their spiritual development. Even if on a personal level, the experience is not one they would choose to have. Those of us who study astrology have also found a correlation between events on the personal, communal, and societal levels and the motion of the planets and their geometric relationships to each other. This validates the Hermetic axiom "as above, so below," and while there is wide divergence in opinion regarding the degree to which we have a say in how this process unfolds in our lives, for people who study it, its relevance is self-evident. In my life, many major events, including illnesses, and seemingly inexplicable emotional states have lined up with the planetary placements and cycles and their connection to my birth chart, even when I had no awareness of them.

I think some manifestations and illnesses arise from a multitude of factors like these, and perhaps they all do. Maybe our offering is always just one thread in a tapestry of creation. Though some teachers insist that we create every element of our experience individually with our thoughts, I have yet to see anyone offer persuasive evidence to support that. This doesn't mean we don't have an amazing ability to manifest, though. This needn't be so extreme.

Many mystics have taught that the causation of creation is beyond the grasp of our intellects. We can't even imagine the size of the universe, and the greatest scientific minds boggle trying to work out quantum physics. Those of us who consistently practice magic can usually see an impact from our work, but this is one gear in a universe of moving parts. We influence a bit of that process (and in some cases, a seemingly immense bit if we limit ourselves to the human scale), but we neither control it nor are in charge of it, save that we, like everything, are cells in the body of Spirit.

Along these lines, I enjoy thinking of humans as being the activities directors on the cruise ships of our respective lives. Though we have an important job planning events, staging performances, and being the "actor" in our experiences, we are not the captain, engineer, or doctor of our ships. Spirit and our higher selves fill those roles, and at any time, we can seek their aid. A consequence of this is that we needn't try to control every aspect of our experience or lives because that is not, and has never been, our work. Many of us carry the stress and tension of that responsibility though, sometimes without realizing it. While it is important that we develop ourselves to be impeccable with our thoughts, words, and actions as best we can, in alignment with our intentions, we can surrender the rest to the higher power of our understanding. We are in good hands, and creation is far too complex of a subject for there to be much value or legitimacy in blaming ourselves for what manifests in our lives, especially if we have not trained in manifestation techniques.

Even if our mental patterns are involved in the manifestation of illness (or other painful circumstances), that doesn't mean we are to blame for that, any more than we would be for causing the trauma that generated those patterns. If this is how our minds reacted to trauma, that is not our fault. The way we react to trauma is not something we do to ourselves. What else were we realistically supposed to have done in the moment with the understanding, awareness, and capacity we had? There is no reason to feel guilt or shame about situations like this if we believe we are in them, which would also not help us heal. From a place of self-compassion, we do the healing work of shifting the patterns, alongside whatever the medical professionals we work with recommend. If the condition doesn't heal, fully or at all, we are not to blame for that either. We can only do our best, and that is whatever it is. Because this topic is controversial, I want to be crystal clear: I am in no way suggesting something like "people give themselves cancer or become victims of war because of their negative thoughts." I have explored this topic with the complexity that I have in large part to avoid such a misunderstanding, while also feeling a responsibility to honor my compelling experiences with manifesting.

Though I do think our ability to manifest in the physical world is an important and exciting subject to dive into, so is the healing potential of inner gardening apart from that. The psychological well-being we can manifest within ourselves is worth exploring on its own and our primary focus here. I think many people have thrown the baby of New Thought teachings—that we are one with Spirit and supported, guided, and able to improve our lives and create by virtue of that—out with the bathwater of concepts from teachers who blame the victim or are anti-science (which is totally understandable, as those concepts are prevalent and in some traditions, foundational). That is the main reason this section is here. An aim of mine with this book is to rescue that baby so some of the benefits at the heart of New Thought teachings can be experienced by more people. Once removed from harmful extremes, I have found them to be profoundly enriching.

That said, I suggest that folks who are inexperienced with magic and manifesting strive not to unnecessarily limit their beliefs about what is possible. Things like the spontaneous remission of illness do happen, and many people have extraordinary stories of faith and energy healing, so it's important to stay open. Sometimes the cure we manifest, though, is the one we "randomly" come across while going about our day, not an apparent miracle, which is why it's important to be receptive to that type of guidance and physically active approach. Curing an illness by acting on manifested information is still a spiritual healing process. Physical action is usually part of magical workings in some form, like how we must attend a job interview even if we manifested it. I also know that when we decide life isn't magical, that belief is projected out of us onto the world, and that becomes the bulk of what we experience. In terms of what we can influence, nothing has the power to manifest within our experience like our beliefs, in how we psychologically perceive reality and with the metaphysical forces available to us, including the belief that magic isn't real. Conversely, when we practice manifesting with intention regularly, we can start to see so much evidence of it that we don't question its reality anymore, and as that happens, we become vastly more powerful.

The healthiest outlook I know to cultivate in this area is what I call "grounded possibility," which is a middle ground between believing that everything that manifests in our reality comes from our thoughts and nothing does. With grounded possibility, we do the commonsense things in situations given the resources and scientific knowledge available to us while staying open to more. If we get sick, we seek aid from trustworthy professionals, and we can absolutely avail ourselves of the power of visualizations, guided meditations, and so on while doing that. If we need money, we don't wait for it to fall from the sky. If it does, wonderful, but if another avenue to it is before us, like a part-time job, we take it (and we can see that as a manifestation). Grounded possibility still leaves an opening for miracles, and I have experienced astonishing manifestations while working within this perspective. There is a huge difference, though, between believing in miracles and expecting that one will happen whenever we will it, to the point where we discard conventional, effective approaches to issues. There is also profoundly less stress and tension in approaching manifesting from the perspective of grounded possibility as contrasted with some of the extreme positions, since we neither blame ourselves for what manifests in our lives nor believe that we should. That said, you are free to believe whatever you want about this, including in greater possibilities than I do. My only recommendation is that the bar not go lower than that of grounded possibility, so there is room for awe, surprise, and unexpected, profound healing.

As I mentioned earlier, divine intelligence is always available to us, providing us with access to insight and understanding beyond our individual minds. This includes a guiding force that each of us has within ourselves, an inner North Star that can help us live in a way that feels satisfying and purposeful to us. As we recognize where the conditioned beliefs we've accumulated over the years cloud our vision and liberate ourselves from them, alongside practicing heart meditation, we can begin to perceive it. Once we learn to trust in what we receive, the inner North Star becomes a helpful beacon we can turn to for the rest of our lives. As we walk toward it, breadcrumbs from Spirit appear that let us know we are moving in the direction of the manifestation of our attainable and beneficial intentions. These breadcrumbs help us understand what to do next, if anything.

No one need take my word for any of this. These experiences are available to anyone who is willing to study manifestational magic or New Thought and diligently perform the techniques they learn with an open mind. You will likely experience some of this organically if you consistently practice inner gardening, heart meditation, and living in alignment with Spirit.

Exercises

Journal about any experiences you have had with manifestational magic, the Law of Attraction, or synchronicity. Have you ever thought of someone right before they called you, for example, or thought of something obscure and then seen it out in the world during the next few days? Have you consciously tried to manifest something? If so, what happened? Reflect on what you believe is possible in terms of manifestation and where that belief came from. If you feel like you can't occupy a state of grounded possibility, what keeps you from that? Is that something you might want to or be able to change?

Once you have practiced inner gardening and meditation for three months, write down every synchronistic event you notice in your life each day over the course of a month. At the end of the month, journal about this experience. If nothing significant comes of this, wait three more months and try it again.

Chapter 3
Preparing Ourselves for the Journey

I see the process of inner gardening as involving three phases. During the first phase, when we are beginners, the information and skills we learn are usually novel. Many folks are skeptical about how well (or if) these skills will work for them. It can feel like a big production to pay attention to the thoughts, emotions, and behavioral patterns we have throughout the day, as well as to question some of those thoughts and affirm new ones in their place. Not to mention to take those thoughts, emotions, and behavioral patterns in sum and try to see if there are any subconscious core beliefs at play in them, which we may then question as well. Many people stop at this phase. In my experience, this often has to do with either not having the capacity or motivation to do this work (e.g., some people are too depressed to do it) or doubting it could help them or in their ability to change. To aid with that, please keep in mind that this work is not nearly as cumbersome as it may seem once we get used to it, which can require as little as a few weeks of solid effort for some people. Additionally, inner gardening needn't be taken to extremes to see benefit from it.

Even some sincere work a few times a week can yield compelling results, provided that work is done consistently.

The second phase comes after folks have diligently challenged their unsupportive thoughts and beliefs and affirmed new ones long enough to be so good at it that it becomes like a reflex. It stops feeling like work to question thoughts and replace them, and the process almost seems to run itself most of the time. Inner gardening gets faster as we go because, despite what some of us may believe, our psychological makeup is usually not that complicated. Painful things happened to us in our lives, we were led by indirect messaging to believe we are deficient, we received harmful messaging directly from others, and so on, and that causes us to think and act in ways that don't support our well-being. On top of that, we've probably done some things we regret that stick with us, often as a consequence of living through those experiences, which also influences how we think and act. With practice, it takes less and less time to recognize these dynamics playing out within us and to challenge the unsupportive thoughts and beliefs involved in that, sometimes eventually happening in just seconds.

The third phase occurs after we've practiced diligently for long enough that we don't have distorted or otherwise unsupportive thoughts the vast majority of the time. Our minds almost never go there anymore because what's the point? We'll just dismantle each thought and belief and affirm healthy thoughts in their place. At this stage, we've also practiced thinking compassionately long enough that our inner monologue and self-talk defaults to compassion. We speak to ourselves like a close friend or loved one most of the time and cut ourselves the same slack, and the effects of this are wonderful.

In my experience, there is no standard speed at which people move through these phases, though the most significant factor in accelerating the process that I've seen is consistent, diligent application of the skills. Every time we have a strong difficult emotion (a difficult emotion is any emotion that feels difficult to you), we have an opportunity to practice this. Sometimes we discover that the thoughts and beliefs involved in an emotional reaction are justified and accurate. We leave those be. Otherwise, we garden within.

One of the pitfalls about the third phase, which can be tricky, is that it can cause us to rest on our laurels, and over time, beliefs that hinder our well-being can creep back in, like weeds overtaking an area in our inner garden. This is usually because we have deep trauma related to a subject, those beliefs were reinforced within us for many years, or we continue to experience environmental influences that reinforce them. In the toughest situations, beliefs often resist being released for all these reasons. For example, one issue we'll explore in this book is body image. Most of us will continue to live in environments with media and advertising that suggest that our bodies are not okay as they are, so it will probably not be enough to challenge the beliefs we have related to this a few times. That may be an ongoing process, and if we have trauma in this life domain from how we were treated growing up, the beliefs will also likely be hard to shake for that reason.

In my experience, healing from trauma is generally like a spiral (and when the process is too intense, it is best to do it with a professional, assuming we can). We work on it, make progress, and seem to be doing much better, and then it comes back up again. If we were diligent in our healing efforts, it usually doesn't return with the same force over our psyche that it used to hold, but that doesn't mean it isn't still extremely powerful. It may also come back with the same force at times, and this doesn't mean we weren't working hard and well. It's just part of the process. Either way, our work remains the same. We dismantle the unhealthy thoughts and conscious and subconscious beliefs that are present within the trauma-based emotional reaction, affirm new healthy thoughts in their place, and take loving care of ourselves.

For issues like these, it is probably good to have a regimen of affirmative thinking that we practice frequently enough for this topic not to fully leave our awareness, provided that feels healthy (and remember: we are affirming the desired change, not revisiting the harmful condition or experiences). This could involve rereading the related chapters in this book every other week, reciting specific affirmations daily, or both. Some of these issues may abide with us for a long time, perhaps even the rest of our lives, but that doesn't mean we can't find profound improvement from where we are, more than enough to make our efforts worthwhile. The healthy thoughts we affirm will become conscious and subconscious beliefs within us, and this will increase our well-being, even if they compete indefinitely with persistent beliefs that originate from trauma.

Navigating Resistance to the Process

Inner gardening is a process that features peaks and valleys, which we all experience to some degree. When we're in valley moments, feeling things like disappointment in our efforts or frustrated by our apparent lack of progress, nothing is gained from kicking ourselves for being down. That usually does little else than make us feel worse, and it can also cause us to lose confidence in our ability to garden within, which we want to avoid because valley moments inevitably occur. They come with the package of working on ourselves. It's critical to be kind to ourselves in those moments while learning from the experience and planning next steps that seem healthy and realistic. Perhaps we feel unhappy about how well we're practicing the tools from this book. If that's the case, we can seek to understand what our lackluster performance is about and resolve to try to do better in the future in a way that takes what happened before into account. If that doesn't pan out, this material may be too much of a stretch from where we are right now or simply not a fit, and that happens. It's possible that we need more accountability too, like getting coaching, or a greater level of assistance in processing our thoughts and emotions, like from going to therapy.

There is nothing wrong with needing either of these things or needing help in general. I benefitted profoundly in my healing journey and spiritual training from working with people who held me accountable and helped me through the rockiest moments of unpacking the trauma I had. Having the secure base of a therapist figure facilitated my opening up and learning to love and trust again. If you feel stuck or stagnant in your healing journey, that can also be a cue to explore other avenues of healing, like bodywork or hatha yoga.

Given the challenges that can come from inner gardening, it's important to consider how to pace ourselves with it. My general recommendation is this: push yourself hard enough that you stretch outside of your comfort zone, but not so hard that this can turn into one more reason to feel not good enough. Be realistic with yourself about what you have the capacity to do as well, and then build from there. Rather than push too hard and stop, it is better to start small with actions we can consistently perform that become a sturdy foundation we can stand upon.

Additionally, recognize that when we stretch outside of our comfort zone, we are bound to have times when we stumble or are uncomfortable because of facing novel terrain, and this can be a sign of progress, not failure. We may not be where we want to be with something, but we might be well on our way there, even if it doesn't feel like that. When we break through to the other side, we recognize that skinning our knees was simply part of the process of learning. Also, it's important to have resting times when we celebrate how far we've come so this process doesn't feel like an endless uphill climb. For some of us, this work includes learning to hear the voice within telling us when to rest (you will perceive it if you make a habit of asking yourself what you need). This journey is for you, and it is about well-being.

We each have a part of us that resists changes in our lives, often even when these changes are positive, which many spiritual traditions call the ego. The ego seeks to maintain our status quo in the name of keeping us safe, particularly when faced with changes that involve the unknown or known pain we want to avoid experiencing again. Most of the time, it would rather stay in an uncomfortable or unhealthy circumstance than risk something worse. This aspect of ourselves was critical in the ancient world, where danger lurked around many corners, but it's far less helpful today. The ego can drain our motivation, make us feel frustrated, impel us to procrastinate, and even make us feel under the weather as it endeavors to keep our world contained in a manner that feels safe to it. It gets stirred up by inner gardening because of how transformative the process can be, but as we persevere with our practices, it usually calms down. It can be quite assertive at any time, though.

Most people don't encounter this aspect of themselves much because they don't make significant changes often. We can see it clearly, though, in the huge resistance so many of us experience when we set New Year's resolutions, especially if those are big stretches outside of our comfort zones. Some of that is just the standard resistance that comes with establishing a new habit or trying to stop an old one, but once we learn to spot the ego, we can see it there too.

Other aspects of the ego as it's conceptualized in many spiritual traditions include that it's our individual personality and the identity created by our minds (i.e., the things that make us feel separate from the divine whole), which is important to explore on a mystical path. For inner gardening, the main part of the ego to be aware of is the facet that seeks to sabotage change efforts, and the most important thing to do about this is stay cognizant that the ego has that agenda. If we decide to read an affirmative talk aloud once a day, for example, and suddenly find that after a few days, we keep forgetting to do it, that's probably the ego. If we start noticing that we're phoning our affirmations in, there it is again. Our work in those moments is to acknowledge what's happening, recognize that the ego is trying to protect us (even if in a way that contrasts with what we want), and affirm our intention for how we want to act moving forward. Then we can create a plan, where necessary, to hold to the path we've identified to support our efforts.

It can also be helpful to ask ourselves if there are any conscious or subconscious fears we might have related to the changes we're making that could be causing us to sabotage ourselves. If we identify some, that is something to affirm about. For instance, I might be afraid of the freedom I would likely feel if I truly loved myself and what I might do with it, and that can stand in the way of my self-love journey, manifesting as procrastination. Once I recognize this fear, I can address it with compassionate thinking and affirmations. We'll explore self-sabotage in greater depth in part 3.

Otherwise, one of the most powerful ways I know to navigate resistance to doing something, including inner gardening, is to clarify why it is important for us to do it. What benefits do we see it potentially bringing into our lives? Why is this a good idea for us? Getting clear about the "whys" behind actions we intend to take can help build energy and motivation for performing them and addressing whatever resistance comes up. When we lack this clarity or feel more ambivalent about doing something, it can be harder to see it through. We will focus on this more in the upcoming exercise to help build motivation for inner gardening.

We mustn't let the resistance we experience stop us from our inner work unless we feel pushed too hard or in need of extra help. For the former, we can take a gentler approach, and for the latter, we can seek a way to get it. I've seen the skills in this book facilitate tremendous healthy change in people's lives, even some with severe persistent mental illness who were written off by others. The common denominator when that happened was diligent practice and application of the techniques, hope for improvement, and a willingness to change.

It's also important to prioritize feeling our connection with Spirit. Spirit is always within us, ready to catch us, support us, and guide us as we align with it. As I mentioned earlier, aligning with Spirit and developing discernment helps us become able to receive information from divine intelligence. The ego can pose some challenges to this though, as it may try to warp what we perceive for its own ends: for example, by telling us what we want to hear (or don't want to hear) to keep us within our comfort zones, in a voice that sounds like our intuition. Divination systems like tarot, oracle cards, and runes can provide a wonderful means of navigating this and honing our ability to receive guidance from divine intelligence. In tarot, for instance, the relatively set yet flexible meanings of individual cards prevent our ego from totally dictating our interpretations, and they give us launching pads for developing our intuitive abilities. Over time, we tend to organically shift from studied interpretations of card meanings to our inner knowing, assuming we make space for our intuitive insights as we practice. As our discernment strengthens through inner gardening, we can trust that the information we receive is from divine intelligence, rather than stemming from egoic fear or desire, social conditioning, anxiety, trauma, prejudice, and so on. Or at least we will have a sense of when the latter factors are at play or could be. I have practiced divination for decades, and when I feel like I'm too invested in the answer to a question I seek guidance about, I still use a tool like tarot or even work with a reader who can be more objective.

> Exercise
> Journal about your motivation for undertaking this work. Why is it important to you to perform inner gardening? What value do you see in it? What results do you hope to gain from it? Put this document in an accessible place and refer to it for inspiration when the inner gardening process is difficult.

Gardening within the Shadow

Inner gardening can include moments that are quite painful. Many if not most of us have a tendency to avoid or deny what is painful and grew up in environments where we weren't taught how to process difficult emotions and painful situations healthfully. We may stuff down the things about ourselves that we don't want to believe, create facades to help us navigate the world (sometimes to the point where we don't realize we're doing that), or suppress the painful experiences we don't know how to deal with. This can all lead to stress and a variety of physical and mental health problems, as well harmful behaviors toward self and others. It also results in a considerable amount of material hanging out in our shadow. The concept of the shadow comes from the work of Carl Jung, and with my clients, I simplify it, conceptualizing the shadow as being the region of ourselves that we seldom see, where what we tend to avoid or deny usually dwells. As we do the healing work in this book, which involves being honest with ourselves and facing areas of life that can be difficult, some of what's in our shadow will likely surface in the resistance we feel to loving ourselves and improving our lives. This resistance can include standard ego resistance, but it can be a consequence of suppressed emotion or buried wounds being exposed too. We may feel a host of difficult emotions: anger, sadness, jealousy, overwhelm, insecurity, and more.

When this happens, it's critical to be compassionate with ourselves and practice self-care as we introspect into our emotions to understand what they're about, being mindful not to fall into the fundamental attribution error with regard to ourselves. I remember how awful I felt when I was getting to know what was in my shadow and realized how jealous and competitive I was. I was told I was less than or worthless so often while growing up that I became oriented in a way to prove that I had value, almost obsessively, but I tended to only see this in myself when I felt threatened. In those moments, I would kind of defensively either shrug off or disregard these thoughts and emotions. It was profoundly helpful to recognize that these thoughts and emotions were there and how they stemmed from my past trauma. As I understood that and addressed them with affirmations and compassionate thinking, my relationship to them, and what I felt, began to change. I went from a state of not even consciously appreciating that I was jealous and competitive to seldom if ever feeling like that, all because of inner gardening and aligning with Spirit.

One way to practice compassion and self-care with ourselves is to treat ourselves like a loved one as best we can, which we can do by imagining we are supporting a dear friend with our exact circumstances. Many of us are harsh with ourselves, yet kind and understanding with our loved ones, so we know how to do that. We just don't do it with ourselves. What might you say to a dear friend in your situation? Does it make sense for them to feel or think as you do based on what they've lived through? How would you treat them? Would they deserve to be cared for? Would they deserve healing? Of course they would, and so do you.

Difficult emotions are a natural part of life. There is nothing wrong with us for having them. The important thing is to learn how to do so in a healthy way. Have you had the experience of being upset and comforted by a friend? Who listened to you and talked you through it until you were soothed and able to see things in a more grounded light? Part of this work is learning how to do this for ourselves, and we can. If you try to do this and feel like it's not working, experiment with talking to yourself like a loved one out loud. That can make an enormous difference.

> ### Exercise
> The next time you feel a difficult emotion, journal about how you would speak to a dear friend in the same situation. Write this journal entry as a letter, and after you finish writing it, write your name at the top and read it aloud to yourself. Afterward, journal about how this process felt and any insights it brought up for you.

Meeting Difficult Emotions with Relaxation, Mindfulness, and Compassion

When our difficult emotional reactions feel overwhelming or debilitating, that is not because it is the nature of most difficult emotional reactions to feel that way. Though some inherent emotional states are extremely difficult, this is what happens when we tend to suppress and not healthfully process our emotions: they build up and can explode in our faces. This can be a consequence of trauma too, and it is also what happens when we exacerbate our emotional reactions with thought, engaging in distorted, unsupportive thinking that blows situations out of proportion. To that end, Jill Bolte Taylor, a prominent neuroanatomist, shared in her book *My Stroke of Insight* that the chemical process of an emotional reaction runs its course in our bodies in ninety seconds or less.[5] What we feel beyond that stems from how we sustain or develop the emotional reaction with thought. When we regularly process our difficult emotions in healthy ways, they are usually not volcanic or troublesome. We become more like young children who cry hysterically, get it out of their system, and move on.

When I work with clients in therapy on healthfully processing difficult emotions, we generally develop the skills of relaxation and mindfulness first. This is to help us soothe ourselves enough to address situations in

---

5. Jill Bolte Taylor, *My Stroke of Insight* (New York: Plume, 2009), 153.

a more centered frame of mind. In a state of heightened emotion, like anger or sadness, we are less likely to really hear the comforting, compassionate words that will help us navigate a situation and see it clearly. The thoughts that feel truest to us are usually ones that resonate with our emotional state, which is part of why we see people have extremely negative thoughts about themselves that feel true while they're depressed but that they don't believe while feeling well. So we begin with self-soothing. Once we feel more calm and collected, we engage with the thoughts and beliefs involved in how we feel.

We covered relaxation in chapter 2. Mindfulness is a witnessing state rooted in the present moment that is non-conceptual and non-judgmental. What this means in practice is that when we are being mindful, we focus solely on being aware, without imposing thoughts or labels onto what we perceive. If we mindfully eat, for example, we pay attention to the process of eating itself as best we can, simply witnessing what occurs. We don't identify with thoughts and feelings like "this tastes delicious" or "I'm starved." Instead, we observe them and whatever else comes up in the experience. Mindfulness practice has its origins in yoga and Buddhism, and it can be performed in a multitude of circumstances.

There is a witnessing presence or awareness within our consciousness that is deeper than our thoughts and feelings. By practicing mindfulness, we acquaint ourselves with this presence. At the beginning of mindfulness practice, many if not most of us have never experienced this part of ourselves on its own. It has always been tied to our thoughts and feelings, forming what feels like a seamless unit. In reality, this witnessing presence and our thoughts and feelings are more like two clasped hands that have never been apart. As we practice mindfulness, which involves observing our thoughts and feelings with some detachment, these hands separate, and as our thoughts and feelings move away from our center, we open to the witnessing presence within. Over time, we experience, as in meditation, that what we perceive within our depths is more fundamental to what we are than our thoughts and feelings. While they fluctuate and wax and wane, this witnessing presence is persistent and something we can turn to when feeling unsteady. Awareness of this witnessing presence is a threshold to perceiving Spirit directly, and some believe this presence is Spirit itself. At minimum, when we connect with Spirit in meditation, we can also usually feel it while we're in a mindful state. The more we practice mindfulness, the more adept we become at it, and the greater our ability to rest our awareness in the witnessing presence within whenever we choose to.

As we learn to see our thoughts and feelings with a degree of detachment, we experience them in a novel manner, and they tend to hold less thrall on our mental state. After all, a bonfire is far scarier if we are inches from it as opposed to watching it from twenty feet away. This new relationship with what we think and feel can help us process our thoughts and feelings in healthy ways, as can the soothing effect that is generally a byproduct of mindfulness. When we step back from what we think and feel and observe it, the intensity of our feelings naturally dies down some, particularly if we remain in that witnessing state, and we tend to feel calmer. The ability to self-soothe and witness that we get from relaxation exercises and mindfulness practice then helps us be with a difficult emotion and move through it rather than be impelled by it into action, which could include harming self or other. We can feel anger, for example, and simply introspect into it rather than angrily text the person who evoked our reaction or we can remove ourselves from the situation enough to explore the anger from a safe distance.

In therapy, I teach clients relaxation before mindfulness, usually via progressive muscle relaxation and breathing exercises. Mindfulness is generally too far of a stretch when someone feels highly anxious, for instance, but it is wonderfully helpful after they calm themselves down some with relaxation exercises. Learning to self-soothe helps us understand that in many if not most situations, self-soothing is a choice and within our power. As I mentioned, the mindfulness techniques we practice then aid us in learning how to get breathing room from our difficult thoughts and emotions. This is not to bypass them, but to facilitate us processing them more healthfully. We don't suppress or avoid what we feel with mindfulness. We just experience it in a different manner. Honoring our emotions doesn't require that we submit our entire being to them.

Once we feel more soothed and collected, we can apply the techniques we reviewed where we examine the thoughts and beliefs at play in an emotion, determine how true they are, understand what they're about, and decide what to affirm in their place, if anything. Until we soothe ourselves, many if not most of us are usually too caught in the emotional intensity for this aspect of the process to be effective. When CBT doesn't work for people, it can be because they weren't taught this order of events. They try to challenge their anxious thoughts, for instance, while feeling extremely anxious, which just feels phony and therefore is unhelpful, perhaps even making the anxiety worse. Another tool that can greatly aid in self-soothing is listening to relaxing music, which we can do while engaging in relaxation exercises and mindfulness practice.

As difficult emotions surface during inner gardening, it's critical to remember that inner gardening fosters our greater well-being, even if it is painful at times. Sometimes a wound must be drained before it can heal, which can hurt quite a bit. This is all just part of the healing process, and the first step in that is usually recognizing that the wound is there. Making a habit of introspecting into difficult emotions is the best way I know to do that.

Otherwise, while it's true that difficult emotions are a natural, healthy part of life, it's also true that we can make matters far worse for ourselves by exacerbating them with thought, and many of us do that. When we think in ways that aren't fact-oriented, accurate, wise, and compassionate, we can pour gasoline on the fire of our difficult emotions: for example, by ruminating about a problem with no end in sight in a manner that is unfairly critical of ourselves or others or otherwise based in unrealistic, unreasonable, or distorted perspectives. Alternatively, we may ruminate in a way that doesn't acknowledge our power to act on behalf of ourselves or we may regularly engage in far-fetched daydreams about how things could've happened differently or might in the future. We can also do this by boarding a train of thought that takes us to dark internal places we've been to many times before and don't realistically need to visit again.

These types of mental behaviors often stem from the modeling and messaging we grew up around or began in response to trauma, and they are normal. Many if not most of us do this to some extent, and that was certainly true of me, though I was on the more extreme end of the spectrum. When I felt anxious about something, I would often fixate on the worst-case scenario and worry about how I would handle it, sometimes for days or weeks. When someone wronged me, I would spend long periods of time daydreaming about what I wished I'd said or done (or would do in the future) to triumph in that situation. I was horribly guilty of thinking I could read other people's minds and understand their motivations, and sometimes would spend hours meandering in a thicket of assumptions that often led nowhere, as it wasn't fact-oriented or accurate. All these habits of thought worked against my well-being, exacerbated my difficult emotions, and were largely if not wholly unproductive. Part of our inner gardening work is recognizing when we do things like this and stopping these habits as best we can. Relaxation, mindfulness, and the compassionate thinking skills in this book have helped many people do this. They have aided me in halting these habits in myself the vast majority of the time, and my life is so much better for that. That said, if the shadow elements that emerge from inner gardening feel too intense or painful for you, I recommend seeking the help of a therapist. We do not have to go through this alone, and working with another may make the difference between learning ideas that feel powerful but that we struggle to apply and harnessing them for profound healing.

Exercises

Practice mindfulness daily until it becomes a state you can enter at will. Doing this can be simple: set a timer for five minutes or so and then simply witness whatever you are doing and the thoughts and feelings that arise within you as you do it. You can also spend moments observing the information

coming in from your senses. Strive not to judge what you perceive or do or to explore your thoughts. Just be in the state
of witnessing as best you can. Some situations in which you
can practice mindfulness include washing dishes, tidying the
home, eating, and going for a walk. To give you a greater sense
of how to do this, if you are mindfully washing dishes, you
would focus on the action of the work while also witnessing
what else comes into your awareness during the process. This
may sound odd, but just try it with that intention and see what
happens. Strive to simply be aware of whatever you perceive.

You can also perform an entire mindfulness meditation
in which, for example, you close your eyes and witness your
breath for a set period of time without identifying with the
practice or conceptualizing any of it.

A Technique for Processing Difficult Emotions

Here is a technique for processing difficult emotions in a healthy way. First,
we go somewhere private and allow ourselves to feel the emotion (or emotions), honoring it for what it is without acting on it. While doing this, we
take care not to judge or criticize ourselves for however we feel, being with
the emotion fully instead and recognizing that its intensity will die down in
about ninety seconds if we don't feed it with thought. Next, we self-soothe
with relaxation exercises and practice mindfulness until we feel centered
enough to explore the emotion. Once we feel ready, we try to discern what
the emotion is about on the surface and deeper levels (and sometimes
this is as simple as "I probably feel down because of the weather"). This
includes figuring out what beliefs and thoughts are involved in or supporting the emotional reaction, where applicable, and we also consider to what
degree we're being reasonable in our thinking. Throughout this process,
we strive to keep our thoughts fact-oriented, accurate, wise, and compassionate, speaking to ourselves as we would a loved one.

When I facilitate this process with clients, I usually ask most of the following questions, many of which are also in the worksheet for challenging
unsupportive thoughts:

- What thoughts and/or beliefs likely evoked this emotion (i.e., what beliefs are in this feeling?)? If it doesn't seem like thoughts or beliefs inspired it, what else might have?

- What desires are present in the emotion, if any? What is it asking for? For example, if you feel angry or sad, what happened that you didn't want to occur, and what did you want to have happen instead?

- What are the facts for and against the thoughts or beliefs you're holding that are involved in this emotional reaction? Include an appreciation of the context of the situation you're in and any relevant history. Does this reaction tie into other experiences you've had in your life? If so, how? Do you remember the first time you had a thought (or thoughts) like this?

- When you get quiet and centered, what does your wisdom say about this?

- What would you say to a dear friend in an identical situation who wanted your honest opinion about it?

- Knowing yourself, what compassionate words would you offer yourself about this?

- What power do you have to improve this situation, where relevant, by shifting your mindset, taking external action, or both? In answering this question, it may be helpful to reflect on the famous "Serenity Prayer" by Reinhold Niebuhr, often paraphrased as: "God, grant me the serenity to accept the things I cannot change, courage to change the things I can, and wisdom to know the difference."

- What can you learn from this experience (assuming this feels like a helpful question)?

During this process of exploration, it may become clear that there are some unsupportive beliefs or thoughts that it would be fruitful to make affirmations about. That can occur at this point, alongside spending some time in meditation to align with Spirit, to whatever degree we can. Then we decide if we want to take any kind of action as a result of this process, and plan how and when to do it. That said, I recommend that people experiencing difficult emotions that have some kind of impulse attached to them wait twenty-four hours before making a firm decision or taking an important action, if that is feasible. Sometimes our perspective changes significantly with time away from the impulse. The impulse itself can also have more to do with wanting to relieve ourselves of the burdensome feeling of a strong emotion than an action being in our best interest.

There are many other methods we can use to process difficult emotions. Journaling has helped me a great deal, I think especially because thoughts tend to look different on a page versus in my mind, and they can be worked with differently there. I find immense value in the clarity I usually get from writing my thoughts out about an issue like I'm drafting a blog post, and then I just never post the piece. Creative outlets like making art, music, and poetry can be beneficial for processing emotion too. We can also try listening to music and watching films that resonate with the emotions we want to process. Some songs and poems have helped me understand my emotions in a deeper manner and experience them more profoundly, which in turn helped me process them.

When we make a habit of processing difficult emotions in compassionate, constructive ways, our emotional reactions tend to even out if they were extreme before. If we were more numb, we tend to feel more, but in a safe, supported manner. The most important thing, in my opinion, isn't that anyone do this in the way I provided here, but rather that we recognize that it's critical to have some kind of process for navigating difficult emotions. Also, this is a case in which over time, the process I outlined becomes faster and less distinct. I don't do all these steps every time. Once they become like second nature, they start to flow in an organic-feeling manner, and what is and isn't needed in the moment becomes self-evident.

Exercises

The next time you experience a difficult emotion, practice this process and then journal about your experience. Also, reflect upon a few times when you felt a powerful difficult emotion in the past and imagine if you had applied this process in those situations. How do you think things may have been different as a result of that?

Keep a mood journal for two weeks, writing down the major emotions you notice during each day. After completing this, reflect on the information gathered and what you can learn from it about yourself and your patterns.

Part 2

The Affirmative Talks

Each chapter in this part features an affirmative talk in which I explore a life domain and common challenges and difficulties people experience within it. I present harmful beliefs that many of us hold to some degree in these areas and some impacts of these beliefs, and then affirm new beliefs and perspectives. These talks see alignment with Spirit, compassion, self-love, and authenticity as being among the most potent healing agents for psychological well-being. Some subjects may include dismantling beliefs that differ from those you were exposed to in your culture, family, community, or society of origin or that otherwise don't reflect your experience. For instance, as a gay Jewish person, there are certain experiences I've had that are particular to being gay and Jewish. Though many of my experiences would still fall under the broader statements in the related chapters that follow, some will not, and I would probably benefit from writing about them specifically. This will likely hold for anyone who has experienced a form of bigotry or oppression in one of the subject areas (or otherwise), and I did not feel that it was appropriate for me to write affirmations that address bigotry or oppression that I haven't experienced. In those situations, write out the harmful beliefs you were exposed to (which is part of the exercises at the end of each chapter) and challenge them using the examples shared in the chapters for guidance. Then incorporate your work into the affirmative talks as a supplement for when you reread them.

Please be aware too that each of the following topics could have entire books written about them. My explorations of them are not meant to be exhaustive, but more to convey a sense of some ways in which we can develop difficulties in the respective areas. Many of the specific issues I highlight have come up in therapy with a significant number of my clients in one way or another, so I imagine others will resonate with them. That said, I also know there are times when the examples I give and perspectives I offer will not apply to everyone equally or sometimes at all, like when I center the experience of people from the United States. If there are additional factors or points

I don't make that you think are important to include, write them out and include them. If you disagree with something I say, voice your disagreement in a manner that helps you move forward with the topic in the direction of well-being. You may also not resonate with the affirmations I share in some sections of the talks. If that happens, write your own in light of the knowledge you have from reading this book and otherwise. It doesn't matter what I believe or find healing. What's important is that you identify thoughts that feel sincere and help you release unhealthy beliefs and feel better and more aligned with the higher power of your understanding.

Otherwise, some points will be made in the following chapters repeatedly or that were made before. This is because each affirmative talk is meant to stand alone and because of what I mentioned earlier about this work being like physical therapy for the mind. It is important to be exposed to these ideas until they seem like second nature to us. One of our goals in this approach is to get the psychological processes behind the illusory truth effect and confirmation bias to work on our behalf. That comes with repeated exposure to the desired new beliefs while feeling that they're true or could be. When addressing a particular issue, I suggest that you read the "Planting New Beliefs" portion of the relevant talk or talks each day for at least thirty days, ideally aloud (you can record yourself and listen to that too or utilize the audiobook when it is available). The more you engage with each talk in a manner that is receptive to the ideas it contains, the truer those ideas will feel for you. As you work through the talks, try to feel the sentiments within them: the empowerment, the alignment, and the harmony.

Finally, some of the ideas presented in the following chapters might be a stretch for you. If they feel too far, this material is not a fit for you at this time, and that is totally valid. Leave it be for a while and work your way up to it with affirmations that don't feel as challenging. If this still doesn't work for you, know that there are plenty of other books and programs to choose from that might suit you better. Also, please note that I have not included trigger or content warnings at the beginning of each chapter. You can assume that if you have trauma in a given subject area, it may surface, as I am going to explore sensitive content (though not in a graphic manner). I also talk in detail about my experience with bullying in the chapter on family and its impact on my mental health, including that I felt suicidal at that time. Please prepare yourself accordingly with a plan for self-care and support, and if you don't already have a sense of what that would entail and feel like it could be something you need, I recommend waiting to explore that chapter or chapters. When compassionate thinking, self-soothing exercises, alignment with Spirit, or other practices bring you to a place where you feel prepared to potentially have some of your trauma surface (or therapy with a professional has), begin that journey.

Chapter 4
Body Image and Body Positivity

Body positivity is the practice of loving and accepting our bodies as they are: appreciating what they do for us and celebrating our appearance. In this chapter, we will explore some of the body negative messaging many of us have received that caused us to have an antagonistic relationship with our bodies. Because this topic can be so loaded for some of us, body positivity may feel like too much of a stretch, and this is part of where the body neutrality movement has come from. Body neutrality is about accepting our bodies and moving the focus away from them, valuing what they do for us in a manner that is divorced from fixating on our appearance. Why be so obsessed with our bodies when we can simply accept them and concentrate on other things instead? Body neutrality may also be a healthier option than body positivity for people who experience body dysmorphia or gender dysphoria or who have an eating disorder. With this topic, my recommendation is to approach it however feels right for you. In a book about self-love, we will unsurprisingly focus on loving our bodies, but if this feels like too much or not a fit for you, know that body neutrality is a powerful, healing option too.

Body image is one of the most common areas of insecurity today. As we grow up, most of us are told in a variety of implicit and explicit manners that our bodies primarily deserve love and affection and are beautiful if they meet a particular standard. Some of us are able to meet that standard or naturally do, but most of us, for a variety of reasons, do not look like that. Generally speaking, what we see a lot of when we are children that is labeled desirable, we internalize as what to aspire to, even if realizing that is unrealistic or impossible for us. Consequently, many if not most of us end up living with dissatisfaction about our bodies for much of our lives, to varying degrees. This issue can be a cause of stress, anxiety, low self-esteem, and depression, among other things. Beauty standards have varied significantly throughout history and between cultures, so it's essentially random if we will live in a culture that views how we naturally look favorably.

Much of what is considered attractive is guided by the fashion world and advertising, and these perspectives are conditioned into us as young people. We are taught to look at what others believe to direct what we think of as beautiful and worthy, and these standards can change quickly. In the nineties, it was considered the height of beauty in mainstream fashion for women to be thin to a degree that is unnatural for most of them. Today, it is to be curvy, but only in a certain way, with some significant variation between cultures and ethnic groups.

Most men once had little to no pressure on them to be super toned or have six-pack abs. Now, that is omnipresent in media and some people even take steroids to achieve a muscular physique. Facial and body hair were out of style in the nineties and early aughts to the point where many men kept their chests shaved. Now, both are fashionable. Once, there was little representation of diversity in media, which affected the self-esteem and self-image of many children from groups that weren't included. There is more representation today, which is helpful, but it can be problematically done, and it often only features members of the groups who fit an ideal body size. Regardless of what the beauty standards of the day are, it is difficult not to internalize them, even when we recognize and live through these fluctuations. On more than one occasion, I've had a client who was strikingly good looking and fit tell me they couldn't stop thinking they weren't attractive enough. Whenever they felt close to being all right with their appearance, the goalpost moved.

Part of this is because of how advertising works. We are bombarded with heavily edited images that can cultivate a sense of inadequacy within us, despite these photos not even containing accurate depictions of people. On top of that, many people also use Botox and have plastic surgery to try to improve their appearance. If anything, the rise of social media has added to this problem because most of the people there are not professional models, and if they can look like that, why can't we? No matter that the main pictures we see are the ones with good lighting and camera angles and that use filters to enhance the desirable aspects of the form.

Food, Sex, and Body Image

Because of the relationship between food and physical appearance, we can't adequately explore body image without talking about food, and because of the relationship between physical appearance and sex in culture, we also must explore sex. Many of us spend years of our lives on diets and planning meals or exercising obsessively, and why? For health reasons? Perhaps to some extent. But mostly? To be desirable, sexually and otherwise. To fit in. To have worth.

Let's be real. Much of this is absurd. Years from now, people will look back at this time and how many of us counted calories and measured our food for decades as if we'd lost our minds. "This is how they spent their lives? They didn't have better things to do?" I can almost hear them saying, "That sounds exhausting and terribly stressful!" And they'll be right. It is. It's stressful whether we're on that rollercoaster of fluctuating personal value or not and feeling guilty or inadequate for not doing more to look better. If we didn't grow up immersed in diet culture, we would see that too, and some of us already do. This is a valuable activity to engage in in general: look at the beliefs that were conditioned into you that seem unhealthy, and then imagine a vastly different and more equitable culture looking back from the future. What might they see and think about them?

Some people might ask, "But isn't it important to focus on health, and isn't being overweight unhealthy? Isn't there an obesity epidemic?" Focusing on health is important, but it's critical to do so in a healthy manner. This means focusing on feeling well and strong within our bodies, not trying to meet an oppressive beauty standard. Some of us will also want a greater degree of fitness than others, and there is nothing wrong with that. In terms of being overweight, that is between a person and their doctor (who understands body positivity in the context of medicine). Otherwise, I believe the obesity epidemic has more to do with systemic issues and societal factors (including body negativity) than self-control and the ability to make healthy choices.[6] If it were mostly about the latter, there wouldn't be such a correlation between it and degree of wealth, culture of origin, and so on. As we release oppressive ideas about body image that we've internalized, practice self-compassion, and learn about nutrition and fitness, we will find a relationship with food and exercise that feels healthier for us and move in that direction as best we can.

I will never forget how my mother, just weeks before she died of cancer, joked of her illness, "Well, I always wanted to be thin." It was totally understandable that she said and felt that—and horrifying. She had dieted for much of her life, beginning when she was a chubby kid who was encouraged to lose weight. She spent many years in a cycle of overeating and crash dieting, which is all too common. Let's be real about that too: being in a cycle of overeating and crash dieting is disordered eating, even if it doesn't meet criteria as a mental health condition. My mother passed her tendency to overeat to me, raising me with the belief that "Childhood is a time when calories don't count" as a reaction to the oppressiveness of her upbringing. By the time I was in middle school, I began binge eating as a reaction to the stress and trauma of being bullied, and by college, I was obese. I lost

6. Alexandra Lee, Michelle Cardel, and William Donahoo, "Social and Environmental Factors Influencing Obesity," Endotext, last modified October 12, 2019, https://www.ncbi.nlm.nih.gov/books/NBK278977/; Adela Hruby and Frank B. Hu, "The Epidemiology of Obesity: A Big Picture," *Pharmacoeconomics* 33, no. 7 (2015): 673–89, doi:10.1007/s40273-014-0243-x.

much of the weight I had gained a few years later, but the dieting that at first helped me lose weight eventually made my binging worse. It catalyzed a cycle in which I would often binge on weekends and then restrict calories during the week to make up for it. I eventually became obese again, then lost much of the weight I gained over the course of a couple years, but my relationship with food throughout that time was agonizing, regardless of what the number on the scale was. So many of us suffer from a toxic relationship with food like this, and I believe that almost never begins with us.

Owning the Pleasures of the Body That We All Deserve

Our bodies naturally know how to eat an appropriate amount of food and stop and when we don't eat that way, it is usually the result of external influences. For example, binge eating disorder begins for many as a direct consequence of restrictive dieting and the deprivation in it, although it persists once the brain develops a habit of seeking the rush of pleasure and release of control that accompanies a binge.[7] This is even likelier to occur with the processed foods that are readily available in the world now, featuring high amounts of fat, sugar, and salt. Many of these foods were engineered to provide optimal pleasure, and they subsequently tend to be craved, some believe to the point of being addictive.[8] Eating them can make healthier, natural foods pale in comparison, and in many communities, processed foods are among the most accessible and convenient. Many of us feel guilt or shame about not having the "willpower" to regulate our eating when companies within the snack industry have literally used science to manipulate our bodies so that we crave their products.

As we grow up in this complicated context of food and body image issues, food can become a source of profound emotional turmoil. Exhausted

7. Kathryn Hansen, *The Brain Over Binge Recovery Guide* (Columbus, GA: Camellia Publishing, 2016), 9–13.
8. Pingfan Rao, Raymond L. Rodriguez, and Sharon P. Shoemaker, "Addressing the Sugar, Salt, and Fat Issue the Science of Food Way," *npj Science of Food* 2, no. 12 (July 2018): n.p., doi:10.1038/s41538-018-0020-x.

by worrying about what we eat, many of us overeat to feel better but then immediately feel worse, as we might gain weight or harm our health. Eating can feel like an indiscretion, like cheating on a spouse, and yet, eating is one of the most pleasurable aspects of the human experience for many of us. Food is also used to comfort us from the day we're born, and it is often a central part of familial and cultural traditions and celebrations. There is nothing wrong with turning to food for pleasure, comfort, and connecting with others, and many see family recipes as a nourishing tie to their ancestors. The problem comes when our relationship with food is dysfunctional.

How would it be, though, if we just allowed ourselves to revel in the pleasure of eating? To focus on each meal with the relish of a lover's touch as best we can? The idea of owning the pleasure of eating terrified me when I first heard it. "What if I just eat myself into health problems and binge every day?" I thought, and I also worried about gaining weight, which is unsurprising given the rampant body negativity where I come from. What I found, though, was that my fears were ill-founded. As I put my phone away, closed my computer, and spent time wholly focused on the pleasure of eating, I felt more satisfied by my meals, less deprived, and more conscious. Eating turned into a meditative experience, and this great source of comfort and pleasure in my life that had seemed irrevocably linked to shame started feeling like a positive experience. As this happened, while I ate a sufficient, nutritionally balanced amount of food and looked at my urges to binge as being a habit that had been reinforced rather than a deeper part of me (which is the essence of the revolutionary Brain Over Binge system by Kathryn Hansen), those urges faded.[9] The way to a healthier relationship with food wasn't to hide from it, but to admit to myself how much I loved it, give myself permission to savor it, accept my body more, and stop dieting. I still overate sometimes, but this usually happens from a place of intention (like on a holiday) and isn't the source of stress it was before.

Otherwise, when it comes to sex, I've had many clients tell me that their libido decreased when they put on weight because they felt less desirable,

---

9. I also found the book *Intuitive Eating* by Evelyn Tribole and Elyse Resch to be extremely helpful in healing my relationship with food and body image.

regardless of what their partner or partners thought. I've had others who never fully connected with their sexuality or explored it because they felt like they didn't deserve to, given their size or appearance. All of this is more culturally conditioned nonsense. We would not feel like this about ourselves if environmental factors hadn't guided us there.

For those of us who enjoy sex, it is one of the best parts of life, and the idea that we wouldn't deserve it because we don't measure up to an oppressive beauty standard is absurd. That is the implicit message so many of us receive, though, when we only see bodies in popular media that fit a particular mold, and the ones that don't are often in decidedly non-sexual or even comical presentations. That's all garbage, and like on trash collection day, it's time to take it out of our inner gardens.

Healing from toxic cultural messages about body image is frequently an ongoing, challenging process. This is in part because the messages have been with us for so long and also because most of us are in environments where we're still immersed in them. I have spent about five months of my life in India, over the span of five trips, where I stayed in an ashram and was sequestered from the kinds of media and other scenarios that influence my body image in America. I noticed that the longer I was there, the easier it was to feel positively about my body. I also didn't see any advertisements for food, and I was amazed by how much less I thought about it than at home, where I see it constantly. When I returned to America, these healthy shifts always faded as I was confronted with the old influences again. Feeling positively about my body required being proactive in response to that.

Otherwise, healing from toxic cultural messages about body image can also be difficult because conventional beauty is rewarded by others and veering too far from those conventions can result in others not treating us as well. As I shared earlier, I have been obese twice, and I experienced this difference firsthand. I believe the answer is not to beat ourselves up to cater to it, though, but rather to recognize the greater truth of our being: that we are worthy just as we are and to let these harmful scenarios go as best we can. The more of us who do this, the freer we all become, and the likelier we are to create a future for our children where this will no longer be an issue.

Weeding the Garden

What I present here and in the following chapters in these sections is exaggerated. They include extreme examples of what many of us believe and what some of the effects of those beliefs can be. In real life, we usually have a mixture of beliefs and our mental picture is not this severe, though it can be, especially in people experiencing depression or low self-esteem. Having said that, many of us will find something of what we believe here, particularly if we are honest with ourselves about the moments when we feel the most insecure. Also, these are just some potential reactions to negative environmental influences. Many others can occur too. I encourage you to think of your own experiences and personalize this as much as possible.

Old Belief — If I do not meet the beauty standards around me, no one will want me. I can't be sexy, and there is no point in caring about my appearance or trying to be desirable. If I am ugly, it is disgusting for me to even have sexual desires.

The more I believe this, the likelier I am to feel terrible about myself in direct proportion to the degree that I don't meet the beauty standards where I live. I treat my body like it is a liability and agent of harm, since I believe it is in the way of me realizing my natural desires. I don't give myself a fair chance when dating (or give others a fair chance) because I believe my relationships will fail. I envision myself spending my life alone. I don't take good care of myself because what's the point? I look for ways to numb the reality of how awful I feel it is to be in my skin. I don't explore my sexuality because I assume no one will want me, and when they do, it's because there's something wrong with them.

Old Belief — If I do not meet the beauty standards around me, I have less worth as a person. It is my fault for not trying hard enough, or I am repulsive and cursed with "bad genes." People will not want to be my friend or value me unless I overcompensate with my personality, work ethic, and so on. I must give unevenly of myself to deserve being in relationship with others, and I can never fully be okay.

As I believe this, I feel deeply inadequate on a fundamental level. Life becomes a race away from my authenticity, trying to get whatever scraps of approval I can from others. I lose touch with my authentic desires because I'm trying hard to do what I think others will want in order for them to value me. I stop advocating for myself, and sometimes even listening to myself, and I feel overwhelmed, stressed, anxious, and depressed. Life is a journey of moving from moment to moment of never being good enough, no matter what I do. Regardless of how proud or happy I am with my accomplishments, I can barely stand to look at myself in the mirror because of the tremendous shame I feel. I feel guilty when I eat and deny myself the full pleasure of food because I think eating makes me worse off and I don't deserve to enjoy it.

Planting New Beliefs

Now that we've explored some of what can happen when we are under the spell of body negativity, let's affirm thoughts to help us release it.

There was a time when you loved your body exactly as it is and accepted it completely. That capacity is still within you today. There may be some parts of your body that you're unhappy with if you have chronic health problems, but that's not body negativity; that's a separate issue. First, let's affirm that we are willing to see our bodies in a new light (or rather, an old one). We have the power to let go of whatever unhealthy beliefs we hold about our bodies over time, perhaps even right now.

> *Affirm — I am willing to see my body in a new light. I am open to believing that how I see my body can change for the better, and I appreciate all the wonderful things my body does for me.*

Allow yourself in this moment to feel a sense of ease and relief regarding your body to the degree that you can. Can you see that if others hadn't taught you not to love it as it looks, this wouldn't have been an issue for you? Can you remember that it wasn't when you were very young?

Affirm — I can release what others have told me about my appearance. I connect with the part of myself that sees my authentic beauty. We only stop liking how we look because of the influence of others. That is not what we authentically see in ourselves. I can express my beauty however I want.

Let's begin opening to the fact that there is an inherent beauty in what we are, as we are, right now. There is hope for all of us to see this, especially as we collectively work to release the unhealthy thoughts and beliefs about our bodies that others gave us. Also, if you like fashion, go for it! There is nothing wrong with the artistic and personal expression that can accompany how we style ourselves. Just do it as best you can from a place that affirms your inherent beauty rather than reinforces insecurity.

Affirm — I know that my body will change, and this doesn't make me less beautiful or deserving of love, affection, and sexual gratification. Every adult deserves these things if they want them, at whatever age.

It is normal for our bodies to change with age. Does this make us ugly? Of course not! Let's celebrate the human experience each step of the way. In the eyes of Spirit, we are ever beautiful. Our authenticity is marvelous and divine. We are all worthy and enough, always. Spend a few moments feeling the Spirit within you, to whatever degree you can.

Affirm — I allow myself to savor the pleasure of eating, knowing that delighting in our bodies is part of the joy of being human.

If you have a relationship with food that is unhealthy, know that it can improve. This may take some time if you've been caught in a cycle of dieting, and it may be difficult to fully release old unhealthy patterns, but you can improve from where you are. Food can potentially become a way for you to feel spiritually connected, rather than disconnected. This is more of our natural state than where most of us are with food now. I believe we can find a way back to that.

Affirm — I am a divine being, effortlessly and endlessly worthy. My body is a reflection of this, made from the substance and structure of Spirit. My cells are composed of material that came from stars, and I am a star myself, like everyone else. The only place I can ever not be holy is within my mind, and I can let go of the thoughts and beliefs that obstruct my view of my sanctity. Spirit is here to support me throughout this process, now and evermore.

And so it is.[10]

Exercises

Journal about the following questions: What messages about body image did you grow up with? How did these messages influence how you felt, thought, and acted? What does body image mean to you? What role do you see it as having played in your life? What role would you like to see it playing in your life moving forward? If you received beliefs about body image that you want to shift, what are they and how would you shift them? How do you think your life could change by believing these new thoughts (i.e., what might their impact be on your feelings, thoughts, actions, etc.)?

If it feels comfortable to you, take a shower and say or think, "I love you," to each part of your body as you wash it.

Try to spend two minutes at the start of one meal each day reveling in the experience of eating, assuming this feels healthy. Close your eyes and focus on the pleasure and sensations, making sure that your phone, TV, computer, and so on have none of your attention. Delight in the experience as best you can. When possible, increase the amount of time, perhaps even to the full meal.

---

10. When concluding a magic spell or affirmative prayer, it is traditional in contemporary witchcraft and New Thought, respectively, to say "so mote it be" or "and so it is." This is not required, but many feel it adds to the experience and process.

Chapter 5
Romantic Relationships

From early childhood, most of us grow up being exposed to the myth of the idealized, fairy-tale relationship, which is generally present in the entertainment we consume. This can form a potent, unhealthy expectation within us of how romantic relationships should be. Even once we are adults who are "supposed to know better," many of us unconsciously expect perfection or an ideal to be met because of a subconscious belief in the fairy-tale relationship. Then, human beings, who will never be perfect or ideal, keep coming up short. As a therapist and among friends, I see this over and over: even though people consciously know the fairy tale is problematic, on a deep level, they still believe in it, and it wreaks havoc in their romantic lives accordingly. Many of us come from homes with divorce too, which can color the way we view relationships in a negative light (e.g., "They are doomed to fail"). The types of beliefs about relationships that stem from experiences like these can make the difference between having a healthy, functional relationship and never seeming to hang on to one.

When we believe in the fairy-tale relationship or one true soul mate, the first sign of trouble after the honeymoon period, like an argument or a nagging flaw, can cause us to doubt that a relationship will work out. Even if we consciously understand that problems are normal in relationships, including arguing at times, subconsciously, we may start packing our bags for an exit. If we accepted the truth though that all romantic relationships take work, this would change.

Another issue related to the fairy tale is the notion that one person should be everything to another. If a partner isn't our intellectual equal, an amazing listener, a mind reader, an eager activity participant, a worthy physical specimen, an ideal sexual complement, and more, then they can't be "the one" because we're supposed to want for nothing. This isn't how it usually works, though. It is rare for a partner to be everything their significant other is looking for, and when we recognize this and prioritize the things that are most important to us, we're likelier to have relationships that last. Many people, for example, find a quality or two in close friends that their spouse lacks (like a shared interest in a passion), and that more than makes up for the difference.

Along the lines of the fairy tale, many believe that amazing sexual chemistry is the strongest indicator of a relationship fit, as if that's like a sign from the heavens. This can cause the converse of the scenario where our bags are packed too readily, with people feeling like they must hold on forever regardless of what happens, save perhaps abuse, because this person rang their inner compatibility bell. Anyone who's been around the block enough times though can tell you that we can have amazing sexual chemistry with someone we have no other compatibility with, and we can also have wonderful romantic chemistry with someone we can't live with. None of this means we can't find a partner or partners whom we're highly compatible with, though, and shouldn't hold out for that. It's just a recipe for failure to seek perfection, and conversely, it's also important for us to have healthy standards and not settle for a bad fit because of strong sexual chemistry or not wanting to be alone.

Accepting Each Other

In the spiritual training program I went through, there was a tenet that bears greatly on relationships. After I introduce it, I will explore how it connects with them. The tenet is that all people have divine, sacred purpose in life as their individual selves, purpose that is complementary. You are here to be you, and I me, in the holy manner that is particular to each of us. For those of us who believe in astrology, the complexities of our respective birth charts reflect and affirm this in helpful, expressive detail. The inner North Star will light the way to realizing our purpose if we learn to follow it, and when we do, we coexist in a manner that facilitates each other's journeys. This sometimes feels good and supportive, and other times difficult and painful, but ultimately, what unfolds is for the best in terms of our collective and personal spiritual evolution.

Only people of an exceptionally high consciousness can have a better intuitive understanding of your trajectory than you, and they are so rare that you may never meet one (or at least know that you did). This doesn't mean we can't have insightful loved ones and mentors in our lives who recognize patterns or other things in us that we don't see in ourselves or who have appropriate, helpful wisdom and advice to share when asked for it. This is different from others knowing what we should do with our lives, though—where we should go, what we're learning, how we should develop, and so on.

In most cases, we each know what's best for ourselves. It may take some doing to release the conditioning we've accumulated that stands between us and our inner knowing, but this knowing, like the spring of Spirit, is always there. Even if we are in a similar position to what others have experienced, that doesn't mean that what they did or learned is relevant for us, as they are on their own path and have a different life, background, and trajectory. Just as this is true of others in relation to us, it is also true of us in relation to them. We can be supportive, loving, and nurturing to others, and we can certainly offer them advice and counsel if they ask for it, but it is not our role to steer the ship of their lives or learn their lessons for them. Chances are we don't even know where they are headed, particularly at the level of the soul, which is necessary information to have in order to understand what is best for someone else. Consequently, it is not appropriate to impose our will or advice on other adults. The main exceptions to this are when someone is harming others or at risk of that or doesn't have the capacity to adequately make important decisions.

This brings us to another common issue in relationships: not accepting people as they are and not honoring their ability to chart their own course (i.e., seeking to impose our will on others). In addition to the fairy tale, many of us grow up with a notion, often reinforced by TV shows and romantic comedies, that we are supposed to change another person or facilitate some kind of realization and growth in them. This then enables the ideal relationship to emerge. Entering relationships with the hope that someone else's character or typical habits will change or that we can guide them in some way is ill-founded though. Aside from the spiritual reasons shared above, it establishes an inequitable relationship dynamic from the beginning. Even when the manner in which we want them to change is something they want too, behavioral change can be extremely difficult. We can't reasonably expect that the people we form relationships with will ever be different from how they are now in terms of self-development. If the current package isn't enough as it is, it's best to move on, as it may never change for the better, and constantly hoping that it will can cause problems on all sides. Also, if we know what we are getting into, we are choosing it, and that is on us. It is unfair to punish people for being themselves. This is fundamentally different from being partners in growth and transformation, which can be healthy and rewarding, but in that situation, people support each other equitably. No one is in a mentorship role over another, and no one places the bond at the heart of the relationship at the mercy of how the growth and transformation process unfolds.

Having said that, relationships do take work, and there is a difference between wanting a partner to develop relationship skills and not accepting who and how they are as people. The skills we have in non-romantic relationships, whether in our personal lives or business, don't necessarily translate to romantic relationships, and some of us may be quite surprised by how much we need to work on being a strong partner. Each party in a relationship can be expected to be open to learning how to healthfully engage, compromise, and provide support to the other or others.

When we enter a romantic relationship, it's like creating a new garden together, but one that features whatever issues each person has about relationships, as these not only factor in but will likely come up. Relationships also tend to surface our deepest insecurities and rawest parts as we let our guard down and expose ourselves to others. They are settings in which wounding from previous relationships can come up too, sometimes being projected onto the respective partners, like having been cheated on in the past and subconsciously assuming that will happen again. Many turbulent emotions and reactions can accompany all of this, and if we didn't grow up around healthy models of conflict resolution and communication, we will probably have to learn relationship skills as adults. Many of us were taught that if you don't have anything nice to say, don't say anything at all, which included offering constructive criticism. Feedback in a relationship isn't "not nice," though, unless it is phrased in an unkind manner. It's normal, healthy, and important to share our concerns about our partner or partners' behavior with them when that behavior is harmful or difficult for us. We can also learn respectful, healthy methods for assertive communication if we didn't grow up with them (some are shared in the next section).

We can all expect that a relationship will include a growth and change process with difficulties along the way when it comes to issues within the relationship. Apart from that, though, how people are may not shift much. Some people are more drawn to personal growth than others, and many let their status quo persist for decades. When people in therapy struggle with this, I often point this out as a line to mind: it is one thing not to like how someone treats us and another not to like how they treat themselves, spend their free time, and so on.

There are going to be areas in any relationship where people are fundamentally incompatible to some degree, and that's totally normal. Some healthy, happy partners have conflict in these areas but find a way to accept each other and make peace in light of their higher compatibility. I attended a wedding once where the bride said in her vows that she had "come to love" how her husband leaves the cupboards open in the kitchen. What was once frustrating became endearing through love and acceptance. My mother loved to travel and my father was ambivalent about it, and what ended up happening was she went on many trips without him. Healthy long-term relationships involve learning how to choose our squabbles and when to say, "You know what, I'm going to close the cupboards myself. It is easier for me to let this go than for you to develop a new habit."

Growing and Developing Together

Building a life together is a process of negotiation and compromise, where we deserve to feel respected, seen, empathized with, and validated. In a relationship, we all have needs like these, which can differ some between people, and wants that are fine to ask for. We get to have boundaries and standards for how we're treated too, provided they're reasonable. On that note, there is a difference between a preference and a need, and it is important to be mindful of that. It is always okay to advocate for our needs. There may be some instances when our needs go unmet, like when a loved one is in crisis and we temporarily don't get enough rest, but most of the time, it is appropriate to champion them. When a relationship is toxic, it is because there is a dynamic within it that prevents a partner from meeting a need. Sometimes this can be fixed, and other times it is a sign to walk away.

With our preferences, it depends on the situation. We may be called to compromise on behalf of the other person at times, and as long as we don't feel taken advantage of, that can be the healthiest thing to do. In the example I gave about the bride, she didn't feel taken advantage of because there were other areas in the relationship where her spouse picked up the slack. Discussing that and coming to an arrangement can be all partners need to do to settle this kind of issue. Conversely, in a situation where one person feels that the bathroom must be cleaned daily, for instance, that is more of a preference than an objective need in most cases. In therapy, we would usually work on this person owning that amount of cleaning, as it would be an unreasonable standard to impose on another. Apart from issues like this, though, it's important to have a sense of fairness with household responsibilities.

In my experience as a therapist, the most significant factor in whether or not partners will have a healthy long-term relationship, assuming they are a good fit for each other, is their willingness to work on the relationship together. The manner in which they commit to navigating the imperfections that arise and to the practice of being in relationship, and how they deal with recognizing that they have different strengths and weaknesses. In the garden of a relationship, one partner is the sun and the other the water (and if there is another partner, they might be the soil, and so on). Though some plants need more sun than water, and vice versa, each is essential for life. No amount of sun can make up for a lack of water, and water isn't a substitute for sun. Each partner has a critical role to play in feeding and nourishing a relationship. When partners work together and start dealing with the problems and accepting the incompatibilities in their relationship, and realize they can weather difficulties like these, the relationship and intimacy deepens. As they undertake the vulnerable work of giving each other honest feedback, taking risks and making mistakes, and apologizing and being accountable, they begin to experience the richer rewards of partnership.

Having said that, it is also my experience as a therapist that one of the hardest questions in life can be whether or not to leave a relationship. At what point are we asking for too much versus not enough? Ultimately, only you can determine this for yourself, but your list of dealbreakers in a partner shouldn't be impossibly long. As we release subconscious beliefs about the fairy-tale relationship, we can realize what is truer: there are many people we could have a healthy relationship with.[11] There are plenty of fish in the sea once we put a healthy hook on our line.

11. Amir Levine and Rachel Heller, *Attached: The New Science of Adult Attachment and How It Can Help You Find—and Keep—Love* (New York: TarcherPerigee, 2010), 103.

Interdependence over Codependence

With a reasonable list of dealbreakers, acceptance of each other's sovereignty over our lives, and a commitment to learning relationship skills and growing together, we can confidently embark on the process of finding or refurbishing a relationship. That being said, now we come to the next issue, which is why do we want a relationship in the first place? What do we think or hope it will bring to our lives?

The fairy-tale template is an ode to codependence. The damsel in distress must be saved by the handsome prince, or in more modern renditions, must save him instead. Without each other, both can't embody their self-narrative, so part of the desire for a relationship is the realization and fulfillment of a hero/victim life role, which is an unhealthy way to think about relationships. Even if we don't buy into the damsel/prince narrative, the fairy tale is bad enough on its own: we are doomed to incompleteness until we find our one true love.

When these are the messages we see in stories while growing up, this is what we internalize, alongside what is around us in the world. As I said earlier, we may not consciously believe in these kinds of dynamics, but that doesn't mean they aren't active within us on a subconscious level. This goes for other narratives too, like that women should sacrifice everything for their families, including their wants and needs. Or that a man's only role is to provide and protect, and men are otherwise free to shrug off household responsibilities. The fact is many of us grew up believing that there is a soul mate out there who will make everything okay and complete us because that is what we were told to expect from a host of different directions. As we start dating, that is what we look for, and the rush of brain chemicals that accompanies new love feels enough like a fairy tale for all the tales of childhood to seize our better judgment. It's like a daydream that we snap out of as we inevitably realize that the person we're dating is a human being, and perhaps (and hopefully) that we don't actually want to be saved or to rescue someone else.

If it were up to me, children wouldn't be exposed to fairy-tale relationship stories at all. We would show them healthy examples of functional, loving relationships, relationships that take commitment, understanding, compromise, and work. Imagine how different dating would be if we went into it fully accepting that problems and incompatibilities would come up and there's nothing wrong with that? While also recognizing that we don't want to hold on too much because of chemistry if significant issues with compatibility are there?

It's cliché to say it, but the deepest fulfillment in life doesn't come from romantic relationships. They do not provide us with internal peace and contentment. Those come from within. This doesn't mean we can't be on that journey of discovery together, though, recognizing as a unit that part of our relationship work is to facilitate each other's individual freedom. This also doesn't mean we can't have profound interactions with our partner or partners that are fulfilling to a great degree, but something will always feel like it's missing, and that's because it is. We can never get from another human being what we can only get from Spirit. Part of a healthy relationship is recognizing this and not holding each other accountable for what the other can never provide.

This isn't to suggest that it's unhealthy to feel dependent upon our partner or partners. Interdependence, as contrasted with codependence, is healthy. It's natural for those of us who want relationships to seek them out, prioritize them, invest in them, and depend on them. This dependence just has to do with the life we build together and our relational needs, and it isn't the core of our spiritual development and sense of self. It also isn't rooted in being possessive or controlling, which stems from insecurity, though we do naturally become highly attached to the people we partner with, even physiologically. We will explore this more in the section on closure in part 3.

When people who prioritize living in alignment with Spirit have a relationship together, it can be glorious. In those equitable dynamics, they support each other on the path of growth and transformation as partners, not rescuers and damsels in distress or perpetual givers and takers. Their ability to align with Spirit becomes something they can share while making love, and that is every bit as staggering and worthwhile as even the hint of it reads. This alignment also helps them navigate whatever difficulties emerge in the relationship, as some inevitably will. We can choose to put the healthy elements of the fairy tale, like romance and passion, in our relationships too by prioritizing actions that feed that fire. There is nothing wrong with wanting all of this, but it can't, and won't, come when we make someone else the hero of our lives or our object for demonstrating how much of a hero we are.

Self-love is the foundation of a healthy partnership, and since most of us didn't grow up with that modeled for us, we can have quite a learning curve with it, and that's okay. We can get there, and we can do it while in a relationship. The work remains the same and simple: we take action in support of our well-being, perhaps through studying material on how to have healthy relationships, communicate effectively, and so on, and we stop any harmful behaviors we engage in as best we can. We also weed the unsupportive thoughts and beliefs in our minds about relationships (and otherwise) while planting and caring for healthy new ones.

Weeding the Garden

Old Belief — My life partner is going to be perfect for me. The relationship will feel right, right away, and it will just work, effortlessly. It'll be clear that we are meant for each other, and we will live happily ever after.

When I believe this, I look for perfection in a partner, consciously or subconsciously. Early on, I may try to convince myself that any ill-fitting foibles or quirks aren't a big deal, but soon I believe they spell doom for the partnership. At the first sign of trouble, rather than bring it up and talk it through, I begin to question whether this is a good match for me, and my concerns fester as I keep them to myself. If there are any issues with the chemistry, I doubt the potential for the future. As things get harder, I take that to mean that we are not right for each other and leave. Rather than develop relationship skills, I assign blame and judge. As the years pass, I miss out on relationships with wonderful people because I decided they weren't good enough for relatively superficial reasons. I am likely to send mixed signals or pull back readily. Eventually, I may cave and marry someone. Not because they're perfect, but because I'm tired of dating, and if I had been less picky earlier on, I may have found a better match.

> *Old Belief — I need a relationship to complete me. Without a relationship, I'm not whole. I can't live a fulfilling life alone. I must be rescued or rescue, fix or be fixed, be a giver or taker, etc.*

When I believe this, the thought of being in a relationship is never far from the fore of my mind when I'm not in one. At the start of a relationship, I overemphasize how good it seems because I'm boiling with hope that this will be "the one." When the person seems like they aren't, I may still cling, because now I'm attached and I don't want to be alone again. I look for ways to be of value to the other person or to receive value from them. I become enmeshed with them, like living on a rollercoaster at times. I become terrified of them leaving me, even if that seems like the right thing for them to do. My biggest conscious fear is that I will be alone, and that clouds my judgment in every romantic relationship I have, every date I go on, every moment of flirtation.

> *Old Belief — I don't deserve a healthy relationship because there is so much wrong with me. I can't make a relationship work. I will sabotage it.*

When I believe this, I unconsciously sabotage the relationships I'm in. I do little things, or ignore little things, that lead to them not working out. I don't try as hard as I could because I feel like I'm doomed to fail, and I miss out on potentially wonderful opportunities because I am convinced they won't pan out. I don't try my hardest because what's the point? And I may be in a string of unhealthy relationships that feel unfulfilling or a long-term one where I accepted far less than I deserve because of how low my self-esteem is. Alternatively, I might send mixed signals without realizing it to keep others at bay.

Planting New Beliefs

When you were a child, you were not obsessed with finding the perfect lover until you encountered stories about that, if at all. You felt at ease with yourself, and you can again. You can release the unhealthy expectations and concepts you were conditioned to associate with relationships, learn relationship skills, and embark on the marvelous journey of spiritual partnership with a lover or lovers. Also, if relationships aren't for you, that's okay too. Being single is equally valid.

Affirm — I am willing to release old beliefs about relationships. I am open to seeing relationships in a new light.

Allow yourself in this moment to connect with the part of you that seeks to join with another in relationship, setting aside the beliefs you've picked up about relationships throughout your life. Can you feel the purity of that desire? That it doesn't come from lack, but rather wanting to cocreate? Not emptiness, but fullness?

Affirm — I recognize that growth and work are part of relationships and that no two people are 100 percent compatible with each other. I understand that in accepting this truth, I can give prospective partners a fairer shot.

Even if we never saw our parents or other role models in our lives work on relationships, that doesn't mean we can't learn how to do it ourselves. Even if we were conditioned to seek perfection, that doesn't mean we can't let that go. When you get in touch with your core, what is it you truly want to love, an idealized image or an authentic human being? What standard do you want to hold yourself to? Isn't there something romantic, intimate, and enriching about sharing all the depth of ourselves with another, flaws and all?

There are many partners who have made relationships that seemed doomed on paper work out and plenty of others who seemed perfectly matched whose relationships didn't last a year. A willingness to work on a relationship and keep the fire of romantic love alive can make all the difference in the world, and that is something we can foster within ourselves.

> *Affirm — I affirm that If I want a relationship, I can have one, and it can be healthy, functional, and supportive of my growth and spiritual development. If I don't want one, that's okay too. I don't need a relationship to complete me. I can experience a sense of completeness and fullness on my own, and I can create healthy boundaries in the relationships I have.*

As we learn to connect with Spirit, we come to realize that there is nothing fundamental that's missing in our emotional experience as individuals. There is no shortage of love, comfort, or peace. All these states are available to us through aligning with Spirit, and we can find ways to prioritize doing that. There is also nothing wrong with desiring to spend most of our lives with others. There's no deficiency within us for wanting to share the human experience with fellow humans. The more rooted we are in our core, the better able we will be to do this authentically, and with healthy boundaries and a recognition of what red flags and yellow lights to mind while dating.

> *Affirm — I deserve a healthy relationship, and I can develop relationship skills and insights to have one if I don't have these already.*

Do you deserve a healthy relationship? Of course you do. As we learn relationship skills, we become able to have healthier relationships, and as I mentioned earlier, most of us start with substantial room to grow in this domain. There is nothing to be ashamed of for being in that position.

During relationship therapy, I have watched many people learn relationship skills, and I have learned them myself. It mostly requires an openness to trying new things and a commitment to practice. Many of us can quickly get used to a lot of what seems arduous and challenging if we stay open, and before we know it, we can smooth out the rough edges in our relationships and enjoy them more deeply. I believe most people can do this to some degree if they are willing to put in the work and look in the mirror, and with all that happening, if a relationship seems like too much work, we can recognize that and move on. One thing I often say in therapy is that all relationships take work, but on a fundamental level they should just work. When we develop relationships skills and something keeps feeling like it's missing in a major way, we can exit that relationship confidently knowing we tried our best and it wasn't a good fit.

When we look at each other through the eyes of Spirit, we see the divine looking back at us. We are holy beings, and it is within our power to live in the awareness of that. The great mystics of history became so self-realized that they never lost sight of this truth. Even if we don't get there or aspire to that, sensing and reveling in Spirit can be part of our everyday lives, and relationships can be a healthy home for this, something we delight in. Spend a few moments feeling the Spirit within yourself, to whatever degree you can, and the next time you see someone else, try to feel it radiating from them.

Affirm — I am a divine being, effortlessly and endlessly worthy. I am full of love that I can give, and I can always receive more. I am holy by myself, and holy with others, and whatever I choose to do with relationships is blessed by the Spirit that I am. I revel in the magic and serenity of this.

And so it is.

Exercises

Journal about the following questions: What messages about relationships did you grow up with? How did these messages influence how you felt, thought, and acted? What do relationships mean to you? What role do you see relationships as having played in your life? What role would you like to see them play in your life moving forward? If you received beliefs about relationships that you want to shift, what are they and how would you shift them? How do you think your life could change by believing these new thoughts (i.e., what might their impact be on your feelings, thoughts, actions, etc.)?

> Write out what you want in a relationship: a healthy, mature relationship, assuming you want one. Even if you're in a relationship now. This will give you a sense of how that relationship measures up. Next, brainstorm steps to help move your relationship in that direction or, if you are single, to find that with a new partner.

Assertive Communication Skills for Romantic Relationships

Here are some techniques I've found helpful for communication within romantic relationships that I generally suggest as a therapist:

First, I recommend that partners have a relationship check-in every other week or so, at minimum once a month. This is a space to talk about the health of the relationship. During this check-in, sharing what we appreciate about each other's behavior is important so that it doesn't just turn into a venue for difficult conversations and feedback, though that is its primary intent. Having this space validates that it's normal to have difficulties in relationships, and as we get used to dealing with these difficulties regularly, it usually becomes easier to navigate difficulty as a partnership in general. These check-ins are also a safeguard against a tendency to keep things bottled up because we know there is a consistent time in which to share. This can prevent issues from festering, which is particularly important if an issue is rooted in some degree of misinterpretation or misunderstanding, as often occurs in relationships.

These check-ins help ensure that partners are vulnerable with each other, and as they feel seen and heard and their relationship isn't destroyed by candor around difficulties, they grow closer together. The check-ins aid partners in developing a sense of comfort around raising challenging topics with each other, as well as recognizing what their patterns of issues are, which makes it easier to proactively work on these patterns. All of this tends to deepen and enrich the relationship.

When we speak with each other in these check-ins, it's important to use assertive communication techniques. These techniques help us communicate effectively while minimizing the likelihood of evoking defensiveness, sadness, or anger in the other or others, making it likelier that we'll be heard. We will review some assertive communication techniques in this section, but in general, it can be quite helpful and transformative to get in the habit before speaking of asking ourselves, "Could what I'm about to say potentially hurt or offend this person?" and if the answer is yes and we want to avoid that, brainstorming other ways to make the point. I also find benefit in explicitly naming what I don't mean if I can see how someone might interpret something that way (e.g., "I'm not trying to suggest that you were being lazy. I just want to understand what happened here").

One of the most popular assertive communication techniques is called "I-statements." An I-statement is a fact-oriented recollection of an event and our reaction to it that helps us convey to another how we feel or what we felt and experienced. These statements are formulated in a manner that excludes judgmental and critical language while fostering empathy. For example, if our partner interrupts us frequently when we talk about something, instead of saying, "Why do you keep interrupting me? That's so rude!" we might say, "When people interrupt me like this, I feel disrespected and like they aren't interested in listening to me." This is usually the form of an I-statement: name the behavior, name the emotion or emotions, and name any other consequences of the behavior, without criticizing the other person. No one can reasonably argue with the legitimacy of an I-statement because the factual event happened (i.e., one person interrupted the other) and how we felt is subjective and ours to determine. Whether our emotional reaction was appropriate may be up for debate, but what it was isn't. This way, someone also isn't being called rude or worse, which could easily start an argument and veer the conversation off course without leading to resolution, perhaps just exacerbating things.

To that end, there is another valuable technique I know called a "parking lot." With a parking lot, we table topics in a conversation for later until we've resolved the issue at hand. For instance, let's say we did call our partner's behavior rude. In a situation like that, many people would respond by deflecting to change the subject as they get defensive, perhaps saying something like, "If you think I'm rude, well, you're selfish. You always put yourself first in so many insensitive ways!" The conversation then falls apart, with little hope for reaching a productive conclusion. With a parking lot, in that moment we stop and say, "We can talk about whether or not I'm selfish after we discuss the interrupting. We'll get there, but let's finish this first," and then that's what we do.

With an understanding of I-statements and having a parking lot, we can then utilize the next technique, which I call "reflect, validate, respond, and resolve." This is an effective communication technique for reflective listening that helps each partner feel heard, seen, and understood. This is crucial because it can be easy to take for granted that we heard someone correctly when we may not have. We can also feel unseen even when it seems like someone understood our words.

In the reflect portion of this technique, one person paraphrases back to the other what the other person said. This is to confirm that they understood the person on a basic level. For example, "I'm hearing that you feel disrespected by how I interrupted you." This quickly shows when people make assumptions and interpretations beyond the content of what was said, which I've witnessed many times. By checking in that we heard the other person correctly, we can nip that in the bud.

When we validate, we share with the other person the sentiments we agree with that they voiced, assuming there are some, and we also validate how we can see where they are coming from, where applicable. For instance, "I can understand how being interrupted like this could feel disrespectful."

Next, we respond. This is our opportunity to comment on what they said or share additional information. In this case, we might say something like, "I didn't mean to interrupt you. I just got so excited about what I wanted to say that I felt like I had to share it immediately." Then the other person reflects, validates, and responds to what was said to them. This might look like, "I hear that you interrupted me because you were excited to share something. I've felt like that myself too. This is also a pattern, though, and I want it to stop so I feel more respected in our relationship."

This brings us to resolve, which is where partners agree upon an action step, assuming that is warranted. In this case, the action might be something like "I will make an effort not to interrupt you like this, and if I do, you can point it out to me in the moment."

While this process may seem clunky, and we needn't necessarily do each step with every point in a conversation, it does help ensure that people feel heard and seen. My experience with relationship therapy is that feeling unheard and unseen are frequently among the main problems people experience in relationships. When we've practiced these techniques enough with an understanding of the philosophy behind them, we start to do them in more organic-feeling ways. Then they flow, and assuming all partners recognize that relationships thrive with a foundation of respect, empathy, healthy communication, and healthy compromise, sailing can become pretty smooth most of the time.

Chapter 6
Self-Love

S ince the self-help boom in the latter part of the last century, it's become cliché to talk about the healing power of unconditional self-love. Some believe it to be a miracle cure for all illnesses, and while I wouldn't go that far, I do believe it is among the greatest forces for psychological healing. It is also my experience that for many if not most of us, a deficit of self-love is one of the core issues that holds us back from realizing the well-being and intentions that are attainable for us. Unconditional love is the primary thing so many of us are seeking too, whether we know that or not, and the most reliable place to find it is within ourselves, as an extension of our divine nature. Even though the healing power of self-love is a cliché concept, my experience is that very few of us have actually tried it, either consistently for a significant period of time or at all.

Whether that's because loving ourselves seemed hokey, silly, naïve, simplistic, or what, the percentage of the total population that has made a sincere effort to engage in loving, nurturing self-talk and self-care on a daily basis is small. That's unfortunate because once we get a taste of self-love, it becomes self-evident how mighty it is, even in its infancy. It's amazingly powerful in helping us decondition ourselves from harmful beliefs, heal from trauma, and establish new beliefs that support our well-being and the realization of our dreams. If you've ever seen someone shine with enthusiasm and motivation after receiving a loving pep talk from a friend, you've caught a glimpse of this. How much should we love ourselves? One goal could be to see ourselves with the same degree of love that a devoted, supportive, and accepting parent has for their children. Imagine how your life would be if this was how you felt about yourself, informing every action you take and as a filter through which you perceive each experience.

To that end, prioritizing self-love helps us make positive changes in our lives. The more we care for ourselves, the more natural motivation we feel to act on behalf of our well-being. For example, we may find ourselves doing chores that normally irk us because we want to provide ourselves with a comfortable home. Loving ourselves also rallies our innate magic behind whatever healthy intentions we set. We are likely to find ourselves presented with action steps and opportunities in support of those intentions, and availing ourselves of them involves considerably less effort than it would've before because self-love helps us release our resistance to realizing our intentions. It is easier to act on behalf of our hopes and dreams when we believe we deserve to have them come true. We start to become so aligned that it's like most aspects of our lives that are within our sphere of influence flow, and loving ourselves helps us celebrate and receive this rather than fear or distrust it. This self-love aids us in better navigating whatever storms arise too because we've become our own best champion, rather than our worst critic, greatest doubter, and so on. Provided we approach this topic in a manner that doesn't feel like overstraining from where we are, its fruits, even with a solid yet small practice, can be glorious and, ultimately, myriad and holistic.

As we focus on self-love, it's critical to recognize that we aren't talking about vanity or narcissism. Those concepts are rooted in comparison and conditionality, and that's not where self-love comes from. This work is about progressively experiencing a truth of being that is deeper than that, in some ways mysterious, timeless, and infinite, yet also immediate, ordinary, and simple.

There is no ego in pure self-love. In the greatest depths, there is no sense of separation from anything at all. This is a state we may only glimpse throughout our lives, if ever, but when we are in it, there is no selfishness that would reduce the freedoms of others or judge them or us for being human. Learning to love ourselves, which can begin with practicing compassionate thinking and taking supportive action on behalf of our well-being, is a process of releasing the obstacles between us and the unceasing love of Spirit that underlies our thoughts.

At first, this usually occurs at the level of personality, as there is often ample psychological healing to be done. Eventually, if we seek to develop spiritually beyond that, we allow the love we connect with to impel and ferry us deeper within during meditation, like sinking into a lake. The supportive thoughts of our innate worthiness and divinity help us enter the stillness at its bottom. After all, we are not affirming that we are special and worthy and unique alone. We affirm that everyone is, and as we affirm the universality of Spirit within our minds, we move closer to a direct perception of it.

Some people differentiate between terms like self-esteem, self-worth, and self-love, and there can be some value in that. For our purposes, though, I find it best to work simply and lump them together. When we find true self-love, there is little question of low self-esteem or self-worth, and the same can be said of the other qualities.

We are each worthy of our own love, simply because we are here, now, on this planet, and many if not most of the problems of the world would not exist if enough of us knew this experientially. Someone rooted in the spring of Spirit won't harm another person unless that harm is unintentional, their capacity is diminished in some manner, or that person is harming them or others. They sincerely want everyone to have a comfortable quality of life and the freedom of self-discovery. This doesn't have to be a world where we compete with each other for resources, or where someone being good at something is only precious if they are better at it than others. Many of us already aren't fully invested in the narratives of competitiveness like these that we grew up with, but in my experience as a cognitive behavioral therapist, some things are important to say, not just know or assume. For example, for me as a person with binge eating disorder, it was healing to say, "Food is a legitimate source of pleasure and comfort." With self-love, it can be crucial to say, "I liked myself until others told me not to." It makes a difference to affirm these sentiments to ourselves, emphatically, until they become the truths of our perceptions and emotional lives.

A Tale as Old as Time

This is the story that most of us have lived, in one form or another, throughout recorded history in much of the world: we come into life loving and accepting ourselves as we are and being capable of expressing whatever emotions we feel. A thought-dependent reality is imposed on us that differs from this, particularly as we move from the universal adoration that generally accompanies infancy into school age. We exist relative to others, and value is ascribed to that. Expectations are placed upon us based on qualities like perceived gender, race, and religion. By the time we are old enough to understand all of this and make up our own minds, the vines of belief within us have grown so strong and are so pervasive that we don't see them. Our inner garden has transformed into one of conditional love, and there comes a time when this is so overwhelming that we likely don't even remember it not being like this and probably struggle to see it another way, at least until we have young children or spend time with children regularly.

When I work on self-love with clients, I usually begin in one or two places based on what they believe. If they are religious or spiritual and believe that life is sacred, we start there. If life is sacred, aren't you too? That's a wonderful foundation upon which to build self-love. If they are atheistic or agnostic, I begin by remarking about things that live in inherent reality, like plants and animals. Does a dog need to prove its value to exist? Don't plants and animals have worth simply because they're here? Of course they do, and so do we. Life justifies itself. This doesn't have to be any more complicated than that. When it is, it's because we've made it so with our minds. Thankfully, what thought created, thought can change.

In our earliest years, we consume messages of conditional love and relative self-worth from our families, communities, and the society we live in. We see this concept play out in TV shows, films, and advertising, and in the relationships and interactions between our family members and how they treat us. Our individual details will vary based on our backgrounds and identities within our society of origin, but the overarching theme is the same: whether we are taught to believe we are better than, less than, or somewhere in between, we internalize the message that these distinctions not only matter but are defining. Our value as people is negotiable and conditional.

The manner in which we digest the emotional and physical violence we grow up around can also profoundly shape our sense of self-worth, behavior, and emotionality. Children are too young to process these kinds of issues, and they tend to stick with us as trauma and in unhealthy psychological and behavioral patterns if we don't find a healthy way to work through them later. It is common for young children, for example, to see themselves as partially responsible for the abuse they experience or witness, which can result in abiding difficulties with self-esteem or trust in relationships. Children are highly influenced by how their parents treat their siblings too, and how they're treated relative to that. This is where we see phenomena like the "middle child" syndrome, and many people believe birth order experiences influence their lives into adulthood.

When we go to school, the process takes a bold turn. Now, we are in a system where our value is not only relativized with others, but it can be quantified. This usually shows up in two areas that are highly prized: academic achievement and sports. There is a third area, the arts, which is also valued, but in something of an odd manner because it's both prized and underappreciated in many parts of the world (e.g., "What are you going to do with an art degree?" is a popular refrain). Additionally, there is the factor of how popular or "cool" we are or how much we fit in, which is not as quantifiable but does bear on how most of us see ourselves and our worth. In any event, the focus shifts considerably from what occurs in our home to how well we perform in the school setting. What happens next generally depends on how that goes.

Some children excel, bite the hook, and spend the next twenty-plus years on an overachievement bandwagon. This is a bandwagon where perfection is an attainable goal if they work hard enough (e.g., getting a perfect score on a test) and, therefore, where their ability, and by extension, worth, can be quantified and weighed against others'. This ill-prepares children for the fact that perfection isn't realistic in most adult circumstances and that holding ourselves to oppressive standards of perfection is toxic. The children who excel often become fearful of any threat to their superiority, which will inevitably come, and chase after accolades to add to their collection. Others embark on an endless popularity contest or dance of posturing, sometimes simultaneously with overachievement. Amid all of this, there is the envy and criticism of peers to contend with, and the potential social consequences of that, which leads some exceptional students to hide or minimize their successes. As much as we may want to experience the thrill and validation of achievement, there is also the innate desire to belong to a group, and the tendency toward some degree of conformity inherent in that drive. Peer pressure, which can come in explicit and implicit forms, is a powerful force to contend with. All sorts of defensive behaviors can emerge in this setting to protect our developing egos and fragile sense of worth.

Many children don't measure up to these standards, and that becomes part of their self-narrative. Academically, this usually ranges in significance depending on the value placed upon education in our family and community, which is also true of sports. The remainder of children fall somewhere in the middle, and some try not to play these games at all, but everyone takes something about themselves from the experience of going to school. It's too much of a part of our lives not to influence us, and many of us receive strong messages from family members regarding performance. For example, instead of receiving unconditional love and the random "I love yous" that drive this sentiment home, we get rewarded for good grades or doing well in sports and may receive little affection aside from that. The truer this is of our family, the likelier we will fall into unhealthy patterns with achievement.

Many of us also start to develop traits, if we haven't already, that distinguish us from our parents. Maybe we're flamboyant or athletic or into the arts. Maybe we're queer or trans and our parents aren't. Many kids have some qualities or inclinations that their parents don't approve of or resonate with, and this can be another issue that affects their self-worth. Instead of acceptance, which is ideally what we'd get from family, there may be judgment and criticism. Conversely, we may mirror our parents in many respects and seem like the "apple of their eyes." This can become its own stifling influence as we tend to continue living in alignment with our similarities with them in light of the love and acceptance that accompanies that. We will likely downplay our authentic, divergent desires and perhaps not get to know ourselves all that well until we are much older. Why rock the boat when we are comfortable and the sailing is smooth?

By the time we graduate from high school or the equivalent to it where we live, we are used to seeing objectives related to performance in concrete terms and having success and achievement be a matter of completing tasks well. Even if we think the school system is deeply flawed, it is difficult not to assume this orientation to some degree. We are also long steeped in the notion that some form of conformity is important for being accepted by others, and being accepted influences our sense of worth, whether we are popular or part of a fringe group. How could it not when our worth feels like a tenuous proposition from such a tender age, well before we can understand and question impulses to seek the validation of others? Even the most radically independent teenagers usually have a portion of their self-worth tied to the acceptance of some of their peers, which may solely be a contingent of fellow radicals. That was my situation. My friends and I were rebellious artists and musicians who bucked convention in many ways, but looking back, we cared about being accepted by each other.

As we enter adulthood, we bring with us what we've learned about our self-worth from school alongside whatever we got from our families, our religion, the films and TV shows we watched, and so on. Some of us may find worth in being perceived as sexy, beautiful, or popular. Others in being smart and capable or giving, and others in being creative, wealthy, or successful entrepreneurs. The insecurities that many of us hold around these issues might not surface unless we feel challenged by another, but when this happens, watch out. People who normally seem confident and even-keeled can be reduced to adolescent competitiveness and pettiness. Why? Because they feel threatened on a fundamental level. Their self-worth is on the line, and that's as deep as it gets.

Then there are the folks who didn't measure up, didn't excel, and don't see themselves as worth all that much. They could be amazing friends and partners and good at their jobs, but they don't believe they are special, so they don't perceive themselves to be. The truth is, though, we are all special. There is no one else like you in the world, and there never will be, and that is worth celebrating. For all of time, from beginning to end, no one else will ever be exactly like you. You are a marvel, and that would be valuable and meaningful enough even if you never did another thing.

Otherwise, we must also consider the harmful effects of advertising on people's sense of self-worth. Billions of dollars are spent each year to make us think we want products that will make us cooler, sexier, whatever. What do we get from jumping through all these hoops? Is the effort worth it? Many people who've reached the summit in these domains say no, or at least that that's not enough. They discover that all the achievement in the world can't make up for a lack of self-love, even if they don't realize that's what they feel is missing. A casual glance into the lives of wealthy and conventionally successful people, whether via reality TV, documentaries, or memoirs, makes it clear quite quickly that money, fame, and success in business do not bring contentment. Comfort, luxury, and exciting experiences? Sure. Perhaps even a sense of satisfaction if people feel like they did something meaningful for others or extraordinary. But deep fulfillment? The peace of true self-love? We can't buy that, and we don't achieve it. It presents itself to us as we learn to let go of externally imposed concepts and become present with what is already within us, connecting with the divine until our hearts overflow. It comes from embodying the authenticity that accompanies self-knowledge.

When we live inauthentically, there will always be a sense that something is off in our lives or a tension and stress that we can't quite place. The more inauthentic we are, the greater this will likely be, though that also depends on how sensitive and self-aware we are. Thankfully, through the work of inner gardening, we can make our way to our authenticity, and there is always a way to feel authentic internally, even if that is challenging externally. For example, some of us may need to act in ways that seem inauthentic to stay safe and attain a comfortable standard of living in a world where we lack privilege, but this is the outer level. These are things like behaving in a certain manner at work to excel in our field, where speaking our minds could derail us. To feel internally authentic while doing this, we can recognize that our actions serve a greater objective of acting on behalf of our best interest given the opportunities before us. There is an enormous difference between the psychological impact of the perspective "I'm being fake at work" and reframing that as "I'm acting professionally to succeed in this job to help my family have a comfortable quality of life." This type of behavior is likely also what we would suggest that a loved one in our position do if they asked us for advice. Applying compassionate thinking techniques like these can help us find a route to inner authenticity in most situations.

So here we are again. We've grown up in an environment full of weeds that have overtaken the gardens of our minds. We were reared to see ourselves as less than or greater than and our worth as conditional, and all of this is harmful. Are some people better than others at certain things? Sure. There are math geniuses, art geniuses, and so on. Do they have more to contribute to fields like science, technology, music, and art? Some do, but they aren't better than other people in a way that would make them more or less worthy of unconditional love. They simply have gifts, and there's a whole spectrum of people along the continuum of intelligence and talent who have valuable contributions to make to this world, even if only in their families. Some people have very little to contribute at all if we defer to standard societal measures, but does the life of an adult who can't work or raise a family because of a disability not matter? Of course it matters. Do they deserve love, acceptance, and a high quality of life? Absolutely, and the part of you that knows that their life has inalienable value also recognizes the inalienable value of your own. It's time to get back in touch with the worthy, loving, and magnificent beings that we are.

Weeding the Garden

Old Belief — My worth is conditional, based on how valuable I am in the various areas of life: how smart, physically attractive, talented, wealthy, and so on. My worth is based on how much better I can be than other people at things.

When I believe that my worth is conditional, I constantly evaluate my position relative to others. I may not consciously do this, but I will notice when I think someone challenges my position in an area or when I feel significantly less or better than. I may dedicate myself to being high achieving to demonstrate my value, feel like I'm never really all that worthy yet coast by, or even feel like I'm hopelessly lost. However things go, I don't feel good about myself on a deep level, and a huge part of my life feels like a race I can never truly win. Participating in this race in and of itself is a losing proposition, and how much I love myself, if that is even something I think about, is at the mercy of how well I see my performance in it.

Old Belief — My worth is based on how much I can do: what I can create and build or what I can do for others. I gain self-worth from checking boxes in life that are placed before me.

When I believe my self-worth is conditional based on what I can do or produce, I find myself trying to demonstrate that I matter in a variety of different ways. Maybe I work a job that has extreme hours and a high salary, spend lots of time perfecting my physical appearance, or become obsessed with some other activity. I may even pick a field of study in large part to impress others and end up in a career I don't like. Perhaps I am a huge people pleaser, as doing things for others makes me feel valuable. I might miss out on excellent relationships because I only date people I feel are "good enough" for me and ignore those who I believe aren't. I may also collect partners like trophies. I have little sense of what I authentically desire, and whether or not I love myself is a matter of how well I think I'm doing in accomplishing what I see as important.

Planting New Beliefs

There was a time when you had no doubt in your worthiness. It wasn't even a question. You loved yourself with such a natural purity that you didn't need to think about it, and you may never have. Even though we affirm novel beliefs in our work together here, we ultimately aren't building something new or convincing ourselves of anything when it comes to self-love. We release what is in the way of us experiencing our innate self-love and align with beliefs that help us tune to and describe it. These are truths that we will hold to be self-evident once we've pierced through the foliage that obstructed our view of the love within.

If nothing had ever suggested that you are not lovable exactly as you are, you would not have come to that conclusion on your own. You would have treated yourself the way you treat things you care for, and to the degree that it was within your power, your life would have been well and comfortable accordingly. It can be again.

Affirm — I am willing to release old beliefs about my self-worth. I am open to seeing my worthiness in a new light.

Any sense that we must compete or be better than others at activities to be valuable was given to us. It was not the truth that we knew when we were young children. Imagine how different the world would be if every child was raised with unconditional love and the freedom of self-discovery.

Affirm — I recognize that I only believe my worth is conditional, based on qualities like my ability to perform or how attractive to others, talented, or wealthy I am, because I was taught that. I see now that I am worth no more or less than anyone else, and that is beautiful. I deserve love.

It is wonderful to contribute to the world, and in a world where so many people suffer profoundly, we must serve. It is critical to do right by each other, so we can prosper now and help future generations. Our ability to do things, though, even noble ones, is not where self-love comes from. We don't have to check any boxes or achieve any goals. We don't have to do anything at all. From a centeredness in the love within, we become better equipped to do what is needed to help others, as we are more able to see and hear them with the lens of conditional value and competition removed. When we don't try to demonstrate our worth through how we act, we can wholly give to others, and receive the love for ourselves that is always present within us as we do so.

Affirm — I recognize that I don't need to be or do anything to give my life value and to prove my self-worth. Doing amazing things and contributing to the world can be beautiful and ful-filling, but this is not where my self-worth comes from. I am lovable just as I am.

On some level, can't you feel the truth of this? Doesn't it sing in some part of your psyche, possibly a very remote one if you are new to this kind of work? Allow yourself to listen to this part of you, like a small sound in a quiet room. Let your awareness move toward it, so that it builds in your experience.

Affirm — It is sacred for me to get to know what I truly am and desire, underneath the messaging I received from oth-ers. I trust that there is guidance within me, an inner knowing about how to make my individual orbit through life, and as I tune in to that, I will perceive it.

Close your eyes for a moment and just feel what is there. What is happening underneath your thoughts and feelings? Your sensations? Is there anything to prove or demonstrate within that quiet perfection? Is there anyone to be better or less than? Stillness is an entry point to profound self-discovery and peace. It empowers us to reclaim the freedom to be ourselves. All the love we need for ourselves is already there, and all the serenity.

> *Affirm — I am a divine being, effortlessly and endlessly worthy. There is nothing I need ever prove to anyone about that. It is the simple truth of what I am. I am already and always whole, magnificent, and worthy of unconditional love, and so is everyone else. It is holy for me to live my authenticity and realize my dreams, but what I do does not define my worth. I accept this glorious truth of my being, today and evermore. I love myself exactly as I am.*

> *And so it is.*

Exercises

Contemplate the following questions: How has your self-esteem been throughout your life? Are there specific negative thoughts you tend to have about yourself, perhaps ones you received from your family, community, or the religion you grew up with? If so, list them out on one half of a sheet of paper or in a computer document. On the other half, list out what would be helpful to believe about yourself now. You may not be able to step fully into these new beliefs yet, but listing them can be a powerful exercise. This sets a trajectory to work toward that your subconscious mind will digest. For example, let's say you received a message growing up that "If you don't clean your room, you're a sloppy person." A belief you might write for yourself now could be "How I clean my room has nothing to do with my worth as a person." How do you think your life could change from believing these new thoughts (i.e., what might their impact be on your feelings, thoughts, actions, etc.)? Note: if you feel like this would be too overwhelming or make coming to a place of self-love feel impossible, don't do it until you've worked with the affirmative talks in this book for a few months.

Otherwise, journal about the following questions: What messages about self-love and self-esteem did you grow up with? How did these messages influence how you felt, thought, and acted? What does self-love mean to you? What role do you see it as having played in your life? What role would you like to see it play in your life moving forward?

Chapter 7
Gender

Gender is a deeply personal issue for me because I was a gender-nonconforming child. I will begin by sharing a bit of my experience with gender and then review some broader perspectives on this topic, but please know that this is too deep and diverse of a subject to be heard about from one voice alone. I encourage you to explore far beyond what I have written if it is unfamiliar to you, particularly listening to the voices of transgender people, thousands of whom have already shared about their experiences on social media, YouTube, and so on. As a child, I loved wearing my mother's high heels, trying on lipstick, and sampling perfume. I preferred Barbie to GI Joe, She-Ra to He-Man, and I had no interest in sports. I used to make myself earrings out of paper and tape, and I always seemed to have an easier time talking and relating to the girls around me than the boys. I was sensitive and emotional as a child too, crying much more often than the other boys, and I loved the arts and music. I insisted on taking a dance class when I was in kindergarten called Little Feet, and I was the only boy, which set the tone for the next fifteen years or so of my life.

My mother frequently tried to push me to play with the other boys and be more interested in "boy" things, and she wasn't alone. I felt like a freak in my community, and many people treated me like one. There was no acceptable word for what I was, like "tomboy" with girls (which itself was met with a raised eyebrow). As I aged and was able to think for myself more, I appreciated that what I liked was just what I liked. I also recognized that other people not getting me was their issue, not mine, though the relentless bullying from my classmates did scar me deeply and resulted in me transferring schools during high school. This was just me, and that's part of the point. Gender can be a process of exploration, discovery, and evolution, but it is an authentic one. Deep inside, we know what is right for us, and if we follow that inner knowing, we will find our way to a manner of navigating gender that works for us.

There are so many toxic messages in our culture about gender, and there is so much baggage. The feminist movements of the twentieth century did extraordinary work to rail against the notion that women have to exist within rigid stereotypes of femininity to be valid as women. They highlighted ways in which gender is socially constructed and broke down myriad barriers, professionally and culturally, though many remain. Today, the transgender liberation movement is breaking down even more. It's continuing the process of challenging rigid, traditional assumptions about sex and gender, which ultimately helps all people in the wake of that lead more authentic lives. There was never anything wrong with me because I loved "feminine" things when I was a child. That was natural, and we are coming into a place in culture in the United States, finally, where large numbers of people recognize and accept that. That said, many communities are still unaccepting and dangerous for transgender and gender-nonconforming people (and people who are both), so it is critical for greater acceptance and understanding to come swiftly.

My loving "feminine" things also needn't have had any bearing on my identification as a boy. What tells us otherwise is toxic masculinity: rigid, traditional notions of manliness that are steeped in misogyny, homophobia, and aggression. Toxic masculinity has come under fire in recent years, with some people loudly proclaiming about how overdue this process of reckoning is. Still others feel like innate manhood is being challenged, and that is hard for them, especially cisgender heterosexual men, because in many cultures, the power and worth of a heterosexual man is tied to how well he embodies stereotypical manliness. Young boys are taught, as I was, that if they don't conform to certain representations of manhood, they have failed as people or are freaks. The sheer toxicity of this has caused immense problems in this world, particularly because this representation can be associated with harmful behaviors, like sexual violence and authoritarianism. If you look at what is being challenged when folks criticize toxic masculinity, though, it's things like the rigidity of gender norms and the domineering power and privilege that is associated with "manhood," not "masculine" traits.

Our Authenticity Is Natural

Some people believe the natural order is threatened by more expansive gender identities being normalized. The flawed premise with this though is if the focus is on authenticity and people being free to be themselves, nature has nothing to fear. What is true is never threatened by the pursuit of authenticity.

Many of us in the gay community learned the hard way how crucial it is to live authentically, suffering the abuse of others as we ultimately realized we couldn't force ourselves to be straight and had to be authentic, despite the great risk living our truths represented. Without the pressure to conform to rigid gender roles, we will express what is natural within us. For some of us, this will look like the conventional representations of gender, albeit manifesting in a manner that is aligned with Spirit (i.e., not one that would threaten the right of others to live their truths). For others, it will be boldly different, and all of that is beautiful because that is the nature of authenticity.

Sometimes there is something in our authentic being that there aren't words for in our culture, and because so much of our lives center around language, this causes tension and difficulty within us. When the language is created, there is relief from these feelings. This is part of what's happening now with gender. For many people, the use of new pronouns and terms like non-binary isn't so much about creating something new. It's giving them language to help them express and better understand what they already feel. This language may facilitate development and evolution, but it's not causal. The idea doesn't create the identity. It helps describe and explore it. It supports authenticity where before there was indoctrination, and it helps move us forward into the great human frontier, the freedom to truly be ourselves and discover what lies beyond what we have known. This includes expansive, novel expressions of gender. For some of us, gender is a process and a dance. It's something we dialogue with over the course of our lives. For some, it's a creative endeavor, and for people who are agender, it may not even be part of their identity, and all of this is wonderful. The sum of human history occupies a tiny portion of a vast, open canvas of possibility within the human experience, and painting outside of that is a remarkable, glorious thing.

That said, gender identity is also not a monolith throughout human history. Cultures have expressed gender in a variety of ways, including many different types of gender identification beyond just masculine and feminine. When this strikes us as odd, it's not because there's anything wrong with it. It's because it's not what we grew up with. A real-life example of this that is relatable to many people is pink being associated with girls and blue with boys. Pink wasn't even a "girl's color" until after World War II, though, and yet some people will treat this subject like it is a sacred hill worth dying upon.[12]

I understand why some people are afraid of the doors of gender being blown off their hinges. This issue has evolved so much in recent years that being transgender only stopped being classified as a psychiatric disorder with the publication of the fifth edition of the *Diagnostic and Statistical Manual of Mental Disorders* (DSM) in 2013. Frontiers are scary. People fear that something valuable and meaningful will be lost or threatened and

---

12. Stacy Conradt, "When Did Pink Become a 'Girl' Color?" Mental Floss, June 23, 2015, http://mentalfloss.com/article/65058/when-did-pink-become-girl-color.

that children will be harmed through negative influences. That is not what happens when we act in the name of freedom and authenticity, though. I'm not saying the process will be flawless, but I know in my core that as acceptance and celebration of gender diversity becomes the norm, this issue will resolve itself. The time has come for each person to live in the fullness of their being, whatever that means, however that takes shape. For us to honor each person's divine right to be themselves. There is no wrong authentic gender identity, only other people's disrespect for and intolerance of freedom.

Weeding the Garden

Old Belief — There is only one limited spectrum of ways to be a man or woman and if I don't fall within that, there is something fundamentally wrong with me. I am defective, and if others don't exist within that spectrum, there's something wrong with them.

When I believe in rigid gender roles (and that sex and gender are the same thing) and don't match up with them, I feel inadequate and flawed. I may overcompensate by modifying myself to reach them, like by forcing myself to participate in sports or adopting certain ways of communicating about the opposite sex, or I may give up and feel like a failure. The opportunities I experience in life, and how I relate to others, will likely feature a genderedness.

Old Belief — Exploring new frontiers of gender expression is unnatural and a product of mental illness and delusion.

When I believe this, I may see anyone who's gender-nonconforming as a disgusting aberration or ill person and a threat to the world I live in. I might try to enact laws and policies to limit their freedom of gender expression, even when I know that can cause catastrophic mental health reactions, because I believe I am doing a service to others in championing traditional gender norms. I will likely raise my children with a strong sense of gender roles and hold them to rigid standards about gender. If I see them as gender-nonconforming, I will work to stifle that. If I notice an impulse to break out of gender rigidity within myself, I will seek to eject it because of the threat I see it causing and what I fear it could imply. There are thoughts and feelings I won't even allow myself to entertain for a moment because of what they might suggest.

Planting New Beliefs

Affirm — I am willing to go beyond limiting beliefs about gender. I am open to seeing gender in open-minded, accepting ways.

There is no threat to our well-being in discovering what we are underneath what we've been told we should be. Many people do derive benefits from tradition and defined roles, but there can be plenty of traditions and roles in life that don't limit our freedom to explore identity or incline us to limit the freedoms of others. Take a moment to think about all the times in your life you received messaging about how you should be because of the sex you were assigned at birth. How light and liberating would it feel to drop all of that and be at peace within your being with whatever feels right to you?

Affirm — I recognize that throughout history, cultures have explored and expressed gender in many ways, and there is no one right, rigid manner in which to do it. I affirm that there is freedom inherent in the human experience to express gender in myriad forms and there is nothing aberrant about doing so.

When people act like rigid gender roles are the truth of history, they ignore history or are ignorant of it. Even if there are themes among large swaths of the general populations within societies, there have always been variations in gender roles between cultures, and there are many accounts from the ancient world to today of people who bucked gender norms. In fact, in many ancient cultures, transgender and gender-nonconforming identities were seen as sacred, which continues among those that remain. It is also self-evident at this point that the negative assumptions foisted upon women in much of the world—not smart enough, capable enough, strong enough—were unmerited. What other incorrect limiting beliefs might our forebears have held? I think there is no greater gift that we can give another person than support in being themselves and following their bliss, as Joseph Campbell famously taught.[13] There is nothing to fear in creating a world in which people are free to explore gender. We will all benefit from the fruits of this process.

> *Affirm — I love knowing that Spirit lovingly accepts my gender identity, which may evolve or even be none at all, and that my inner knowing is enough to guide me along this journey.*

The Spirit within us never judges us as inadequate or unworthy. It supports us in the exploration of what our hearts call us to become, and scientific progress has made it possible for people to affirm their gender when it differs from their sex at birth, which is a profound blessing. One that we have only seen the beginning of in terms of what is possible with advancing technology. The more open we are to pursuing what we feel emanating from within, the more beauty that can enter the world. The point isn't for any of us to express our gender in particular ways, but to feel free to do so however we choose, and to afford others full acceptance in doing the same. Imagine how wonderful that world will be! Let's speak it into existence now.

> *Affirm — I am a divine being, effortlessly and endlessly worthy. Whatever gender expression I embrace is an extension of that. It is holy for me to live my authenticity and follow my inner knowing, and I know what that is better than anyone else. I am whole, loved, and sacred exactly as I am.*

> *And so it is.*

13. Joseph Campbell with Bill Moyers, *The Power of Myth* (New York: Anchor Books, 1991), 113.

Exercise

Journal about the following questions: What messages about gender did you grow up with? How did these messages influence how you felt, thought, and acted? What does gender mean to you? What role do you see it as having played in your life? What role would you like to see it play in your life moving forward? If you received beliefs about gender that you want to shift, what are they and how would you shift them? For example, maybe in your home you received a message that "Women aren't supposed to be tough like this." A belief you might write for yourself now could be "Women can be any way they want. There is no one set way or gold standard for womanhood." How do you think your life could change by believing these new thoughts (i.e., what might their impact be on your feelings, thoughts, actions, etc.)?

Chapter 8
Sexuality

I realized I was gay in the mid-1990s, and I'm amazed at how far many societies around the world have come in their acceptance of queer sexual identities since then. It is normal now in a large number of households for a child coming out of the closet to be a virtual non-issue and for gay marriage to be equivalent to heterosexual marriage. That was unthinkable when I realized I was gay, which gives me hope, but I also recognize that there is still much work to be done.

Amazingly, the Kinsey scale of sexual attraction, which was first published in 1948, was around for decades before same-sex attraction became normalized in most people's minds, regardless of what the science said.[14] This scale rates sexuality on a spectrum from totally heterosexual to totally homosexual, with seven options, and Kinsey's research demonstrated that a significant portion of the population experiences homosexual attraction. For many years, the popular estimate was one in ten, though the actual figure is unclear, especially since there is a great difference in identification

---

14. Kinsey Institute, "The Kinsey Scale," accessed August 12, 2021, https://kinsey institute.org/research/publications/kinsey-scale.php.

between generations. A recent Gallup poll found that 20.8% of Gen Z identify as LGBT, contrasted with 10.5% of millennials, 4.2% of gen X, and 2.6% of baby boomers, with approximately 96% of those folks identifying as lesbian, gay, bisexual, or otherwise not heterosexual (i.e. queer, loving the same gender).[15] These numbers may still be low, as it's hard to know what people's true sexual identities are when we live in a society where many don't feel free to experiment or be forthright with their desires.It wasn't until 1973 that homosexuality stopped being formally considered a mental illness in mainstream psychology with its removal from the *DSM*. When I was in middle and high school, "gay" was the go-to pejorative for almost any situation, and it was the ultimate sin of masculinity to be sexually attracted to another man. There was no greater popular insult at that time in many circles than "gay."

From religious intolerance to threatening rigid gender roles to simply feeling confused, many people found cause to get upset about homosexuality. Homosexuality exists throughout the animal kingdom on a large scale, though. It has also shown up in many ways throughout human history. We see something similar with this to what we saw with gender: regardless of the historical precedent, here is a rigid box to fit in, and if you don't, you're a threat to others or defective and less than. It's amazing that we can be this small-minded regarding something that's so prevalent in the natural world and history. Even among communities of same-sex attraction, skepticism about the legitimacy of bisexual and pansexual identities has existed, which thankfully has changed a fair amount in recent years, though there is still some stigma and lack of acceptance.

Sexuality is also about more than just being gay, straight, bisexual, pansexual, and so on. Some people are asexual, which means they don't have a significant sexual attraction to others or are not highly interested in sex, if at all, and asexuality is a legitimate orientation. Among people who identify as sexual, there are varying degrees of sexual interest and engagement. There are different proclivities toward fetishes and ways of connecting

---

15. Jeffrey Jones, "LGBT Identification in U.S. Ticks Up to 7.1%," Gallup, February 17, 2022, https://news.gallup.com/poll/389792/lgbt-identification-ticks-up.aspx.

with others too (being dominant, submissive, both, etc.), which are all part of a magnificent world of pleasure and intimacy that is ours to discover. As a therapist, when I work with clients who identify as sexual and voice enjoying it, I will sometimes remark that good sex is probably one of the best things in their lives, which they recognize as true. I do this because that is not the message they usually grow up with, and it is powerful to acknowledge this fact and affirm it. The shadow of religious denigration of free sexual expression reaches wide upon many, often even if we didn't come from religious families, resulting in a combination of guilt and shame about our desires. We may feel guilty about being attracted to people other than our spouse or shame about unconventional sexual interests of ours or the amount of sex we want to have. Most of this is healthy to release.

That said, not all sexual desires are healthy. Some, like what inspires pedophilia and incest, result in devastation when they are acted upon and must be addressed accordingly, ideally with professional help. It is also important to recognize and heed the deeper call for healing when we find ourselves turning to sexuality in a manner that extends from insecurity or reinforces or deepens trauma, which may be connected to things like a lack of self-love or fear of intimacy.

Sexual Exploration Is Healthy and Holy

Most sexual exploration is totally healthy. What is labeled as perversion is usually just creativity and enjoyment in sampling different things. Who's to say there's anything wrong with exploring if it's not hurting anyone? Why shouldn't people just try what they want to? If it feels good to them, wonderful. How exciting to identify new ways of celebrating and enjoying the human experience! As effective prophylactics against sexually transmitted infections (STIs) are readily available and most STIs are treatable, why not adventure?

I don't believe that we fully understand human sexuality. Most people have been cut off from its potentials for thousands of years because of factors like religion telling us that our desire or pleasure is wrong in some respect, that there is nothing holy in lust and the simple joys of delighting in the body, as if anything created by Spirit that feels this amazing could be inherently wicked. In some mystical traditions, sex is a pathway to the divine, a direct means of cosmic consciousness. Until we reach a place where we put no judgment on sexual desire, I don't think we will fully understand human sexuality. The way of the future is freedom, not restriction and holding falsehoods about the human experience that only exist when we believe in them. We owe future generations the work of pulling these weeds from the gardens of our minds.

Imagine for a moment if everyone had full freedom to explore their sexuality. If there was no negativity at all around experimenting with different genders, roles, and fetishes. If everyone felt affirmed in whatever they wanted to try, and when something wasn't for us, we simply accepted that and moved on to other things. Imagine if everyone held enthusiastic consent as a requirement for engaging with another person sexually, seeing it as one of the highest virtues. Or if couples felt able to celebrate each other's desires without feeling threatened by the possibility of exploring outside of the relationship, assuming that felt healthy and appealing to both of them.

There is room in life for all of us to learn about our authentic sexualities and to pursue whatever organically comes from that. This includes owning the pleasure of sex to the fullest degree we want to, and it's okay if that's not at all. Our bodies are sacred. Our sexuality is sacred. Allowing sexual energy to thunder within us is sacred, and sex is not the only way to do that. Asexual people still have access to sexual energy (and "sexual" here refers to the energy involved in sexual reproduction, which is not limited to procreative sex or even sex at all), and I recommend that anyone who is curious about this learn about the yogic practice of *brahmacharya*, which includes a means of sublimating sexual energy through celibacy and meditation. From primal, animalistic experiences to tender lovemaking to cosmic revelatory orgasms: the palette of sexuality is ours to explore, and if it weren't for the restrictive notions of sex, pleasure, and desire that others imposed on us, we would know that. It's time to let these restrictive notions go and find out how wonderful and electric being human really is, luxuriating in whatever feels healthy and authentic to us.

Weeding the Garden

Old Belief — There is something shameful, guilt-worthy, or wicked in my amount of sexual desire or lack of sexual desire and that of others.

When I believe this, I think there is something wrong with me if I'm "too horny" or not horny enough. This can cause a variety of internal stresses. I may not speak up about my desires in relationships, and I might feel guilt or shame about the amount I masturbate. I may also look down on people whose amount of sexual desire seems greater or lesser than mine, possibly even shaming them.

Old Belief — There is something wrong with the unconventional desires I have for certain sexual activities, roles, or types of partners, which also holds true for others.

When I believe this, I feel shame or guilt about the desires I have that I feel are inappropriate or even wrong. I may repress myself for years or my entire life, or I might act out because of this repression in ways that are harmful to me and threaten some of my relationships and sense of self-worth. When I do this, I judge myself harshly for it. I also likely look with scorn upon others whose sexual expressions feel inappropriate and wrong to me. I may even shame or guilt them. I feel trapped within a rigid box of sexual identity that stifles my sexual energy.

Planting New Beliefs

Affirm — I am willing to release old beliefs about sexuality. I am open to seeing my sexuality in a new light.

Consider for a moment what your sexuality might look like if no one had told you anything about sex other than basic sexual education and to enjoy it with other people who enthusiastically consent or by yourself.

How might your development have differed? What might you have tried that you didn't? How much sex might you have had by now?

Affirm — I recognize that sexual desire is a natural part of life and that anything that tells me otherwise operates out of alignment with the natural order.

Sexual urges are a healthy, natural aspect of being human. Sex is part of inherent reality. It is one dimension of the human experience that has nothing to do with society, culture, religion, and so on, except that like our relationship with food, our relationship with it can be shaped by external influences and how we think. Deep down, part of us knows what we want sexually, and if we are detached or disconnected from this part of ourselves, we can reestablish a connection with it with practice and care. Do your best to quiet your mind and ask: What do I want? Be present with whatever surfaces. Get in touch with this inner voice that speaks of joy and ecstasy.

Affirm — I recognize that the amount of sexual desire I have is likely different from others, and this is healthy, natural, and normal.

Much like our appetite for food, our appetite for sex varies, and in all of that, there is nothing amiss. If you feel like you want to have sex all the time, revel in it. If you never want to have sex, revel in that. Wherever you fall along the spectrum, it is fine and good as long as it is authentic, and we each have the means to get in touch with what is authentic for us. Much of the process of sexual reclamation begins with aligning with what feels natural, and that's exactly what these desires are.

Affirm — It is sacred for me to explore my sexuality and get to know what I desire and enjoy. It is also sacred and healthy for me to develop my sexuality however I choose.

Humans have created a palette of sexual options of the thought-dependent variety, and we are each invited to take our fill of them. It's amazing and unfortunate that such stringent ideas of right and wrong were imposed on most of us regarding this. Begin to let that go now: whatever you are attracted to in terms of gender, fetishes, and fantasies is beautiful and valid. There is nothing wrong with you for being sexual, naughty, and whatever else sounds good. Revel in what sets your body and soul afire. This is your life, and it can be as adventurous and orgasmic as you want.

Affirm — I am a divine being, effortlessly and endlessly worthy. My sexuality, whatever it is, is an extension of that. I celebrate my life upon this earth and all the joys available to me. I open to the fullness and richness of the human experience.

And so it is.

Exercises

Journal about the following questions: What messages about sexuality did you grow up with? How did these messages influence how you felt, thought, and acted? What does sexuality mean to you? What role do you see sexuality as having played in your life? What role would you like to see it play in your life moving forward? If you received beliefs about sexuality that you want to shift, what are they and how would you shift them? How do you think your life could change by believing these new thoughts (i.e., what might their impact be on your feelings, thoughts, actions, etc.)?

If you identify as sexual, brainstorm ways to celebrate your sexuality. Go wild if you want and think outside the box. If you put no limits on yourself beyond enthusiastically consenting partners, what would you do? Can you plan to incorporate some of this in the coming days or weeks? If so, how and when?

If you identify as asexual, brainstorm ways to celebrate your asexuality. What value and beauty do you find in it? What meaning does it bring to your life? Beginning with what feels natural and authentic about it, what do you find sacred about your asexuality?

Chapter 9
Career and Productivity

Notions about career and productivity can vary considerably depending on where we're from in the world. I know people from many countries and have witnessed how divergent our perspectives on career, productivity, and achievement can be. Most Europeans I've met, for example, didn't have the relentless and hardcore focus on career achievement that many people from the United States have. They didn't have the sense that most of their time must be spent being "productive" either, as many Americans do, which isn't to suggest that they weren't active in their careers and with other projects. They also enjoyed a considerably larger number of vacation days per year. Many were stunned when I told them that it's common in the United States to have as little as two weeks of paid vacation a year, and a large percentage of people who have more than that don't use all their vacation time. Not only that, but it is sometimes an expectation here that if we want to advance in our careers with a given company, we won't use all that time, despite it being a "benefit" of the job.

Even within the United States and different regions of countries, concepts of career and productivity can vary greatly. My relatives who live in rural areas have a different notion of what career achievement is from me, who grew up in a highly educated, career-focused Washington, DC, suburb and was told by my father that "If you do a half-ass job, you'll have a half-ass life." We all must get our money somehow, though, and decide what to do with our time, so it's important to explore this topic and dismantle the beliefs we hold about career and productivity that work against our well-being. It's also important to find a relationship with career and productivity that supports our well-being as best we can, to the degree that they are parts of our lives.

Many of us grow up around the notion that the structure of the average work schedule in the United States—work for four focused hours with one fifteen-minute break, followed by a lunch, then work for another four focused hours with a fifteen-minute break—is a normal and healthy way to work. Not just once, but five days a week, fifty weeks per year, for decades. No one may have ever told us this directly, but with it being the norm, if someone doesn't challenge it, we can easily absorb it as a realistic standard. In all my years of working and having therapy clients, I've only met a few people who could pull this off. Even people who work longer hours tend to structure their time differently or at least have some variety in what they're doing. I do not believe it is normal for most humans to be able to focus and maintain productivity like the "typical" work schedule suggests. When we believe that it is, though, and don't measure up, we can experience a constant underlying sense of dissatisfaction with our work performance, and I've had many clients who felt like that. Even if we successfully complete our projects and our boss is pleased with our results, there's a nagging sense of "I should be doing more," and this keeps us from feeling as satisfied with our work as we rightfully could.

This is a good example of why it is important to take a step back from societal or cultural expectations and ask ourselves if they make sense, rather than just go with them because they are traditional. Sometimes they are ill-fitting relics from a different time, and they may have never been healthy at all (like the commonly held notions that we should work when we are sick, despite our bodies clearly telling us to rest, or "clean our plates" at meals, despite our bodies telling us we're full). As the field of psychology grows and we gain greater insight into our nature via research, we develop a better grasp of what is healthy and realistic in areas of life like work. We can already see the benefits of this research improving the quality of work environments in some progressive companies that integrate it into their business models, often resulting in employees feeling more satisfied in their jobs.

The Expectation of a Dream Job

Many children are raised with a notion that there is one thing for them to do professionally, a "dream job" that's like a career destiny. As we grow up, we'll each identify some magical path and then the sun will shine upon us all our professional days because "if you love what you do, you'll never work a day in your life," as the saying goes. I remember when I was in fifth grade, the teachers tasked us with deciding our future careers, which they published in the class graduation book. The suggestion was that we'd each find a wonderfully fulfilling career that was tied to our purpose in life, and, at least in my family, no one refuted this. This is just one example of what can happen to children though. Depending on the degree of privilege we grew up with and the opportunities afforded by our society, we may or may not have heard a message like this anywhere other than school, and perhaps not even there. Our family may have placed considerable pressure on us to choose a specific type of career because of factors like financial opportunity, prestige, and stability, or placed little to no pressure on us at all. Perhaps we were told that we might as well not even aspire to much because "Things like that don't happen for people like us" or "Who do you think you are?"

Though some people do feel like they find their dream job, or at least dream field of employment, the notion that we each have one major professional contribution to make doesn't hold for many people. Many also go through life without ever feeling that their job is all that satisfying or purposeful. The narrative of a "dream job" fosters a belief in children that they should seek self-worth in the capitalistic structure around them and can incline them to feel disappointed in themselves if that doesn't work out, as if they are to blame for that. It is a wholly imposed narrative, not found throughout most of history or in many parts of the world today. It's like the harmful ideal of the fairy-tale relationship, and it belies the fact that many if not most of us can find a variety of jobs that could feel fulfilling to us to some degree, which has a lot to do with how we think about work in general. It also disregards the role of external factors in our work experience. Toxic work environments and managers are what many people dislike the most about their jobs, for example, far more than the work itself (i.e., even a "dream job" at a nightmare workplace will probably feel awful).

The concept of a "dream job" can cause us to look down on certain types of work, and it doesn't acknowledge the disparities of opportunity between people from different backgrounds. Some of us have very limited opportunities through which to shift our circumstances in terms of what is available to us in our society, and the way to maximize those usually involves education, which we largely complete before becoming adults. Children are too young to fully understand the stakes their performance in school holds. Are they then to blame as adults for being normal kids if they didn't do well in school? How people fare academically often has a lot to do with the influence of their families and communities. The current system greatly favors the privileged in a cycle where privilege feeds itself, and it doesn't do anywhere near enough to even the odds for children who don't come from privileged backgrounds. The notion of a "dream job," and the worldview inherent in that concept and its lack of recognition of privilege, can help keep people asleep to the stark realities faced by large swaths of others.

The Professional World Is Thought-Dependent

Some people think of careers as being central to the human experience (and that how hardworking we are is a measure of our virtue). They aren't. Aside from having to act to meet our basic needs, everything about the professional world is thought-dependent. It needn't exist, and we would all be fine if we'd never heard of it. I'm not denying that work can be fulfilling and provide us with some sense of purpose, particularly in what we can give to others in service and create to improve and enrich the quality of our lives. But how many people sincerely feel that way about their jobs? How many would still do what they're doing if they didn't need the money? On a different note, how many of the people who likely would stay where they are grew up with the privilege and encouragement to readily explore career paths? I find my work as a therapist and writer fulfilling, but I also have the benefit of working for myself and setting my own schedule. No one is lazy or defective for not wanting to punch a clock five days a week most weeks for fifty years or so in a job they feel ambivalent about in order to provide themselves or their family with a decent quality of life. Not to mention one where they feel underappreciated or even set up to fail or exploited by their employer or the work conventions of their country, which are part of a system that has no inherent place in human life.

None of this means that we don't have a natural motivation to do something with our lives besides meet our basic needs and enjoy ourselves. Many of us do. For example, I believe that curiosity, creativity, innovation, and exploration are authentic human drives. Yearning for expansion is inherent within the human mind and spirit. I believe that without the carrots of exorbitant wealth and power on one end, we would still make amazing discoveries and launch bold creative endeavors. Not only that, but those actions would likely be healthier for us and more organic, as they wouldn't be contaminated with greed, which has caused us to leap before we adequately looked many times. Just consider what we've done to the environment and how worker benefits have degraded over time in the name of profit over people.

Despite what anyone may have told us, there is nothing we need do with our lives to have value, and what we need to feel fulfilled is inherent within the human experience: the love we can feel, what we can share with dear ones, the joys and awes of taking in the natural world and connecting with Spirit, and so on. There are also millions of people in the world who are unable to work, either temporarily or permanently. Are they less valuable as people because of that? Of course not. That has nothing to do with their worth.

There is plenty of magnificence to go around in human life exactly as we find it. I believe that if we started with that foundation, we would feel healthier as a collective. Instead, there is this sense among many that we must go, go, go, and do, do, do, and "make something of our lives." While there's nothing inherently wrong with ambition and productivity, it is harmful to tie that to our sense of self-worth. That is a hamster wheel that none of us need get on. If you authentically love being ambitious and productive, though, go for it, and the same is true for things like loving challenges and friendly competition. This is your life, and whatever remains once you've weeded unhealthy beliefs from your inner garden is yours to own and celebrate. Success is 100 percent yours to define, and at the end of the day, your conscience is what you will answer to as you reflect on how you lived. When we clarify our values for ourselves, examining our beliefs and how we deeply feel about things, we are better able to live in a way that feels meaningful and successful to us over the years and at the end of life.

Making the Most of Where We Are

Unless we are prepared to live in a revolutionarily different way from the society we find ourselves in and see a course to that, the professional world is a space where it is wise for us to make the most of where we are as best we can. This includes owning our power to improve our circumstances. What is feasible for us can vary based on factors like the amount of privilege we have, but I believe most people have some power to find improvement from where they are. Even if we didn't do well in school as young people, for example, that doesn't mean we can't get some kind of education now that expands our professional options or that there aren't other opportunities available to us. Many people go back to school later in life and start new careers that they enjoy. While private schools are often exorbitantly expensive, at least in the US, between community colleges, state schools, and trade schools, there are educational options in many fields where people can avoid high, long-term debt. When I was a psychiatric case manager, I helped some clients return to school who previously felt that was impossible for them. We broke the process down into action steps, created timelines, and brainstormed success strategies. Eventually, they graduated and that was a huge turning point in their lives. Even if we don't see a way to improved career conditions, that doesn't mean we can't manifest one. It's amazing what can happen when our belief in our possibilities goes from "I can't" to "maybe I can."

Sometimes we also just have to make the most of how things are in our jobs while working to change conditions for the future. I had a supervisor once who said we can expect to dislike twenty percent of any job, and hearing that benefitted me greatly, including helping me extricate myself from the "dream job" narrative (i.e., "Even in an ideal job, I can expect to dislike twenty percent of it"). I also derive comfort from the gratitude I feel in appreciating how much better of a position I am in than most of my recent ancestors were in terms of resources. They had far less of a say in what they did professionally and lived in much worse conditions. I have found ample value over the years in using my jobs as avenues for personal and spiritual development too, which was something I learned to do in my spiritual training program. For example, most jobs offer opportunities to develop qualities like concentration, active listening, and acting with intention. I also practice karma yoga, the yoga of selfless action, which is a manner of working that involves performing each task as attentively and mindfully as we can while cultivating detachment from the benefits and rewards of the work. When practicing karma yoga, we strive to release all extraneous thoughts and be fully present with whatever action we're taking. Though detaching from benefits and rewards might sound like it could decrease productivity, my experience is that I am more effective in what I do when I practice karma yoga and work can become meditative. If you want to dive deeper into this topic, there's a chapter about turning work into part of a spiritual path in my first book, *The Little Work*, and a classic treatise on karma yoga is the Hindu scripture the Bhagavad Gita.

The professional world is such a substantial part of most of our lives that if we solely hate or resent it, we are bound to suffer a great deal. In the interest of our well-being, it is important to strive to see our work in other ways. That said, it's not beneficial to acquiesce to an environment that's harmful toward us and future generations either, and none of what I share in this chapter is meant to suggest that we should willingly subject ourselves to a toxic work environment if we have other satisfactory options. In those situations, it's critical to leave them when we can. The path to improved professional well-being, in my opinion, is to take the reins of our minds, decondition ourselves from harmful beliefs, own our inherent worthiness, and then from that vista of strength, do what we can to better things for ourselves and others.

Following Our Bliss

As technology continues progressing and eliminating jobs, my hope is that large swaths of people will accept that this means wealth must be redistributed, and there's nothing wrong with that. Without having to worry about earning money to survive, we would be freer to follow our individual muses of purpose. I believe they would lead us to remarkable places because I know the creative force within the human spirit. It is one that would be served, rather than hindered, by freedom from undue restriction. Imagine if everyone's needs were met, and for those who wanted more, they could work for it, but out of choice, not necessity. Imagine if we all had the encouragement to connect with our authenticity and go wherever it led us, and then do whatever we felt was best in light of that. No toxic productivity telling us we must do, do, do to be valuable and no ill-fitting jobs that we resent. Just the inner North Star guiding us on.

It is an inherent truth of humanity that we have diverse talents, and sometimes our station in life depends on how these talents are valued during the time and place we live in. Centuries ago, the life of an actor was no lavish affair. Today, movie stars are paid more than almost any other profession. If someone had a beautiful singing voice a thousand years ago, that may have been nothing more than a delight for their family. Today, it could lead to fortune and worldwide fame, or a sense of disappointment in never having experienced these things despite being talented enough to. The connection between talent and career is novel in most cases, not historic, certainly to the degree that we see it now.

There are people who naturally excel in math and science (and this was true before math and science were discovered), the humanities, and every field that we have brought into existence through the mind. Talent and drive within those areas innately coexist for most people, in a way that makes exploring our gifts satisfying on its own. This needn't be forced. If we are left to follow our bliss, living in a world where technology affords us greater freedom of self-discovery and the time and resources to follow our dreams, we will be fine. Particularly if we can liberate ourselves from the notion that our career is tied to our self-worth. Some of us will find a way to have our natural talents be our careers, while others won't. Some of us will maximize our potential, while others will leave theirs undeveloped. That's all right too. Having a career that maximizes our talents isn't a requirement for a contented, satisfying life, even though that can be fulfilling. It's also fine to spend our lives devoted to things we aren't that talented in but love anyway. Must we be good at something to pursue it? Like art or music? If we love it, that's what really matters.

In the end, what does Spirit ask of us? I believe our greatest duty is to be kind to each other and ourselves, to care for each other. If we teach our children how to find and follow their inner North Stars, that will guide them, and the world they create will be magnificent and loving. No one will ever need to work a job they hate again and everyone will have the opportunity to develop, utilize, and offer their talents. Think of it for a moment, and what amazing, enriching, and exciting lives they will lead together in service of the greater good. This is not an impossible dream.

Weeding the Garden

Old Belief — If I don't meet my society's definition of "hard-working," I'm lazy or defective and have less value than others.

When I believe this, I feel like something is fundamentally wrong with me if I'm not able to meet the standard expectations my society places upon me. I probably look down on others who don't meet them or don't meet them as well as I do. As we explored some earlier, modern concepts of work are not universal. They are thought-dependent and vary from society to society, culture to culture. As Jiddu Krishnamurti purportedly said, "It's no measure of health to be well-adjusted to a profoundly sick society."[16] When we don't mesh well with a societal push to be hardworking, we're not the problem. This doesn't mean it isn't fruitful for our well-being to find a way to make peace with having to work and do our best with the opportunities we have. There's a difference though between doing that and internalizing unhealthy beliefs about ourselves related to productivity and work. When I believe I am bound by standards of productivity and don't meet them, I feel inadequate, possibly to some degree for most of my life.

Old Belief — The perfect career exists for me, and I will readily be able to find it and thrive in it.

When I believe this and see myself as having access to opportunities, I quest for the perfect career, and I feel disappointed if I don't find it. Each job I have becomes an internal struggle of wondering if this was the right decision or if there's something else I'd rather do or be better suited for, unless I hit the jackpot of finding a career that fits my talents well and feels satisfying. I have difficulty feeling happy where I am because I wonder if I should be somewhere else (which is also often how people feel about relationships).

When I believe this and don't see myself as having access to opportunities (or my access is limited), I may think that the life I was meant to lead eludes me. I might feel that I've been thwarted and cheated by circumstances and therefore am unable to realize my true potential. It becomes difficult for me to feel satisfied with whatever I end up doing for work.

---

16. Mark Vonnegut, *The Eden Express* (New York: Laurel, 1975), 264.

Planting New Beliefs

Affirm — I am willing to release old beliefs about work, career, and productivity. I am open to seeing these topics in a new light.

Take a moment to think through everything others told you about work and productivity and what examples were around you and goalposts were placed before you. Imagine if none of these were there. What do you think you would do, career-wise? Let yourself fill in this canvas in your mind.

Affirm — My value as a human being is nonnegotiable. It has nothing to do with what I produce or how successful I am in my career. Success is mine to define, and I needn't even define it or work with that concept.

As we tap into our abiding sources of value, we stop looking outside of ourselves for our self-worth. If you want to have a big, bold career, pursue one. If you don't, don't. If you want to constantly be on the go doing things, do that. If not, no problem. All of this is up to you. Just make sure that you are the one defining success for yourself. This is your life, and you are free to determine both what you value and how you act based on that.

Affirm — My talents are mine to offer others as gifts, and my inner knowing will guide me to a fulfilling way of doing that, which may be great or small, if that is right for me.

I believe we all have gifts to offer others and to enjoy on our own. Some of us will be the next Einsteins and Mozarts, and there's a whole spectrum between that and talentless for people to fill, and in all of this, everything is as it should be. Some of us will find or create careers that use our talents and others won't. This has nothing to do with how successful or valuable we are, and it need have no bearing on our sense of self-worth.

As we connect with Spirit, inner guidance comes to us. We begin to feel our way through the choices before us in a process that is integrated with the wisdom we've accumulated and the discernment we've honed. We get a sense of what would feel healthy and helpful to do, and we find the motivation to do it. The bar of achievement increasingly becomes relative only to the dreams we authentically hold and the goals we make in light of them, against the backdrop of our opportunities. Our relationship to the thought-dependent cultural constructs of others about work and in general need have little to no bearing on our inner experience or sense of self-worth. This is available to you. Getting there mostly takes practice.

Affirm — I am a divine being, effortlessly and endlessly worthy. Whatever I want to do with my life that is healthy for me and others is wonderful. I have nothing to prove to anyone and nothing to earn. I am enough as I am, and in knowing this, I trust that what is good for me to do will become clear as I focus on receiving my inner knowing.

And so it is.

Exercises

Journal about the following questions: What messages about career and productivity did you grow up with? How did these messages influence how you felt, thought, and acted? What do career and productivity mean to you? What role do you see them as having played in your life? What role would you like to see them play in your life moving forward? If you received beliefs about career and productivity that you want to shift, what are they and how would you shift them? How do you think your life could change by believing these new thoughts (i.e., what might their impact be on your feelings, thoughts, actions, etc.)?

Journal about your career trajectory: what it is and what you want it to be, if anything. Incorporate some of the concepts from this affirmative talk and your answers to the journaling exercise in the previous paragraph while doing this.

Chapter 10
Money and Material Goods

Money and materialism are extremely loaded topics for many people, and how could they not be? Immense disparities of wealth exist throughout the world. Financial lack and the consequences of it are at the heart of so much suffering, from seemingly little things, like not being able to partake in the latest trends, to huge ones, like not being able to afford healthcare or adequate housing. I can imagine people years from now looking back on this time with amazement that some societies could be so wealthy yet have such huge wealth disparities, observing with horror that we had the technology and resources such that no one need live in poverty, be homeless, or lack healthcare and we let these problems go unsolved for years. That's the world we live in, though. Hopefully, if enough of us realize this and advocate accordingly, it will change soon. It could shift quickly if a critical mass of us get on board with this cause. Until then, we are tasked with doing our best with where we are.

Many people see money as "the root of all evil" and hate it accordingly. This kind of belief will yield a host of difficulties, psychologically and metaphysically, given how central money is in much of the world and how awful it feels to hate something, particularly something that's part of our everyday lives. I'm not saying we must love money, and certainly not the systems of privilege it is wrapped up in, but it is beneficial for our well-being to make some kind of peace with it: for example, by affirming that money isn't inherently good or bad or that money and greed are separate issues. It doesn't matter what you believe in particular. Just find something that helps you establish material well-being for yourself in alignment with your ethics, ideally something that facilitates changes in the broader society so it can become more equitable.

From early childhood, an onslaught of influences condition us to want certain things. When I was growing up in the 1980s, there was a popular TV show called "Lifestyles of the Rich and Famous" that was all about how fabulous and amazing it is to be rich. My friends and I dreamt of having mansions and fancy cars, which we talked about sometimes. I don't think anyone in my family ever said to me that I should try to make as much money as possible and live a lifestyle that reflected that, but the greater cultural message about that was clear. We see this today in the reality TV world, in the entertainment industry, and on social media, where influencers parade lavish lifestyles before us, featuring designer clothing, luxurious homes, exotic travel, and high-end gadgets that are like capitalistic carrots. Not to mention the ads that greet us seemingly everywhere with content tailor-made to make us believe we not only want certain products, but need them in order to be cooler or sexier or we're missing out without them. There are so many messages trying to manipulate our desires, and yet when we get in touch with our authenticity, many of us realize we could care less about most of what they push us toward. We don't actually want what we were told to want.

That's what happened to me. As I embarked upon inner work in my early twenties and started releasing old beliefs that didn't fit me, I realized I didn't want much of what I was conditioned to want. A huge mansion sounded like a lot of space and work for a single person, and the difference between $2,000 sheets and $20 sheets didn't matter to me. As soon as I stopped caring about these lavish things, they lost their value for me, fading like any element of a thought-dependent reality will without our reinforcement of it. I didn't feel like I was missing out on these things because I sincerely didn't want them. This has helped me follow a career trajectory focused more on what feels meaningful to me rather than what will net me the highest income.

Owning Our Authentic Wants

Though my path led me away from luxury, there is nothing wrong with wanting well-made products and high-end items. There's something to be said for the beauty and intention of fine craftsmanship and the application of art in material goods. That said, we all have a duty to work toward creating a world where none of that comes at the expense of a comfortable and equitable quality of life for all. The way things are now being "the way of the world" is just an idea many of us were conditioned to believe. As with the other topics in this book, concepts of money and material goods, including their value and worth, varied considerably throughout history and are just as flexible now as they were then. This is another area where we have the freedom to explore a topic and determine the role we want it to play in our lives.

In recent years, many people have found profound benefit in approaching material goods from an animistic perspective, perceiving a spirit or non-human consciousness within them and treating them with care accordingly. This outlook was common in the ancient world and lives on in some cultures today, and cultivating it can begin simply, with a practice of consistently saying "thank you" to the items in our lives.

Relatedly, there is nothing wrong with finding comfort in material things. Items we associate with loved ones and fond memories, for example, can conjure enriching and profound states of mind, and this takes on an even deeper level if we see them as inspirited or recognize that they, like all things, have a divine essence. While it's important not to be so attached to them that losing them could threaten our sense of self-worth or security, this doesn't mean we can't enjoy and celebrate them. We just continue doing the work of seeking a sense of abiding serenity and love within while participating in the physical world in a manner that extends from that.

Regarding how much money to aim for, compelling research suggests that as long as people have enough money not to have to worry about it while being able to afford a comfortable quality of life, their overall life satisfaction doesn't change much if they are wealthy.[17] Aside from the fact that not having enough money can be stressful, difficult, and agonizing at extremes, the old saying is true: money doesn't buy happiness.

When it comes to money and material things, the bottom line in inner gardening is for each of us to figure out what we authentically want, to get in touch with our cores and separate our authentic desires from the external influences that cloud our view of them. It doesn't matter what we want as long as we don't harm others in the pursuit of it to the best of our ability. When we undertake the work of discovering our authentic wants, it becomes clear to many of us that much of what we want has little to do with money at all. It often has more to do with the quality time we share with loved ones, what we give back, what we explore within our minds, creative endeavors, and the simple pleasures of life.

Weeding the Garden

Old Belief — More is better when it comes to money because luxury is crucial for success and life satisfaction.

When I believe this, I judge myself and my family based on how much money we have. From a young age, I may see myself as less than if my family doesn't have a lot of money, and if I'm unable to turn the financial tide in my life as I get older, this feeling will likely abide within me. If I have a lot of money, I may look down on others who don't as being less than, as if I'm somehow inherently better than them or more worthy. My

---

17. Andrew T. Jebb, Louis Tay, Ed Diener, and Shigehiro Oishi, "Happiness, Income Satiation and Turning Points around the World," *Nature Human Behaviour* 2, no. 1 (January 2018): 33–38, doi:10.1038/s41562-017-0277-0.

choice of career will probably relate to how much I value money, as well as the things I want to buy.

Old Belief — I'm inadequate if I don't have a lot of money. I'm missing out on the important things in life. Money buys happiness.

When I believe this, I chase after money as much as I can or feel inadequate when I don't. I dream of being able to afford luxurious things, and when I can't do this, I feel cut off from abundance. I may feel like I'll never truly be happy or satisfied and believe that life is against me. However much money I make might never feel like enough, and when I feel unhappy, I may attribute that in part to not being where I want to be financially, even with a comfortable income. When I believe that wealth defines my success and satisfaction and don't measure up to my desired standard of it, I feel like a failure.

Planting New Beliefs

Affirm — I am willing to release old beliefs about money and material things. I am open to seeing money and material things in a new light.

Imagine for a moment if you'd never seen an advertisement in your life. What do you think you would want? What do you feel you need of the things that you have? What might you want to let go of? What have you bought only to realize it brought you little satisfaction? Items that only exist outside of the natural world aren't required for living. This doesn't mean they can't be helpful or wonderful. Some make us quite comfortable and far safer than we'd be when left to the whims of the elements! They aren't mandatory parts of the human experience, though. We don't need them to feel satisfied and fulfilled in our lives.

Regarding money, many people simply see it as energy, and no more fundamentally bad than any other form of energy. This enables them to harness it in their lives while also working to shift the oppressive systems money is wrapped up in. There are societies in the world with a partially socialist orientation too that still have money and generally thrive. If that's not true where we are, we can work toward a more equitable society while not having as much of an antagonistic relationship with money itself.

Affirm — I recognize that I am free to decide what I want in my life, separate from the input of others. I love knowing that something can be valuable to another and not to me, and there is nothing wrong with that.

As we move through life, our desires may change, and that's totally fine. What we appreciate one year may mean little to us the next, and none of this bears on our self-worth. It also doesn't matter what other people do unless they're harming others. Let them enjoy what they like while we enjoy what we like.

In her popular book *The Life-Changing Magic of Tidying Up*, Marie Kondo shared that her recommendation for clients who declutter their homes is to primarily keep items that "spark joy."[18] This can include many different types of items—sentimental ones, fun ones, goofy ones, luxurious ones, whatever—but this approach creates a beautiful atmosphere. That can be how your home feels and the way you operate with material things in your life too.

Affirm — Happiness doesn't come from having lots of money. It is a state of satisfaction I can experience within by aligning with Spirit and feeling good about the choices I make.

The true abundance of life has little to do with material goods. It's about how we feel, and how we feel is generally a product of how much we live in alignment with our values and Spirit, and there is no price tag for that. The more we do it, the less we care about the fluctuating circumstances of the outer world and the luxury we are or aren't able to afford.

You have the ability, right now, to be free of conditioned desires. It is with you every moment of your life. It's simply a matter of realizing this

---

18. Marie Kondo, *The Life-Changing Magic of Tidying Up: The Japanese Art of Decluttering and Organizing*, trans. Cathy Hirano (Berkeley, CA: Ten Speed Press, 2014), 41.

and doing the work to sustain that realization. This may not be easy, but it is always available. You needn't feel like you "need" these manmade things. When we align with Spirit and live from there, we tend to enjoy material things in a fun, uplifting way. We can delight in creature comforts, have exhilarating adventures, and celebrate lavishly with loved ones and then leave that be what it is, knowing ourselves to be so much more.

Affirm — I am a divine being, effortlessly and endlessly worthy. I take charge of my material desires, aligning them with my authentic, inner knowing. I love that the satisfaction of Spirit is always available to me, and the best things in life are free.

And so it is.

Exercises

Journal about the following questions: What messages about money and material goods did you grow up with? How did these messages influence how you felt, thought, and acted? What do money and material goods mean to you? What role do you see them as having played in your life? What role would you like to see them play in your life moving forward? If you received beliefs about money and material goods that you want to shift, what are they and how would you shift them? How do you think your life could change by believing these new thoughts (i.e., what might their impact be on your feelings, thoughts, actions, etc.)?

Think about what your "magic number" is for money, where you have enough to feel financially comfortable. Only do this after sifting through your wants and determining what you authentically want, separate from conditioning. Is this a number you can reach on your current career path? If not, what actions might you take to help get you there?

Chapter 11
Family

When families are functional and healthy, they are often among people's greatest sources of joy, love, and fulfillment. Sadly, many families are not this way, and few topics are more loaded and relevant for many of us during an inner gardening process than family. As children, our families are the foundation of our universe. The undeveloped and immature minds of childhood lead us to turn our parents and loved ones into seemingly mythic figures. It's not until our late teens or early to mid-twenties that we can usually appreciate that our parents are human beings, just like us, with understandable and natural strengths, weaknesses, and flaws. The stories of childhood are slow to die, and this holds not only for our parents, but for all close family members.

The spiritual teacher Ram Dass once said, "If you think you're enlightened go spend a week with your family," suggesting that this is one of the greatest tests of our spiritual development and emotional maturity.[19] After all, our family members not only know how to push our buttons:

19. Ram Dass, "Ram Dass Quotes," Love Serve Remember Foundation, accessed September 29, 2021, https://www.ramdass.org/ram-dass-quotes/.

they were often the ones who installed them, which is a frequent saying in recovery programs. Conceptualizations of identity tend to persist in families too, which can be quite frustrating. For example, the youngest child who was treated like they didn't know much while growing up and who goes on to become a Rhodes Scholar might still be treated like they don't know much.

Few wounds sting like the wounds of childhood, and few linger as prominently. Part of this is because wounding that occurs before we're mature enough to healthfully address it gets processed poorly and etches itself into our minds accordingly. This is particularly true if traumatizing events occur repeatedly, which can create deep grooves within us, and also if we continue seeing the people involved in them, which is one thing that generally distinguishes family trauma from trauma from peers at school. Wounds of childhood are also conceptualized at the child's level of understanding. This often results in skewed, harmful core beliefs in our minds, some of which may be so deep we don't realize they're there. Many if not most of us learn unhealthy habits from our families too, in terms of how to see ourselves and others and how to act in the world, relationships, and with ourselves.

Our parents were also unable to teach us things that they didn't know. If they weren't raised to treat family members with unconditional love, for example, they wouldn't know how to do that just because it sounded like a good idea to them. If they didn't grow up around models of emotional maturity, they may have big gaps in their emotional development and, consequently, have been unequipped to facilitate emotional maturation in their children, and this is true of many people. They may not have even realized there was anything wrong with simply repeating what was done to them in their childhood homes. The field of family psychology, and psychology in general, has grown tremendously in the last fifty years, but that doesn't mean everyone's caught up with it.

Most people continue to play out the unhealthy patterns of their families, and that likely happened with us to some degree. Experiences of familial harm and the way they connect with our behavior and outlook is frequently one of the main things unearthed in therapy, which is where many people first notice the depth of the cycle of violence. Harm is passed from person to person, generation to generation. Hurt people go on to hurt others as a reaction to their own pain, making past harm the primary cause of future harm. In my experience, internally and as a mental health professional, this is usually true, with some exceptions related to things like diminished capacity, burdensome circumstances, and not being aware their actions are harmful.

This isn't to suggest that we have no free will and people shouldn't be held accountable for their actions, but it's not just or accurate to decontextualize people either, falling prey to the fundamental attribution error. As I wrote earlier, there is also no need to rush to compassion in a healing process related to harm from a family member (or anyone), and forgiveness is something that happens subconsciously. Our work, when we feel ready and not before, is to pave the way for forgiveness by recognizing the various factors that shaped that family member and inspired their harmful behavior, leading to the moments when their life intersected with ours.

My Story of Family Healing

This is the story of how I was able to do this work in my own life with my relationship with my mother. I debated considerably about including some of the specifics I share because of not wanting to tarnish her memory, but I feel like it is important to be honest and hope the greater exploration I provide keeps that from happening. The story starts with the bullying I experienced in my childhood, which escalated once I reached middle school. There, I was dehumanized almost every day at school for three years, with other students calling me homophobic slurs so frequently you'd think they were my name. This was after being bullied for being gender-nonconforming in elementary school harshly enough that I would miss class to meet with the guidance counselor. I still remember her teaching me how to stand up to the bullies and how little anything I tried made a difference. In eighth grade, at thirteen, I became suicidal and two of my friends turned me in to my middle school's guidance counselor because they were worried about my safety. In her office, she asked me if I was depressed, and as I steeled myself to lie and say no, I exploded in tears. I uncontrollably sobbed for the better part of an hour. She called my mother and shared with her what my friends had said, and when I got home, my mom angrily told me I needed to learn to "roll with the punches," which was one of her favorite sayings, and criticized me for not being stronger. She offered no comfort, and this set the stage for our frequent screaming matches in high school once I grew teeth of my own.

I was livid with my mother for years about the way she treated me that day and all the other times when her anger, denial, or avoidance got the better of her. She frequently pushed back firmly on my choices, particularly the queerer ones, and constantly rewrote my life into something she could feel comfortable with. This included eventually acting like the same trauma and hostile environment that led my middle school guidance counselor to strongly recommend that I transfer schools hadn't been as bad as it was, which infuriated me. I was mad that she seldom apologized for anything too, even when she was clearly in the wrong.

I was also hurt that she pulled away from me and my sister as we entered middle school. Parenting seemed like a chore that she'd rather not be bothered with, even though I never questioned that she loved me. For all the pain and fighting, I knew I was the apple of her eye. It was only years later, weeks before she died, that I learned she was diagnosed with leukemia when I was in elementary school. She recalled how she distanced herself from me and my sister because she didn't want the loss of her to be too much for us to bear, hoping to at least live long enough to see us graduate from high school. No one thought she'd live on until we were in our thirties.

I also came to understand that my mother carried the trauma of having a father who died when she was nine and a mother who suffered greatly after that and lashed out at her for years. She grew up in a home where yelling was normal, and her parents thought it was better to be blunt than nurturing and supportive in order to build resilience, which she simply continued with me. I recognized that as a Jew, she struggled to fit in at times while growing up, and being born during the Holocaust escalated this to a high degree and brought its own fears and concerns. As I understood how difficult it was for her to navigate the painful realities of her life and how she was never taught how to by the adults around her, I understood why she was so quick to disregard, deny, or push away the painful realities of mine. In light of her early experiences, fitting in became very important to her, and I believe that is part of why it was so hard for her to accept a child who didn't. When I learned in graduate school about the nature of denial as a psychological defense, and how it can even occur unconsciously, my understanding of her deepened even more.

Also, because I was bullied for ostensibly being gay, I felt too ashamed to talk to my parents about it, so the call from the guidance counselor was the first she'd heard of my depression, and I think she didn't know how to handle it. She didn't have the coping strategies that I eventually learned from self-help materials and healers, most of which didn't even exist when she was young or weren't widely available. She knew little of psychology and mental illness too, which was shrouded in far more stigma then than it is now, much less how to raise a gender-nonconforming child, a topic that has only begun receiving mainstream attention in recent years. I came to recognize, when I was ready to be understanding, that the way she treated me was an extension of what she knew, and given her perspective, it was what she thought was best. She wanted me to have a successful life. It's just that she wanted me to have the successful life of her envisioning, not mine.

We often see this with parents. "They had the best of intentions" and "They wanted a better life for their children" frequently indicate a fairly specific trajectory that the child may not want at all and experiences substantial stress trying to follow. When we consider where our parents were coming from, though, it is usually clear why they wanted the things for us that they did, and this often reflects a history of familial hardship in some form or a rise out of it. Some of us reach the summit of our parents' hopes and expectations and realize it largely satisfies us. Others feel ambivalent about it, and some of us rebel against it. For all of us, though, the greater route to an overall "better life" is the one that authentically fulfills us. I don't believe that anyone who lives with authenticity as their compass and has a comfortable quality of life feels less satisfied than someone who largely lives based on the imposed desires of others yet is more financially successful and higher achieving, assuming their families don't shun them.

It's become cliché to be told to look at our parents and say, "They were doing the best they could." The reason that's a cliché is because in most cases, it's true, especially when we view situations holistically, considering our parents' understanding and awareness alongside their circumstances and capacity. This may not be what our pain wants to hear, and honoring where we are in processing that pain is why the work of compassion isn't something we rush or force, but it is usually true. It's important to include the context of circumstances and capacity here because both can greatly influence our behavior. We may observe a parent, for example, who seems to understand right from wrong better than their actions would suggest. When we examine their life circumstances, though, we can appreciate how holding down three jobs while trying to raise two kids as a single parent stretched their patience further than it could take. Their life stressors diminished their capacity to behave well, and situations like that must be acknowledged when trying to understand people's behavior. We might also have a parent who has an untreated mental health condition that inclines them to act harshly toward others, like borderline personality disorder often does.

My mother didn't want to harm me. She sought to raise me in a way where I would be tough enough to weather a world that had challenged her, as it had challenged her mother and countless others before. As a Jew, she stood in a long line of resilient survivors, and like most of the fruit of surviving, some of the habits that came to her were healthy and others weren't. She passed on what she learned from the various aspects of her upbringing to me, who decided to stop the cycles of harm at play in that, as all of us are tasked with doing today in the ones we find ourselves in. Not just for ourselves, but for future generations, and one way we can do this is by doing what we've done throughout this book: recognizing the unhealthy patterns of thought, belief, and action and challenging them, dismantling them, and replacing them, over and over until they erode away.

I was thirty-one when my mother died, and because I had done a ton of work on myself, a substantial amount of which involved my relationship with her, there was no unfinished business between us, at least on my side. I had discovered years before that underneath my anger at her, there was pain. The pain of being hurt by many people for most of my childhood and of a boy who just wanted to be loved, understood, and accepted as he was, in particular by his mom. Because I'd learned to give myself that love, understanding, and acceptance, to find it within, I didn't need it from her, and a certain degree of acceptance was there, at least regarding my sexuality. I had also long since stopped looking for the apologies that were probably never going to come, and I didn't need them either. Were there echoes of pain? Sure. I imagine if she said the wrong thing too many times, she could've triggered me like she used to, resulting in a tearful rage, but forgiveness had happened. I rarely thought about our tumultuous past, and when I did, it didn't bother me. The wound had healed, and as she died, with my hand in hers, I only wished her well.

Healthy Boundaries and Healthy Children

Some of us experienced horrifying treatment in the home, well above and beyond the kind of difficulties I shared here. Our parents may have raped us or beaten us brutally, kicked us out of our houses and excommunicated us from our communities for being queer or trans, and more. We may never forgive that. Sometimes the understanding that comes is essentially that our parents were very ill, ignorant, or wounded, and we do our best to move forward with our lives. While we may carry this trauma with us in a stinging form forever, that doesn't mean we can't still have a healthy, largely contented life. It just may not involve our parents.

There is no requirement when having compassion for others that we welcome them into our intimate lives again or become anyone's doormat or punching bag. Sometimes the healthiest thing to do is be compassionate from a safe distance, and we get to decide what feels safe enough for us. There may also be no healthy manner in which to have a relationship with someone, and if that's where we are with a family member, I believe that Spirit can provide us with a way to make peace with that.

Like all subjects in this book, how the topic of family manifests within us depends on what's in our minds, not the minds of others. In terms of our sense of well-being, it doesn't have to matter how our family members see us. We can't control that, but we can guide how we think of ourselves and how much we value their opinion.

Many people resonate with the concept of "chosen family," where they make friends who effectively become family members. This can be a beautiful bond to share, and there are myriad ways we can enjoy connecting with each other. The canvas is open for us to dream and fill.

When it comes time to raise our own children, the main recommendation I have is to apply the underlying concepts within this book. Children need to be accepted as they are, know they are unconditionally loved, and, ideally, be given the freedom of self-discovery. Some of the latter will vary depending on the circumstances and opportunities within our society. With the former, we can take care to show them love and affection simply because we love them, rather than mostly as a reward for good grades or other victories. This will help them understand that our love is unconditional.

It's also important to model for children that we are fallible human beings. Even though they won't understand adult psychology until they are older, if their parents never apologize, either to their children or each other, that is what the children will learn to do. It's critical for parents to realize that above any other influence, their children learn how to be human beings from them. Our kids absorb the way we demonstrate emotion, responsibility, and accountability. Fortunately, it is far better for our children if we model imperfection in a healthy manner than strive for perfection, and this takes ample pressure off of us.

I once knew a life coach who said she struggled with arguing with her teenage children for years before deciding to adopt a coaching approach with them. Rather than tell them what to do, she leaned into their knowledge of right and wrong, and what seemed healthy and unhealthy to them. She found this revolutionized her relationship with them for the better, and that most of the time, they knew what was best, and having them say it themselves was powerful. If they acted against that, as teenagers are wont to do, sometimes skinned knees are a necessary part of maturation. We can neither learn lessons for others, nor get them to value what we do and see the world and themselves through our eyes. We can accept them as they are, though, nurture the legitimacy of their authentic desires, and take whatever protective actions are necessary to ensure that they're safe as their young minds mature into adulthood.

Weeding the Garden

Old Belief — My parents messed me up for life and that is totally their fault. They should have done better and known better.

When I believe this, I may feel immense shame or guilt if I don't measure up to my family's expectations or try to shame or guilt other family members if I feel like they don't. I make major life decisions to try to please my family, perhaps including my vocation, where I live, and even the person I marry. Much of the shame and guilt that many people experience in life stems from their relationship with family and is excessive. When I believe I'm failing my family, I am hard on myself and struggle to enjoy my life.

Old Belief — My parents should have done better and known better. They messed me up for life. I am trapped in what my family believes about me.

When I believe my parents should have known and done better without appreciating their context, I see them as fully culpable agents of harm in my life. I exist in an adversarial relationship with them, even if just internally. When I believe I am messed up for life, it becomes monumentally harder for me to do anything about the patterns of unhealthy behavior and emotional reactivity that wreak havoc in my life. This belief forms a barrier against my healing, and I run into the same issues over and over again. When I believe I am trapped in what my family believes about me,

I feel stifled within my own being and upset when I see them. I feel like I can't get the kind of support and love I want from them, and that I'm not seen for who I am.

Old Belief — I must micromanage my children's worlds and make their decisions for them to keep them safe.

When I believe I must micromanage my children's lives, I do everything I can to insulate them from any potential difficulty or harm. I try to impose my beliefs on them and make decisions for them, including in areas where they are probably best left alone, like the subjects they want to study and whom to choose as friends. In my fear, I do not let them authentically explore who they are, which is one of the worst restrictions we can place upon a person.

Planting New Beliefs

Affirm — I am willing to release old beliefs about family. I am open to seeing family in a new light.

Family stories, conditioning, and experiences can be among the hardest to work through, but it is possible to move forward from where we are. We can feel lighter and freer than we do now. The power to do this is within us, and Spirit supports us in our healing, endlessly. Our inner knowing will aid us in processing what we need to and identifying helpful resources.

Affirm — I can shift the stories I have about family. Family can be about whatever I want it to be about. My perspective can change from what I've learned.

It doesn't matter if we come from a rigidly traditional family or one that was fluid and flexible: we get to decide how we carry that within us. Our mental agreement with the stories of shame and guilt that linger with us is what anchors them in our experience. Sometimes they can be hard to release and take time to, but this doesn't mean we can't do it. Even if not always fully, to a great extent. Also, you get to decide what family means to you. You have the power to give it whatever role you want in your life.

Affirm — I can see my family members as flawed, like all human beings, and move forward from the experiences of my childhood. I do not need anything from my family to validate me or for my self-worth, including to be seen as I am today.

Many of us primarily harm others out of ignorance or immaturity. Sometimes people just don't know better or have blind spots where they currently are in their development, or they lack the capacity to do better because of other factors in their lives. We have the ability to see our family members as human beings though with strengths and weaknesses, struggles and pain. We need not worry about forgiving them and "getting over it." That is not our work. We can try to understand them when we feel ready, figure out what boundaries would be healthy for us, and then move forward in light of that, and we are always worthy and full of love exactly as we are. No one ever need give us love and acceptance for us to know that is true.

Affirm — I can raise my children to be empowered, with an understanding of what is healthy and unhealthy. I can pro-vide them with unconditional love and the freedom of self-discovery.

There is no greater gift that we can give a child than unconditional love and the freedom of self-discovery. Isn't that what you wanted? There is no need to impose ourselves on children in any kind of rigid way, aside from what we must do to keep them safe and healthy. We can love them, support them, teach them ethics, and then trust in their budding wisdom as they enter young adulthood. Children whose parents repress them often rebel. I certainly did. But children who have the freedom to discover themselves? What is there to rebel against? This doesn't mean no rules. It does mean rules that are explained, with increasing complexity as each child's mind develops, and any valid rule can be explained.

Don't you want to know who your children really are? Don't you want them to feel comfortable sharing that with you? Whatever path they choose will be right for them if they follow their inner North Star, and that is also true of us.

Affirm — I am a divine being, effortlessly and endlessly worthy. I can find a healthy sense of family in my life in some way if that is important to me, and if it's not, that's okay too. Everything I need to feel loved and whole is always available to me.

And so it is.

Exercises

Journal about the following questions: What messages about family did you grow up with? How did these messages influence how you felt, thought, and acted? What does family mean to you? What role has family played in your life? What role would you like to see family play in your life moving forward? If you received beliefs about family that you want to shift, what are they and how would shift them? How do you think your life could change by believing these new thoughts (i.e., what might their impact be on your feelings, thoughts, actions, etc.)?

Consider the role(s) you have in your family, attending to the various family constellations in your life. Do you feel like your role(s) is appropriate? Do you feel unseen or underappreciated in any way? Do you feel like you haven't been given a chance to be accepted as an adult? If you answered yes to any of these questions, what steps might you take to try to shift these dynamics, either with others or in your mindset?

Chapter 12
Home

With clichés like "Home is where the heart is" and "A man's home is his castle" floating around, home is an issue that merits exploration here. Our living space can have many effects on us. One thing I like to say is that it's helpful to surround ourselves with what we want to become because our subconscious mind digests elements from our environment, which can affect how we feel and what we think, believe, and perceive. Consequently, decorating homes with items that reflect our intentions for well-being and otherwise can support these intentions manifesting (and our living space can also hinder them manifesting if we are surrounded by things that push against them). The items we choose for this help remind our conscious minds of what our priorities are, rendering our home as an excellent venue for helping us create a reality that feels healthy to us. This can make a critical difference because our priorities become a large part of the substance of our lives, to the degree of our personal power. For most of us, our home is our main opportunity to mold a part of the world in the way we want (in accord with the people we live with), to the degree that our resources allow, and this can be a wondrous thing, even when it is small and simple. We can make our homes feel safe and nurturing, for example, by featuring items that feel nourishing and uplifting or help us feel a sense of spiritual alignment.

Many of us have firm ideas about how big our homes should be, or how clean, or what items should go in them and how. Some of us were also raised to believe that a core part of success in life is owning a home. When we have these ideas, it's critical to reflect on where they came from and if they feel right to us today. Your home is yours, not your parents', and not your community's. It can be whatever you want it to be. It's far more important to please yourself and feel comfortable within your home than to please others.

So many of us grew up with the cleanliness of our rooms being tied to how good we were as children. Factor in sayings like "Cleanliness is next to godliness" and there's a ripe opening for significant feelings of shame and guilt if our home isn't as clean as we think it should be. A sink full of dishes suddenly feels like an indicator that we've failed as people. Cleaning a house and upkeep can take a lot of time, though, and many of us don't have the arrangements previous generations did. For example, it was often the case before that one member of the household would work in the outer world while the other took care of the home. An offshoot of this is that many of us grew up in homes that were pristine, or our grandparents' homes were. As we become adults and work full-time jobs, many of us are too tired for that when we get home, and there is nothing wrong with us because of this. That said, sometimes little cleaning "hacks" can go a long way, like always handling faucets and stove knobs with a kitchen towel so they don't get dirty and spending a minute wiping down the shower with a sponge after each use.

However you want to keep your home is ultimately your decision, and this also holds for how you furnish it. If it feels good to you as it is, you need do nothing else. If it doesn't, consider how you might want it to change and how it can support your intentions in life. Many people on a spiritual path benefit from creating altars in their homes, or even having a meditation or temple room. Some also study means of aligning energy within spaces, like the ancient Chinese practice of feng shui. Artists and musicians often benefit from having spaces dedicated to the arts. The most salient point here is to recognize that the home is a powerful opportunity for anchoring us in our intentions and supporting us in the realization of them.

When I was in my spiritual training, we made goals every New Year's Day, which is a practice I have continued since leaving that program. One of my favorite goals I made was to turn my home into a sanctuary. This goal was all about filling my home with items and arranging them in a manner that gave me the sense of being in a temple, and it was extremely helpful having that stated intention as I embarked upon the process of establishing a home. I knew I wanted a living space that helped me feel centered and aligned when I entered it, and when I achieved this goal, it felt amazing. Interestingly enough, many of the items I ended up displaying were things I already owned, but how I chose to arrange them made a huge difference. I don't know that there is anything quite like a nourishing home, and we each have the freedom to determine for ourselves what that means to us.

Weeding the Garden

Old Belief — My home needs to be spotlessly clean, and if it isn't, I'm lazy.

When I believe this, I feel bad about myself when my home isn't pristine. I may also judge myself when other people's homes look cleaner than mine. The state of my home becomes directly tied to my self-esteem, perhaps even being a source of shame or guilt.

Old Belief — My house needs to be huge and full of expensive items or I'm a failure in life.

When I believe this, I am dissatisfied with my home unless I meet an ideal. I feel like I should have more than I do (unless I'm wealthy), and I likely blame myself for that. I'm also likely not to fully enjoy what I have because I'm constantly aware of what I lack.

Planting New Beliefs

Affirm — I am willing to release old beliefs about home. I am open to seeing my home in a new light.

It's exciting to know that we are each free to do what we want with our homes. Our space could have lots of fun knickknacks or almost nothing! There is no problem with whatever we decide to do with our freedom. If your home feels good to you and the people who live in it, however it is, that is enough.

Affirm — I recognize that my home can look and be however I want it to, and as long as that is healthy for me and the other people who live there, there is nothing that needs to change.

Our homes can be glorious reflections of the world we seek to create. We can fill them with inspirational and themed spaces in support of the intentions we want to manifest in our lives. The primary limits are our imaginations and the resources available to us. Beyond that, we are free, and what a joy to live this freedom! Your home is your corner of the world, all for you and your housemates. How fantastic!

Affirm — I am a divine being, effortlessly and endlessly worthy. I can use my home to reflect my awareness of this, or not, and I am free to do what I want with my home without judgment. None of this affects how divine and worthy I am.

And so it is.

Exercises

Journal about the following questions: What messages about home did you grow up with? How did these messages influence how you felt, thought, and acted? What does home mean to you? What role do you see home as having played in your life? What role would you like to see it play in your life moving forward? If you received beliefs about home that you want to shift, what are they and how would you shift them?

How do you think your life could change by believing these new thoughts (i.e., what might their impact be on your feelings, thoughts, actions, etc.)?

Think about your dream home. What would it look like? Allow yourself to dream as big as you want. Once you have a clear image of this, journal about ways to incorporate elements of it into where you live now.

Reflect upon the items in your home. What do they mean to you? Why do you have them? What is their relationship to the intentions you have for your life?

Think about ways to surround yourself with what you want to become and how to put things in your home or rearrange what you have to support your intentions. What might this entail?

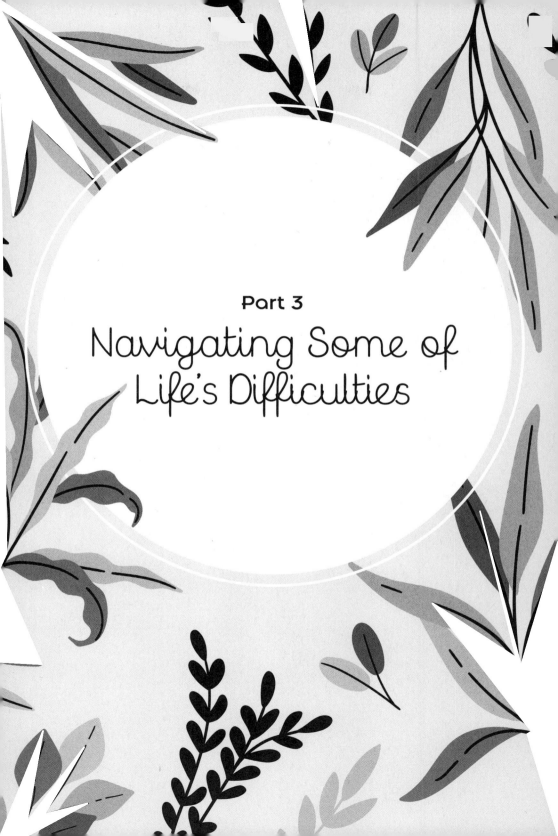

Part 3

Navigating Some of Life's Difficulties

In this part of the book, we will explore some of the difficult emotions and experiences we face in life and ways to navigate them in alignment with the system presented here. I have seen many spiritual teachers and approaches struggle with how to deal with adversity, sometimes favoring a form of denial or avoidance, which we will focus on in the next chapter. In my experience, this denial and avoidance is unnecessary, as there are many ways to honor the reality of being human while walking a path of healing and spiritual development. In this part, I will review the techniques and concepts that have helped me do that, with specific, detailed attention to some of the areas I have witnessed people have the most challenges with.

My recommendation for this part is that you reread the sections when you experience the emotions or situations featured within them. This is to help you healthfully process these emotions and situations and establish healthy habits with them. Doing this consistently should start to shift your emotional reactions and mindset to align with the concepts presented here over time.

Chapter 13
What Is Spiritual Bypassing?

S piritual bypassing is a term coined by psychologist John Welwood for "a widespread tendency to use spiritual ideas and practices to sidestep or avoid facing unresolved emotional issues, psychological wounds, and unfinished developmental tasks."[20] In my work, I broaden the definition of spiritual bypassing some, conceptualizing it as the attempt to avoid or deny natural elements of the human experience in the name of spirituality or when we use spirituality as a means of avoiding or denying the difficulties within our circumstances. It is a big problem in many spiritual communities, and it is critical to keep it out of our inner gardens as best we can because even when it feels helpful in the short run, it ultimately works against our well-being and can sometimes negatively impact others. One example of spiritual bypassing is teachers who imply or outright say that part of the point of spirituality is to never feel difficult emotions like anger, guilt, grief, and fear again, despite these emotions being innate parts of the

20. Tina Fossella and John Welwood, "Human Nature, Buddha Nature: An Interview with John Welwood," *Tricycle: The Buddhist Review* 20, no. 3 (Spring 2011): 1, https://www.johnwelwood.com/articles/TRIC_interview_uncut.pdf.

human experience. This can result in students of theirs shaming or guilt-ing themselves when they feel these emotions and trying to push these emotions away or pretend they don't feel them. In practice, this often leads to suppressed emotions that can then turn into physical and mental health problems, eruptions of harmful behavior, and more, since our emotions don't simply disappear because we want them to. An emotional reaction may run its course within us in ninety seconds, but this doesn't mean if we just ignore or brush off what we feel, it will go away. That may be true with low-stakes events, like being startled for a moment, but not when a reaction stems from harmful core beliefs or unprocessed painful or oth-erwise difficult experiences. With the cause of a reaction left untreated, it will likely abide. This can create a tender spot in our psyche if one isn't there already, one that can fester over time with neglect. If we deal with an issue head-on instead, we may be able to process it fully and leave it in the past, or at least move in the direction of healing.

Another example of spiritual bypassing is that we can use a spiritual path to reinforce low self-esteem rather than help us heal from the trauma that caused it. For instance, by seeking to renounce or renovate our ego in a way that makes us our own punching bag. Instead of dealing with our self-loathing, we find justifications for subtly maintaining it as we hold ourselves to standards of unattainable perfection in the name of finding enlightenment or being pious. The spiritual path becomes as much about not wanting to be ourselves as finding truth or serving the divine, if not more so. Spiritual practice is seen more like medication for treating our unworthiness than an affirmation of our innate divinity or connection with the divine. Unless someone is there to point this out to us, it can be hard to see. We may think we are diligently releasing our ego or living in alignment with religious law when more than anything, we are cut off from ourselves if not actively causing ourselves harm. An additional exam-ple of spiritual bypassing is someone who disregards the practical reali-ties of their life in the name of spirituality. For instance, when someone believes that approval for a credit card means they manifested that money, only for them to blow through it and then become saddled with debt.

It's one thing to believe there is more to reality than meets the eye and that we have some power to influence what manifests in our lives and another to use spirituality to avoid facing what's already here. To turn spirituality into a hiding place from difficulty, often without realizing that's what we're doing. Spirituality that doesn't spiritually bypass integrates the realities of human life without attempting to sidestep them, which enables us to thrive as best we can where we are. We needn't retreat into a fantasy world, which is another form of spiritual bypassing. When we do, we are likely to wind up with more problems than we went in with, particularly if we linger there over time.

One manner of assessing if we're spiritually bypassing, which can be hard to discern because it's true that spiritual practices can revolutionize our lives in uncommon ways (including how difficult emotions manifest for us), is to examine our lives. How has our spiritual path influenced and changed us? If we find that we are unable to have a difficult emotion or experience without falling apart, fear any negative thought, try to force ourselves to feel grateful and positive no matter what's happening (which is sometimes called "toxic positivity"), or struggle to understand our emotions, and we can connect this to our spiritual studies, we are probably spiritually bypassing to some degree.

As I share this, I want to be clear that this isn't something to judge or criticize ourselves about. We learn to spiritually bypass from other people, and it's so prevalent that's it's normal to have engaged in it. It is also natural to turn to spirituality to help us cope with difficulties in life, and spirituality can provide strength and aid to us in navigating adversity. We just want to be sure that moving forward, our spiritual path helps us approach problems in a manner that allows us to embody our humanness rather than avoid or deny integral aspects of it. Also, to take care not to attempt to use spirituality as a means of hiding from the difficult parts of our lives, which will not help us deal with them. Importantly, spiritual bypassing in some cases is less about what we believe and more about what we do with our beliefs. For example, it is a common Christian belief that "God has a plan for my life," and a common Hindu belief is that much of what manifests in our lives results from karma from previous lives. These beliefs could be used to spiritually bypass if, for example, we said "I shouldn't grieve because God has a plan for my life," or "I shouldn't feel angry that this didn't work out because it is my karma. I will try to make myself feel grateful instead." In both cases, that would be denying our humanness if we organically feel grief and anger, respectively, but the beliefs themselves do not inevitably lead to that behavior. It is where we take them that matters most, and there is a profound difference between comforting ourselves with a spiritual belief, like to help us find hope or relief from fear, and denying what we feel or other realities that come with being human.

An irony with spiritual bypassing is that when we push back against elements of the human experience, we block ourselves from having the spiritual experiences that are deeper than its surface. Yogis teach of experiences of consciousness that are beyond our likes and dislikes and sense of "I" and "mine." When we become attached to only feeling good or having positive thoughts, that locks our consciousness at the level of what we think and feel, the limited perspective of our personality. In other words, trying to force ourselves to think and feel in ways that we associate with being spiritual can prevent us from experiencing the depths of how spiritual we inherently are. We may catch glimpses of these depths, but that will be it unless the lightning bolt of grace strikes us.

When we learn to accept the spectrum of thoughts and feelings in the human experience, we can go deeper within our consciousness than the level of thought and feeling, like an anchor sinking into the ocean. This usually occurs first in meditation, but the way to get there, in my experience, is to harness compassionate thinking to make peace with the realities of being human and forge a healthy relationship with the difficulties in life as best we can. When we do this, we become able get up from the floor more quickly during times of trouble, release the shame or guilt we may feel about having been down there, and generally lead healthier lives. Considerable tension leaves our minds as we stop trying to force ourselves to be other than we authentically are, and all of this in turn helps us deepen our spiritual practice.

Throughout this book, we've considered the power that comes from replacing old beliefs with new ones. A critical element of that process is knowing what those old beliefs are, and determining this usually involves introspecting into how we think and what we feel. We can't introspect into what we feel, though, when we deny that we feel it. It is better to face the shadow, even if doing so is extremely painful, and learn what it can teach us about ourselves than to avoid it and run in fear from it throughout our lives, never really knowing the freedom and power that we have.

There is a false dichotomy in some spiritual traditions that looks at life in terms of light and dark, as if we should only embody light in each moment of our lives. That is what spiritual maturity supposedly is: all light, all the time. Darkness is inherent in nature though, and everything inherent in the natural world is sacred. The dark of the new moon, the womb, and a dense grove at midnight, for example, are holy, enriching things for us to experience. Much of life begins in darkness, within the soil of being. When we meet darkness from a place of spiritual alignment, that doesn't take us out of our spiritual connectedness. That deepens it. Our sense of our spiritual self expands and integrates the holy dark, and this opens the pathway within us to mystery. As Lao Tzu wrote in the *Tao Te Ching*, "Darkness within darkness, the gateway to understanding."[21]

Having said that, in the name of serving itself, the human ego has concocted tremendous violence and suffering, resulting in behavioral patterns that are like a sickness within our species. That is not the holy dark, and we must heal that sickness. That is what evil is, and it only exists when we are out of touch with our divine nature. It is neither inherent to human life the way that darkness is, nor found in the rest of the animal kingdom. Violence exists there for survival and as an expression of instinct, but malice? Tyranny? This is something we've done to ourselves, and even if it wasn't, that wouldn't mean we can't move beyond it. Compassion and alignment with Spirit are the antidotes I know of for the wickedness of the human

21. Stephen Mitchell, *Tao Te Ching* (New York: Harper & Row, 1988), 1.

ego, while the darkness we find in nature is simply part of life's harmony, critical to be with and integrate.

Modern technology and science have made it possible for humankind to live with a degree of comfort and security that would've been unfathomable to our ancestors, insulating us from most of the perils of nature. This allows for us to experience life in a fundamentally different manner, as the ego needn't go to the great lengths it had to in the past to survive amid the harshness of its surroundings. We get to decide if we will harness technology and science to serve the ego's fear and greed or the greater good of all. A world of profound freedom, creativity, and discovery is available to us if we have the wisdom to build it together.

In the following chapters, we will dive deep into the topic of difficult emotions and experiences. Earlier, I mentioned that depending on how we think, we can pour gas on the fire of our difficult emotions and experiences, exacerbating them beyond what they need be. Part of our work in inner gardening and ensuring that we don't spiritually bypass is to avoid doing that, embracing the reality of difficult emotions and experiences in a healthy manner. To do this, we can use the approach we reviewed in the first part of the book. This starts with learning to accept what we feel without judgment. Criticizing ourselves for our emotions isn't going to help us heal and be well. We can soothe ourselves instead, mindfully witness our emotions, and admit the truth of where we are, offering ourselves compassionate, encouraging words as needed throughout this process. Then, we seek to understand what we feel: we look at the beliefs and thoughts involved in our emotional reactions and assess if they are true and helpful. If they aren't, we dismantle the old beliefs and thoughts and affirm new ones. If they are, we recognize that, appreciate that, and learn from them. At this point, we figure out what to do about this moving forward, if anything. Over time, this process helps shift our emotional reactions in a healthy direction.

Gardening within our minds generally results in a state of being where we have a positive experience of life most of the time. This doesn't come from trying to force ourselves to "be positive," though. It emerges organically from becoming aware of what's in our inner gardens, weeding them of what is unhealthy or unhelpful, planting supportive thoughts, and meeting life's difficulties with effective coping strategies, all while prioritizing alignment with Spirit. The difference between that and "I must only think positive thoughts and feel happy all the time" is immense. There's a composting dimension of inner gardening too, which we'll explore in this part of the book, where we make use of difficult experiences to help us learn and grow, though only at a time and pace that feels healthy to us. This whole process generally results in us feeling freer, with a greater sense of ease and appreciation, as well as being more content, but not because we avoid tough emotions or situations. Rather, because we come to trust, through inner gardening and spiritual alignment, that we can handle them well the majority of the time.

Exercise

Journal about the following questions: Have you observed spiritual bypassing? If so, what are some examples of it that you've seen? Is it something you've struggled with? If so, what brought it into your life? Having read through this chapter, how might you see that aspect of spirituality in your life differently? Are there ways you can see these concepts about spiritual bypassing being helpful for you?

Chapter 14
Listening to Anger and Guilt

Anger is a natural emotion. There is nothing wrong with any of us because we feel angry sometimes. Though there are certain habits of thought that may incline us to experience anger inordinately or unnecessarily, which we'll explore some in this chapter, anger itself is part of being human. When we learn how to be with anger and channel it constructively, it can become a powerful force for positive change in our lives. This provides a stark contrast to the destruction it can wreak when we let it loose reactively. Some of the worst episodes of anger I've witnessed were from people who identified as spiritual and suppressed their "negative" emotions for so long that they had no idea how to have a healthy relationship with anger. Rage came up, for example, and they lacked the tools with which to process it, leading them instead to lash out at others to a dramatic degree or to harm themselves in direct or indirect ways. Tools for processing difficult emotions like anger are readily available to us, though, and we've learned some of them already: relaxation, breathing exercises, mindfulness, exploring our thoughts, and compassionate thinking.

Anger signifies an unmet want or need. We desired for something to happen, perhaps many things, and it didn't, and the emotional consequence of this is that we feel angry (we may also feel sad or disappointed). Whenever you feel angry, sad, disappointed, or frustrated, ask yourself what you wanted to have happen differently, and don't stop at the surface if you feel like more might be going on. For instance, let's say your romantic partner didn't respond to a text message of yours promptly. The desire there can be simple: "I wanted them to respond promptly." What if you feel enraged, though, not just frustrated? When we have an emotional reaction that seems disproportionate to a situation, that usually means something more is going on within us. Though this can stem from factors like having low emotional bandwidth due to shouldering burdensome circumstances, it often indicates there's more happening within us psychologically beyond the specific situation: there are layers of desire. For example, perhaps your partner has a habit of treating you in ways that feel unconscientious to you. Underneath the immediate desire for a quick response is a deeper one, like "I want to be treated respectfully in my relationship," and perhaps deeper still, "I want to feel valued by the people in my life, and I seldom do." Even the example of navigating burdensome circumstances contains deeper wants; they just aren't about the romantic partner and instead are something like "I want fewer demands on my time," "I want a break," and so on.

A disproportionate emotional reaction can also indicate that some emotion about one circumstance is being transferred onto another. For instance, if someone feels mad about how they're treated at their job but is unable to voice this at work because of the potential consequences of doing so, that may lead them to snap at their spouse to a greater degree than they otherwise would've. In this case, the deeper desire is about their job (i.e., "I want to be treated well at work"), while the surface one has to do with the interaction with their spouse.

After we discover the desires within our anger, we can consider if they are wants or needs. If they're wants, we can determine if they're reasonable. If they are, we can then try to get them met, either currently or in the future. If they aren't reasonable or it makes more sense to compromise with the other party in this situation, we may just work to let them go. If they're needs, they're definitely reasonable, and identifying them can help us advocate effectively for ourselves. In cases where we're angry on behalf of others, like in the face of injustice, discerning the wants and needs in our anger can help us strategize how to be supportive.

When we don't glean this information from anger, it can be totally externalized onto the other (e.g., "I can't believe my partner's such a rude jerk!"). This may lead us to lash out and make the other party feel defensive or hurt, which will probably not help us get what we desire from the situation, especially if we haven't identified what that is. Certainly not as well as when we say something like "When people don't text me promptly, I feel disrespected, and there are several things that have happened that made me feel disrespected in this relationship. For example…"

The key with anger, in my experience, particularly when it's extreme, is to process it in a safe setting using self-soothing techniques and introspection. Once we know what we wanted and what to do to help make that happen in the future or accept that it didn't, we can strategize how to move forward. When I work with people in therapy who struggle with anger, it is often helpful to break this process into steps and once they are adept at the first one, we move on to the others. The first step is usually training themselves to leave the situation when they feel angry, like creating a new reflex response. After that, they learn ways to self-soothe, like breathing exercises, progressive muscle relaxation, and mindfulness, which they apply while feeling angry. Once they have a handle on self-soothing, we practice introspecting into the anger to understand it, strategizing how to effectively utilize that information, and finally, doing this without having to leave the situation.

Many of us grew up believing that anger is unseemly or something to stuff down and try to disregard. A healthy belief about anger to affirm is that it is a natural part of life and one we can use productively if we commit to approaching it with understanding. It holds critical information for helping us improve our lives and those of others (and also, for recognizing when we're being immature and could stand to let some baggage go). It can energize us to make positive change too, especially when we clearly recognize the healthy desires within it.

Affirm — I am a divine being, effortlessly and endlessly worthy. I can have a healthy relationship with anger, experiencing it in my life primarily in a manner that is beneficial for me, harnessing it as a means of gaining insight into my wants and needs and providing me with energy to advocate for myself and others.

And so it is.

Exercises

Journal about the following questions: What messages about anger did you grow up with? How did these messages influence how you felt, thought, and acted? What does anger mean to you? What role do you see anger as having played in your life? What role would you like to see it play in your life moving forward? If you received beliefs about anger that you want to shift, what are they and how might you do that? How do you think your life could change by believing these new thoughts (i.e., what might their impact be on your feelings, thoughts, actions, etc.)?

Consider outlets for anger that feel healthy to you. Some people find benefit in beating pillows or screaming to vent their anger. I personally like to perform rituals or sing along with songs that help me express it. We can also recite poetry or watch films that help us process it.

Shame versus Guilt

Shame is what we feel when we believe something is fundamentally wrong with us, usually in the context of our behavior or an aspect of ourselves. For example, if I believe I can never make a relationship work because I'm broken as a person, that's shame. Because of being raised with certain religious beliefs, many gay people feel like they're fundamentally defective, which is also shame. Someone might feel shame if their family members told them they'd "never amount to anything" or if they don't perform as well as most of their peers in school or in the workplace.

Shame is not one of the emotions that we honor, for at least two reasons. The first is that it fundamentally misrepresents what we are. Though we can have behavioral problems and other internal challenges that make our lives difficult and cause us to do things we regret, that doesn't make us fundamentally bad or broken as people. We are still manifestations of Spirit, still divine, and we can come to know that and experience the healing and peace of it. The second reason is that shame creates a state of powerlessness and hopelessness with regard to change. If my take on relationship skills, for instance, is that I'm a lost cause, how able will I be to develop them? I may have a high aptitude for them and never know that because my feeling of shame is a wall between me and this potential.

We dismantle shame through challenging the beliefs we have that keep it active within us and aligning with Spirit. We are all worthy and divine in our cores. The parts of us that are out of alignment with that are the direct result, in most cases, of our experiences growing up and our reactions to them. That is not the truth of what we are. That is what we survived made manifest, and we can go deeper than that. As we do, shame falls away, particularly as we forge a healthy relationship with guilt.

Guilt, in contrast to shame, is the bad feeling that emerges within us when we believe we haven't met a standard we hold for ourselves. This standard may be wholly our own or have come from others. The operative word with guilt is "should." When we feel guilty, there will always be at least one form of an "I should," "I shouldn't," "I should have," or "I shouldn't have" that inspires the feeling, provided the guilt is personal. Sometimes we feel guilty about broader issues, like societal circumstances, which stems from shoulds like "This should be different," "Our country should do more," and so on. We may also have conflicting feelings of guilt because of contradictory shoulds. For instance, like the tension between "I shouldn't hurt their feelings" and "I should stick up for myself," when we know an action would likely hurt someone's feelings but not taking it would dishonor us.

Some guilt in life is healthy and important. In its purest form, guilt is the voice of our conscience alerting us that something we're doing, did, or are thinking of doing doesn't align with our values. We don't want to spend any more time in guilt than we need to though beyond what it takes to hear this voice and heed it, but we all benefit from it being there. That said, sometimes this voice is polluted by the ill-fitting perspectives of others, and that is part of why we garden within.

To ensure that our guilt is the voice of our conscience rather than more of a reflection of other people's opinions, we can introspect when we feel guilty, identifying the shoulds behind the guilt and determining if we believe they are healthy for us to hold. If we decide that a should is not healthy for us, we can strive to let it go. For example, maybe we feel guilty about standing up for ourselves because someone in our family told us that a person like us should stay silent in most situations. In this case, we would work to release the should and affirm a new standard in its place since it is important that we feel comfortable standing up for ourselves.

Because many people have drawn the connection between the word "should" and an increased tendency toward self-judgment and criticism, which can pave the way for shame, we want to avoid affirming it within us. Consequently, I suggest using the word "intend" instead of "should" when replacing shoulds. In this case, we could affirm that, "I intend to speak up for myself in most situations, aside from when I feel unsafe or not well enough to or it is unwise to do so." Where shoulds can easily feel oppressive and perfectionistic, intending feels more tentative. It recognizes that sometimes we have bad days or encounter warranted exceptions. Relatedly, when we feel guilty, instead of taking the thought behind it at face value, as in "I shouldn't have done that," I recommend adding "I feel," like "I feel like I shouldn't have done that," followed by an exploration of the greater context of the situation. This helps make space for compassionate thinking that acknowledges that we are imperfect human beings who are part of a bigger picture of factors.

As another example, let's say we were mean to someone when in a low mood and think, "I should be nicer. I don't want this be how I behave." We can turn around and affirm, "I intend to be nicer to people in the future. I treat others respectfully as best I can." Sometimes guilt relates to actions from the past that stick with us, a sense that we "should have" done something differently. We'll explore this in the section on closure.

Though we want to take care not to shame ourselves, it is beneficial to have standards for our behavior and listen to the guilt we feel when we don't meet them. Healthy standards that we identify and think through that aren't rigid or impossible to meet help us live in alignment with our values, which builds a sense of integrity and character within us over time. If we are mindful of being compassionate with ourselves, shame will not result from this process. We will also find ourselves struggling less and less with decision-making because that is a natural consequence of having clarity about what we think of as right and wrong or better and worse in terms of our behavior and otherwise.

Additionally, it's important to be aware that guilt, like anger, can have multiple levels to it (i.e., we may feel guilty because "I should be more productive" and "I should be a better person" are both active within us). We may also feel little moments of guilt or disappointment with ourselves throughout the day that don't register much until we pay more attention, yet negatively impact our mood to a significant degree, especially over time. Whenever you notice yourself feeling dissatisfied or uncomfortable with how you're living or what you're doing, ask yourself if there is a "should" of some kind involved. At the beginning of inner gardening, we may find loads of shoulds within us, as they tend to be heaped upon us while growing up. "I should be less talkative." "I should be more attentive." "I should be less accommodating." "I should be more engaged in politics." As we find these, we consider them in light of our perspective as an adult, and then affirm what we want to believe in alignment with compassion and our intention of well-being. This will help ensure that we primarily feel guilty in the future when that guilt truly aligns with our values.

Old beliefs we may have accumulated in our lives about guilt might include that it is a healthy way to motivate children or, conversely, that there is no value in it. A healthy belief about guilt to affirm is that after we examine and renovate our shoulds to become intentions that align with our values, guilt is a natural alert from our conscience that aids us in living lives we can feel good about.

Affirm — I am a divine being, effortlessly and endlessly worthy. In coming to know myself as divine, I release whatever beliefs I hold that cause me to feel shame. I also accept the guilt in my life that is healthy while releasing that which is not. I appreciate having a natural aspect of myself that helps me live in alignment with my values.

And so it is.

Exercise

Journal about the following questions: What messages about shame and guilt did you grow up with? How did these messages influence how you felt, thought, and acted? What do shame and guilt mean to you? If you received beliefs about shame and guilt that you want to shift, what are they and how would you shift them? How do you think your life could change by believing these new thoughts (i.e., what might their impact be on your feelings, thoughts, actions, etc.)?

Chapter 15
Chronic Mental and Physical Health Conditions

Note: nothing in this chapter is meant to be taken as a replacement or substitute for medical treatment.

S ome spiritual teachers believe that mental illness isn't real the way physical illness is. They teach that it's all a product of how we think and if we shift our thinking in a healthy manner, it will go away. I won't deny that in some cases, especially with something like a mild situational depressive or anxiety disorder, that can happen. Also, many if not most of us can make substantial improvements in how we feel through practicing supportive thinking skills like those in this book. As a therapist, everyone I've worked with who had mental illness and the capacity and motivation to give CBT and mindfulness skills a solid try benefitted from them.

At the same time, it is irresponsible at best and reckless and harmful at worst to suggest that mental illness is something we are always able to wholly heal, particularly with positive thinking alone. Navigating mental illness is often far more complicated than that, especially once we start talking about conditions like bipolar disorder, OCD, and schizophrenia. Some of us must take medication to manage our symptoms for the rest

of our lives or have a tight, heavy regimen of coping strategies, boundaries, and self-care techniques in place to appear "normal" while inside,
we labor arduously. Sometimes we later find that such a regimen ends up
being insufficient too.

This was my experience, as someone who has had symptoms of mental
illness since early childhood. To set the stage, I've had a daily meditation
practice since 2005. It has revolutionized my relationship with my mind,
as has doing healing work like what's in this book, alongside intensively
studying spiritual scriptures for years, which renovated much of my mindset. That's a wonderful way to plant new information in the garden of our
minds: rereading inspiring books with a sense of receptivity and reverence.
I also had some eye-opening spiritual experiences that changed the way
I experience thought-dependent reality, making it feel far less real to me,
which I will discuss more in the next section.

While this enabled me to function highly in most areas of my life, it
didn't make my mental illness go away. I became far more adept at managing my anxiety, and it diminished considerably much of the time, but it
was still part of my experience most days. The waves of depression came
less frequently and tended to be less deep, sometimes with many years
between them, but they still came, and sometimes they were as deep as
ever. I still had moments, occasionally, when I got knocked on my butt.
They were quite humbling. Since I have also accepted my humanness with
compassion, though, they almost never rattled my world like they used
to. I trusted that they would pass, and they passed more quickly, and I
rebounded from them faster because I didn't judge myself for being in that
position. That's one of the greatest keys with mental illness: not judging
ourselves for having it or being wherever we are with it.

That said, during the coronavirus pandemic, my symptoms escalated
to a degree where I could not manage them on my own, and I started
taking psychiatric medication for the first time since 2004. I feel no shame
about this. Mental illnesses are legitimate illnesses, and if we need to take
medication, sometimes or always, there is no reason to feel bad about ourselves for that. Not only do I not feel shame about this, but if I could go

back in time, I would never have tried to walk this path without medication. The reason I felt impelled to was largely because I bought into some of the social stigma around mental illness and teachings about it rooted in spiritual bypassing. That to a degree, this was a personal failing of mine to fix or at least that I could prove I was powerful enough not to need medicinal help (that was a way of demonstrating I was worthy). To be fair, many people who took psychiatric medications back then to the degree I was prescribed them appeared to be emotionally numb and not very alert, and I didn't want that for myself. Mostly, though, I sought to prove I could make it without medication, and I listened to the spiritual teachers and holistic healers who made that seem like what I should do.

While I did go many years without medication, at what cost? Managing my symptoms required immense effort and some life-limiting boundaries, and at times I still experienced extreme symptoms. Had I been on medication this entire time, I probably wouldn't have experienced those extreme symptoms or needed to make such a substantial effort or establish those boundaries. I don't regret my life choices, but I wouldn't do it this way again. I sincerely hope anyone facing my type of circumstance sits with how much social stigma and other external factors are influencing their decision-making before electing whether or not to take medication. At this point, I think I will be on medication for the rest of my life, like how a person with type 1 diabetes takes insulin. I see the medication not as unspiritual or my need for it as a personal or spiritual failing. Rather, I see it as the manifestation of my intention to heal. Sometimes taking medication is the next step on our journey, an opportunity from Spirit for a healthier life.

As I share this, I know that for some people, finding an effective medication regimen is a long process, one filled with disappointment and undesirable side effects, and I get that. My medication journey has had some serious missteps, and what I take now isn't perfect, though it is quite helpful. My main point is that for some of us, medication truly is a need, and we can let ourselves off the hook for that. We are legitimately ill, and we require appropriate treatment. That said, it is also my experience with persistent mental illness that the medication process is not always, or even often, as simple as finding a medication that suddenly eradicates our mental health symptoms. Inner gardening is still important, and the application of CBT skills can greatly influence our symptoms while on medication. I think part of the reason mine works so well is because I actively practice inner gardening. What the medication doesn't take care of, I can usually manage on my own. Many of my clients who felt better after learning these skills were also taking medication for years before working with me and stayed on the same regimen during our work together.

Medication can do a lot, but it will not teach us how to challenge unsupportive thoughts and think in healthy ways or alert us to the value of exercise and ensuring that we engage in enough socializing and pleasurable activities. It also won't fix problems with low self-esteem or in relationships, heal trauma, or totally insulate us from the effects of toxic situational factors. This is something I share with my clients who take medication when describing the value of CBT. I want to be clear here that I am not suggesting that if our medication isn't working effectively for us, it's because we're not taking care of ourselves well enough. This is a far more complicated topic than that, and I would never blame my clients who struggle with practicing CBT skills for that difficulty. Working on ourselves is not easy, and CBT is not for everyone or a fit for everyone's current capacity level. We can only do our best. I'm saying that when we find a medication that is a good fit for us, it may be more effective when used in tandem with CBT skills. The best results I've seen when working with people who have persistent mental illness have come from the combination of CBT skills and medication.

When we have a chronic illness, be it mental or physical, it is important to be careful with our expectations. This is particularly true with the notion of becoming cured, which isn't usually a healthy subject to focus on unless that is likely to happen. Focusing on being cured can easily turn the healing journey into a cycle of disappointment and shame if we decide that our chronic illness can be cured and it is our responsibility to find a way to do it. We may be someone who does get cured and feel good about ourselves, but we may also feel cured for a time only to have an episode that reminds us we're chronically ill and makes us feel worse about ourselves than we did before. Not just worse because we're symptomatic, but because now we're a failure too, or the coping skills and techniques that seemed like they helped us were a waste of time because here we are, not cured. This can make it much harder to use those skills in the future. After all, since being cured was our goal, they didn't work, despite the fact that we found benefit from applying them. Our healing journey becomes one disappointment after another because we constantly don't meet our objective.

Instead of assuming this black-and-white orientation, we can focus on improvement, with an understanding that setbacks often occur with chronic health conditions. If we find our way to a cure, wonderful. If not, that's okay too. We place no expectation on ourselves about that. We try different things and assemble a helpful set of coping tools, and then we use them as best we can. With compassion for ourselves, we will hopefully continue improving, and focusing on improvement above being cured won't prevent us from getting cured, as some might worry. If that is something we're concerned about, we can affirm that we remain open to the possibility of being cured, even if it's not our main focus. Dwelling in possibility is fine. It's holding unlikely expectations and blaming ourselves when they aren't met that causes problems here. Whatever improvement we can find with our symptoms is worth the effort, and I believe we can all find some improvement from where we are, at least in terms of our internal experience.

On Depression

As we explored earlier, one of the foundational tenets of CBT is that our emotions follow our thoughts and beliefs. Much of the time, my experience is that this is true. Emotional states can seem to come out of nowhere, though, or at least not be an extension of what we're consciously thinking about. Depression, for example, can stem from the weather, distressing items in the news, watching sad movies, difficult life situations, and more. All these factors may weigh on us in a kind of collective or significant manner, but not necessarily one we consciously think into being. Depression can also be something we are biologically predisposed to or a consequence of poor treatment and trauma earlier in life and the depressing subconscious core beliefs that resulted from that, which we may not be aware of.

Once depression is active within us, our conscious thoughts and actions generally feed it. For instance, it's common in depression to have excessive feelings of guilt and low self-worth, and then to stop taking good care of ourselves and our home and to become less active and attentive in our relationships. This then feeds the depressed mood and low sense of self, launching a vicious cycle of deepening depression that can be like sinking into a tarpit. This cycle tends to result in a decline in interest or pleasure in doing things alongside the worsening mood. It's critical in those moments, regardless of how we feel, to recognize that shaming and guilting ourselves, and seeing ourselves, others, and the world through the distorted fog of depression, will likely continue the vicious cycle of depression.

For this, CBT can be helpful, provided we receive it from a skilled therapist and have the energy for it, or another form of psychotherapy that feels supportive to us. If you can't participate in CBT directly, I recommend getting a CBT workbook to help move through this process and learn specific skills, which can still be quite effective.[22] Fundamentally, though, we challenge the depressive thoughts we have by asking if they are fact-oriented, accurate, wise, and compassionate and then affirm supportive thoughts. In our depressed state, it may be hard to believe these supportive thoughts, so we just do our best with this and take care of ourselves as well as we can. We try to appreciate that if our thoughts, actions, and circumstances don't feed the tide of depression, it will usually go out on its own in time or at least not be as high. Relatedly, as we explored in the section on behavioral activation, even if we don't feel like socializing, exercising, or engaging in pleasurable activities or household chores, it is important to try to

22. I recommend the *Cognitive Behavioural Therapy Workbook for Dummies* by Rhena Branch and Rob Wilson.

make ourselves do some of that. Ideally, at least one activity each day, big or small. Self-care is a must, and though it may feel empty and unhelpful at first, this tends to change with persistent effort. Researchers have even found that for some people, exercise is as effective in mitigating mild to moderate depression as antidepressants.[23]

Some affirmations that may be beneficial during depression include the following:

- Depression is an illness that waxes and wanes. I will not feel like this forever.

- Research suggests that many activities can help with depression, even if it doesn't feel like they will in the moment.[24] I can do my best to make myself go for a walk, watch entertaining films, and spend time with loved ones or pets.

- Depression is an illness that tells us things about ourselves that are not true. It highlights the worst in ourselves, others, and life. I can work to recognize that those thoughts are the voice of depression, not my own.

- Depression can lead us to feel like we have less energy and capability than we have. It can also make us doubt ourselves. I know from experience that I am capable of doing at least some things well.

With a depressive disorder, anxiety disorder, or any other mental illness we have, learning about it can also prove highly beneficial: how it tends to work, what types of symptoms it generates, and so on. When we have this knowledge, we are likely to be more able to see it as a legitimate illness

23. Harvard Health Publishing, "Exercise Is an All-Natural Treatment to Fight Depression," Harvard Medical School, February 2, 2021, https://www.health.harvard.edu/mind-and-mood/exercise-is-an-all-natural-treatment-to-fight-depression.

24. David Ekers, Lisa Webster, Annemieke Van Straten, Pim Cuijpers, David Richards, and Simon Gilbody, "Behavioural Activation for Depression; An Update of Meta-Analysis of Effectiveness and Sub Group Analysis," *PLoS One* 9, no. 6 (June 2014): e100100, doi:10.1371/journal.pone.0100100.

rather than as a reflection of our inner monologue or truth, or as a sign of our weakness, and to get some mental space from it.

All of this can help us cope with depression if it is something that recurs in our lives. That said, when depression (or anxiety) occurs for situational reasons or is escalated by them, sometimes great relief will not come until our circumstances change. For example, if we are in a toxic work environment or relationship that causes us a high amount of stress and exhaustion, we may need to leave it to see a big improvement in our symptoms (although it is still critical to engage in what self-care we can). Inner gardening can only do so much when the demands on our nervous system are high or we are in a consistently painful situation.

This is an issue that is highly relevant to the topic of spiritual bypassing because some spiritual teachers, as well as CBT absolutists, would argue (or at least strongly imply) that ultimately, the way we think about our circumstances determines how they affect us, so we should be able to make burdensome circumstances totally okay for ourselves. While I agree that in many situations, we can improve how we feel to some extent by thinking supportively, and we can certainly exacerbate how we feel by thinking unsupportively, the degree of mental mastery required to completely shrug off a highly burdensome circumstance is at the level of a being like the Buddha, assuming this is even possible. From that vista of consciousness, this would also be organic, not forced. It would be rooted in a profound, experiential understanding of life and the mind, not denial or avoidance of what is felt or a belief that we must only think positively.

As I alluded to in the last section, I have had experiences of consciousness that fundamentally changed my relationship to thought-dependent reality. Beyond watching my perception of reality shift through compassionate thinking and affirmations and experiencing inner stillness during meditation, in 2007, I became able to silence my mind at will most of the time. This ability appeared in me after tuning in to a grove of trees while on a walk one morning following an intense experience of light and surrender in meditation the day before. It enabled me to experience inherent reality apart from thought-dependent reality, and when I am in that state, thought-dependent reality feels like a mirage in comparison. As I experienced this, though, I appreciated that there was nothing anyone could've said to explain to me what this state was like that would've made me understand it, and I think that is true in general. There are some things we must live to understand. Those experiences were like a flowering too, a gift of grace in the wake of letting go, not a consequence of will from acting on judgments about how I should be.

So I know firsthand that we can have spiritual experiences that reorient our experience of thought-dependent reality in a core way, but I also believe that these experiences must be had to be more than conceptual, and we can't force them to happen. Performing spiritual practices can create inner conditions that make these experiences more likely to occur, but like all ripening, they have their own organic process that will be whatever it is. What I experienced was indescribably blissful and has provided me with a deep, abiding sense of peace, freedom, and connection to Spirit. Becoming able to step out of thought-dependent reality did not make everything in my life feel wonderful all the time though, heal all the trauma of my childhood and adolescence, or instantly eradicate the unhealthy core beliefs in my subconscious mind. I gained a new tool and vantage point for gardening within and experiencing myself, an astonishingly powerful one, but there was still work to be done.

After experiencing silence, I never looked at thought-dependent reality as I had before, but some thoughts, particularly the intrusive ones from OCD, felt as compelling as ever to me at times. I think this is just the nature of OCD, and that is part of the point. In inherent reality, we are human beings living in a world that has pleasure, pain, and illness, and consequently, when thought-dependent reality goes away, pleasure, pain, and illness are still part of life. All the mental illness that we see in the world may not stem from inherent reality causes, but some of it does, or at least is more nature than nurture. The fact that mental illness is in the mind does not mean that it is necessarily a product of thought-dependent reality. Also, when it isn't innate and is caused by our nervous system being overburdened by our circumstances, I believe that is more of an inherent reality effect than a thought-dependent one, aside from where we exacerbate the situation with thought.

When we adopt the belief that it is appropriate to hold ourselves to the standard of making any situation totally okay with mental discipline, which inevitably comes from external influences, we set ourselves up for harm. Not only are we apt not to reach it, but we will also not process our emotions healthfully because of the denial and avoidance in that. We will likely disregard the messages coming from within urging us to get out of something like a toxic relationship because we are too busy trying to prove we can handle it, as well as not hold situations as accountable for the harm they cause as we rightfully could. We will also probably feel like we are failing at something we should be able to do, alongside some guilt or shame about not being more enlightened. After all, if we were really spiritually mature or adept at CBT, we would be able to think our way into feeling comfortable with whatever is happening, right?

When we recognize instead that it is normal to feel burdened by that which is burdensome and meet ourselves with kindness, compassion, and care, we are likely to find some improvement in how we feel. If our spiritual and healing practices pave the way for a breakthrough in our experience of consciousness that fundamentally changes how burdensome circumstances feel to us, that will come on its own in divine right timing. I do believe that spiritual enlightenment is real, and if that is sincerely where we end up, or at another vista of consciousness that allows us to be at ease in any circumstance, then there is no spiritual bypassing in that. But if instead, that is where we think we should be but aren't such that we deny the reality of where we are, then there is spiritual bypassing occurring. When that is the case, I believe we are best served by honoring where we are and working with the options and tools that are available to us.

On Anxiety

Anxiety is one of the most common mental health symptoms people experience, with approximately 19.1 percent of adults in the US meeting the criteria for an anxiety disorder each year.[25] Anxiety is a sense of intense fear and worry, usually about a future event that seems threatening. It feels like we won't be able to handle that event, which can then trigger our fight, flight, or freeze system to varying degrees, sometimes in a manner that feels paralyzing. Some anxiety is normal in life, like feeling anxious about receiving the results of a medical test or giving a presentation. Relatedly, my experience as a therapist is that people who don't have an anxiety disorder tend to have the most anxiety during times of uncertainty, ambiguity, or before doing something they know they fear or are intimidated by. Clinical anxiety extends beyond this, to the point where anxiety can become a debilitating part of everyday life, and anxiety disorders can fixate on almost anything. They can turn seemingly insignificant activities like grocery shopping, going to work, driving on the freeway, or speaking at a party with strangers into terrifying experiences. They can make us writhe when remembering the past, as if distant dangers are still a threat to us, or incline us to believe that an itch on our arm is a symptom of a deadly illness or that we can't trust what anyone in our lives says. We can even feel anxious for no discernible reason, requiring us to introspect into the anxiety to determine what it's about. Sometimes we discover that anxiety like this stems from trauma and there are subconscious core beliefs at the root of it. Other times it may remain a mystery.

Anxiety disorders can originate as a reaction to scary or stressful life events and circumstances and can co-occur with issues like perfectionism and desiring constant control. They can also have no clear cause. As with depression, I recommend participating in CBT for anxiety or another form of psychotherapy that feels supportive, or at least getting a CBT workbook if therapy isn't an option.[26] Much of that work tends to focus on learning self-soothing techniques, practicing mindfulness to help us gain space from distressing thoughts and feelings, exposing ourselves in incremental safe doses to that which we feel anxious about, where applicable (which helps

25. National Alliance on Mental Illness, "Mental Health by the Numbers," last modified March 2021, https://www.nami.org/mhstats.
26. I highly recommend *The Anxiety and Phobia Workbook* by Edmund Bourne.

erode the anxious reaction), and challenging our anxious thoughts in the ways we've learned throughout this book.

These are the two affirmations that helped me the most with my anxiety:

- I have effective coping skills.

- Feeling anxious like this is a symptom of an anxiety disorder. It doesn't mean the story anxiety is telling me is true.

The first affirmation occurred to me when I noticed that when push came to shove in my life, I handled adversity well. I was able to navigate significant difficulty and be resilient. Anxiety just made me feel like that wasn't the case most of the time. As I affirmed to myself each day that I have not had effective coping skills, that thought began to pop up when I was anxious, like a reflex. Eventually it substantially reduced my anxiety much of the time.

The second affirmation emerged as I appreciated that my anxiety, like most clinical anxiety, often recited stories in my mind about something (life, the world, myself, etc.) that were untrue. Intellectually, to some degree, I could see that they were far-fetched, but they felt as true to me as anything else that struck me as true. By reminding myself that the very experience of this is a symptom of anxiety, and that just because something feels true, that doesn't mean it is, I became less and less susceptible to these stories. It was critically important not only to question the stories anxiety told me, but also to highlight the greater fact that it is the nature of an anxiety disorder to instigate fear with untrue or far-fetched scary thoughts. Doing the former without the latter often felt to me like fighting with quicksand, which tended to make the anxiety I felt worse. In my experience, the best way to win anxiety's game is to stop playing it. When we meet anxiety on its own turf, it is much easier to lose.

These affirmations helped mitigate my anxiety such that it went from being severe to moderate or mild most of the time, and there were some symptoms, like feeling anxious about flying, that totally healed within me. Generally speaking, the combination of breathing and relaxation exercises, mindfulness, quieting my mind, regular physical exercise, healthy boundaries, avoiding caffeine, challenging anxious thoughts, and these affirmations aided me in moving through anxiety quickly and getting on with my day. That said, I feel like these affirmations were critical in that outcome. Before working with them, I mainly focused on relaxation exercises, mindfulness, and challenging my anxious thoughts when I felt anxious, and that wasn't enough. I needed to digest the sentiments in these affirmations too, and as I did, they became the clear missing ingredient in my treatment. It's amazing what can change when we identify a helpful thought to believe. Once I started taking medication, my anxiety diminished considerably, and paired with these skills, it mostly appears at subclinical levels now.

If you experience anxiety or depression that seems to be rooted in trauma or connected to it, you may benefit from also affirming directly about that: for example, with an affirmation like "I comfort the wounded parts of myself, offering them love, acceptance, and reassurance." As you affirm this, do your best to connect with Spirit and feel the support, security, and healing power of the divine to whatever degree you can. Depending on the severity of the trauma, other healing practices, like guided meditations, bodywork, and trauma-focused therapy may also be called for.

Chronic Physical Health Conditions

Physical pain and discomfort are inevitable parts of life, and as we age, they tend to figure more prominently for us. We can have parts of our bodies and processes within them stop working as well as they used to and a host of other health conditions. Some things also don't heal at the physical level once they are damaged in a certain way. This is just reality, and the more we accept this and make peace with it as best we can, the easier it generally becomes to deal with.

As I mentioned earlier, I have several chronic physical health conditions. The two most prominent ones are a digestive disorder that regularly gives me difficulties and a spinal condition that causes me daily pain. I also experienced a debilitating chronic illness in my late twenties for about two years and at the time of this writing, I am treating a health condition with no clear diagnosis that appeared in the spring of 2021 and has been disabling at times, though I have found substantial improvement most days. Applying what I know about mindfulness and supportive thinking skills has made a huge difference for me in navigating these conditions and thriving as best I can. One of the central steps in that process is accepting the health conditions I have as they are the majority of the time. I almost never fight against the fact of their existence because I know that will just cause me more pain. I'm a human being and I have my low moments, and I think wrestling with the reality of our pain is healthy sometimes as part of grief and acceptance, but I'm also aware that habitual thoughts about how awful my situation is will make me feel worse. For example, I don't dwell in thoughts like "It's so sad that I have been sick in one form or another for most of my life." When I have thoughts like these, I acknowledge them and honor the pain within them, but I don't feed them beyond that.

Once it was clear to me that my chronic health conditions were not going anywhere, I grieved their effect on my life and harnessed compassionate thinking and alignment with Spirit to move toward acceptance. It is my lived experience that the more I accept and make peace with them, the less they bother me. As I apply mindfulness to my symptoms, this is even truer, and there is ample research on the efficacy of mindfulness as an intervention for chronic pain.[27] Importantly, acceptance doesn't mean we don't hope for improvement or work toward it. It means we are not locked in battle with the reality of what is. I believe that to a degree, acceptance is a skill, a way of looking at life. As we hone it in the various areas of our lives, we become better able to accept the myriad transitions and circumstances that we encounter in the future. This makes us more effective in navigating them, since much of the time and energy we would've spent fighting with reality can now be used in beneficial ways, including making whatever improvements we can.

---

27. Peter la Cour and Marian Petersen, "Effects of Mindfulness Meditation on Chronic Pain: A Randomized Controlled Trial," *Pain Medicine* 16, no. 4 (2015): 641–52, doi:10.1111/pme.12605.

Some healers and teachers speak of the difference between pain and suffering, which connects with what I just shared. Pain is simply part of life. It comes with the package of having a human body. Suffering is the way we extend or exacerbate pain through focusing on it or thinking about it, or when we induce pain with thought: for example, by thinking about a former lover and crying or even by watching a disturbing film and feeling upset. What CBT skills show us is that we have power over the films we play in our minds, or the monologues that occur within them. We don't have to watch or listen to painful ones over and over again. We can say to ourselves, "I've done this before, I know where this is going and how it makes me feel, and I'm not doing this again today." Becoming able to do that and have the unsupportive thoughts stop can take considerable work, but it is an attainable goal in many situations. This is particularly true if we are diligent with our meditation, mindfulness, and affirmation practice. We don't have to water certain parts of our inner garden, and by taking care to not to, they will wither, and we will suffer far less. Even when we lack the ability to stop an unsupportive thought process, we can affirm compassionate thoughts alongside it, which may also be helpful. This is the degree to which I agree with spiritual teachers and CBT absolutists who believe we can mitigate burdensome circumstances with thought.

Most people will probably always have days when negative thoughts get the better of them, though. I think that's just part of what happens when we have a difficult circumstance like a chronic health condition, and there is nothing wrong with that. One facet of not spiritually bypassing is owning the reality that some aspects of life feel bad and tend to be difficult to navigate. We aren't failing as spiritual seekers or people on a healing path by allowing this to be true. As with everything else in this part of the book, though, we don't want to throw extra logs on that fire. We let our pain be what it is and not a speck more as best we can by practicing self-soothing techniques, prioritizing our connection with Spirit, and taking care to tend to our inner gardens and plant supportive, compassionate thoughts there.

Our Best Is Enough

As we weed our inner gardens and consider what thoughts are support-ive and unsupportive, it's important to be compassionate with ourselves regarding any thoughts and beliefs of shame we have about having a chronic health condition, be it physical or mental. It is normal to grieve our body or mind not functioning as it did before and the consequences of this in our lives or other ways we are not able to do what many others can. That said, it is also critical to affirm that this doesn't take away from our worth as people. Being unable to do certain things as well as we could or want to or at all doesn't make us any less valuable than anyone else. As we learn to connect with the heart and Spirit through meditation, that revolu-tionizes our understanding of this.

For some of us, this notion will be easier to digest than for others. One of my cousins was paralyzed from the neck down for most of his adult life, following an accident. He never walked again. We didn't see him often, but I know this was excruciatingly difficult for him and his immediate family. Even the suggestions in this chapter may have been too much for him, and if that is where we are, that is valid. The grief around a chronic health con-dition, like all grief, is not something to rush or force, and sometimes we are in too much pain to do anything more than bear it. All any of us can ask of ourselves is that we do the best we can from where we are and that we try to make peace with what that is while accepting our humanness, taking care not to turn our healing journey into an arena of shame.

If you are able to meditate and cultivate a supportive internal environ-ment, do it. If your symptoms are too strong, you are not defective as a person because of that. Just do what you can, when you can, and strive not to water the weeds in your inner garden. Do your best not to criti-cize yourself for being wherever you are with your healing and acceptance journey. The main affirmations I would use for a chronic health condition are something like "I am willing to learn how to accept this and experience whatever healing I can" and "I enjoy my life as much as possible and know that I can find fulfillment and connection."

Many spiritual masters have taught that being brought to our knees by life circumstances can humble us in a way that opens us to spiritual revelation. This has been my experience too. I have found that when I turn to Spirit to help me cope with my health conditions and other difficulties, surrendering to the degree that I can, I experience an intimacy with the divine that would be challenging to discover otherwise. There is an urgency in the seeking that is harder for me to muster when life is comfortable, and Spirit answers that urgency accordingly. It was during one of those periods, following a dark night of the soul, that I first experienced my mind go totally silent for a prolonged stretch of time, which felt somewhat like waking up from a dream. This is not to suggest that everyone must see this subject in this manner or that everyone will have my experience (or that this makes everything okay all the time), but it is the truth of my path. When we offer our pain and suffering to the higher power of our understanding, it is received, and so are we. Our bodies and minds might not necessarily heal, but the peace of the soul can be revealed to us.

Affirm — I am a divine being, effortlessly and endlessly worthy. The state of my health has no bearing on that. I am fully divine and whole in each moment of my life.

And so it is.

Exercises

If you have a chronic health condition, what came up for you while reading this chapter in terms of emotions and thoughts? If some information was helpful, what was that and why do you believe it was helpful? What are some thoughts you can think to aid yourself in coping with your health condition(s)? What might you say to a loved one who is dealing with your identical situation and has come to you for support?

If you have a chronic health condition and are not in the habit of engaging in self-care consistently, try to plan out two to three things you can do this week, large or small, that feel fun or otherwise nurturing or nourishing.

Chapter 16
Self-Sabotage
and Transitions

In my experience, self-sabotage can appear in unconscious and conscious ways. Unconscious self-sabotage often comes from the aspect of our egos we explored in part 1 that doesn't want our lives to change because it feels threatened by that. The ego can kick up a high level of resistance, manifesting in a variety of forms. We may feel tired, unmotivated, frustrated, or distracted, suddenly forgetting what we intended to do for months, and so on. The list is virtually endless. Generally, it is helpful to know that this part of us is there so when we experience this resistance, we don't just take it at face value and let it derail us, holding to our intentions instead.

Subconscious beliefs can also sabotage us. For example, beliefs like that we don't deserve success or that any romantic relationship we have will inevitably fall apart. These types of beliefs usually become evident when we examine the patterns in our lives and contemplate where they might come from. For instance, someone notices that they opt out of taking most risks, and then they reflect upon this and realize that after being aggressively bullied in their preteen years, they tend to believe that people will let them down and that they will fail to protect themselves. Consequently, they defend themselves by staying with what is familiar.

When we have a pattern like this that keeps popping up, we can assume that something more is going on than what's happening at the surface level. In the example above, the person may not have realized that avoiding risks was a pattern for them until they considered if there were themes or cycles in their behavior. Once they notice this pattern, though, it becomes clear that risk avoidance must stem in part from a deeper belief or story within them, which likely originates in past experiences. They weren't just making healthy, conservative judgment calls. The person in this example may then sit with the facts of their risk aversion and after contemplating their life, recognize that someone who's lived through what they did would be unlikely to trust in general: other people, themselves, life. This could easily incline a person to be risk averse.

Doing this work might seem like we need to sit in a therapist's office for hours to uncover these subconscious beliefs and stories, but it's usually straightforward. First, think about what tends to not go well in your life that, theoretically, you have the power to have go well. For example, a string of failed relationships or ongoing difficulty taking next steps in your career. Factor in considerations of your context: for instance, are you stressed from being overworked? Tired from managing too many things? We must recognize the potential influence of environment and circumstance on our behavior. If these kinds of factors seem to be the cause of the issue, we can stop this inquiry process and strategize action steps accordingly, like increasing our self-care, planning to find a new job, and so on. If not, reflect on the major events and influences in your life and how they could've created this kind of pattern within you, either because you're mirroring behavior or messaging you saw or reacting to that or something else that occurred around you. Draw connections between the past and the pattern and consider what stories or beliefs logically might stem from your past experiences and perpetuate the pattern, as we explored early in the book. Also, a major event or influence doesn't just mean something that seems huge in an objective sense. It can be anything that felt major to you, something that sticks with you over the years and appears to have shaped you.

Once you identify the subconscious belief (or beliefs) or story behind the self-sabotaging pattern, like "I am afraid of success" or "I refuse challenges because I'm afraid that I'll fail at them," create an affirmation to move your thinking in a healthier direction. Commit to act differently in light of what you learned (using baby steps to avoid overstraining, where applicable), keep the intention for change in your mind however you need to, and water your healthy new thought. Be sure to acknowledge your humanness and treat yourself kindly if resistance comes up, recognizing it as such. With time and persistence, you can shift this pattern.

Next, there is the matter of conscious resistance. This is when we know something is challenging for us and our thoughts seem to get in the way of us following through. For example, we know we're afraid of relocating, despite feeling that moving would be good for us long-term, so we keep putting off applying for a job where we want to move to. In this case, we can look at the belief or story, question it, and affirm what we want to believe in its place. For instance, perhaps the belief is "I won't be able to handle a massive transition and successfully launch a life in a new city." We can challenge this belief with all the examples of resilience in our past and affirm that we have the power to make the most of our new circumstances. We can also affirm to ourselves the fact that humans have a great capacity to adapt to change quickly.[28] We may feel like we don't, but we do, particularly if we prioritize releasing our thoughts of resistance to the change once in a new environment. We can create a strategy for being social and engaged when we move too. As we do this, we will likely begin to feel some improvement with regard to this situation.

Self-sabotage is one of the main reasons people don't realize their intentions in life, once we factor out difficulties related to things like ability, capacity, opportunity, and privilege. It is also one of the primary reasons

28. Thomas DeMichele, "Humans are Quick to Adapt to Change," Fact/Myth, last modified July 16, 2016, http://factmyth.com/factoids/humans-are-quick-to-adapt-to-change/.

why centering self-love in our healing journey is arguably the best thing we can do to improve the overall quality of our lives, which we explored some earlier. As we affirm the types of beliefs in this book—that we are loved and worthy as we are, that we deserve healthy relationships, and that we are willing and able to work to improve our lives—we will start to heal and move in that direction. The motivation to do so naturally emerges from our increasing love for ourselves.

Affirm — I am a divine being, effortlessly and endlessly worthy. I have the ability to release the resistance that arises within me to realizing my healthy intentions for my life. Spirit supports me in doing whatever is good for me.

And so it is.

Exercises

Journal about the following questions: Are there ways you see self-sabotage happening in your life? If so, what are they and what strategies might you implement to help address them? Why and how could making changes here benefit you? There is no pressure in this exercise to act on these strategies. This is about building awareness.

Reflect on the major changes you've made in your life and when you've tried to set goals. Do you see any self-sabotage or ego resistance in that? Perhaps it was subtle at first, but does anything become clear as you contemplate this?

Closure

Some things are harder to weed from the gardens of our minds than others, and this is particularly true for most of us when the subject is closure. We may have done something that harmed others, others might have harmed us, we may have unanswered questions, and so on, and this sticks with us, sometimes for many years. Perhaps even the rest of our lives.

The first thing I know to do when struggling with closure is to practice compassion, which includes trying to understand the big picture of the situation. As I shared earlier, I wouldn't rush or force this, but when we feel ready, we can analyze it in our minds. What causal factors were at work in this situation? Where was everyone coming from? Remember the fundamental attribution error: many of us have a tendency to hold ourselves and others as being personally responsible for situations to a greater degree than is probably fair. What was the full context? How does the situation look from that vantage point and the wisdom we have today? Can we see how the person or people involved were probably doing the best they could with the understanding, awareness, and capacity they had, in light of their circumstances?

We also extend this courtesy to ourselves. What was going on with us when we hurt someone? Can we imagine a situation in which we realistically would not have done that, given the state of our inner and outer life at that time? We may be able to, but even that doesn't mean we don't deserve compassion. People make mistakes. Sometimes life and circumstances strain us and we make desperate or unhealthy choices. Other times we disappoint ourselves but still couldn't manage to do better. We all have weak moments. Must we be branded for the rest of our lives because of this? I say no. Our work is to learn from our experiences, strive to do better in the future, and make amends to the other person or people if it is appropriate to do so. We are all allowed to be human beings, and as I shared in the first chapter, our task is recognizing that with compassionate understanding, not forgiveness. Forgiveness will come on its own when it's time. We just have to do our best to understand, on an intellectual and emotional level, when we feel ready to.

When an issue sticks with me, I have found benefit in putting these explorations in writing, which includes listing out compassionate thoughts and lessons learned related to the situation. Many people find that writing about what they can learn from a situation helps them process it, and I often talk this exercise out with therapy clients when they go through breakups (I share the questions I ask in the exercises at the end of this section). I did this with a couple of situations that nagged at me, and over the years, I returned to these documents when the situations resurfaced. Reading through them helped me make peace with what happened, and having my thought process written down meant I didn't need to rehash it.

This also prevented me from looking back on the past with rose-colored glasses, since the perspective from the moment was captured. Otherwise, I have also found benefit in reading online about other people's experiences with situations like what I went through. If you feel like you harmed someone and it's unwise to contact them or you can't for some reason to make amends, consider writing them an unsent letter in which you explain the whole situation. Expressing how you feel as if you are communicating with them, even if they never see it, may prove helpful.

Many of us struggle with getting closure after romantic relationships end or loved ones die. We may wish we said or did something differently or that they did. In situations like these, I think one of the most important things to do is accept that they are over. In my experience, a tendency to sit in "what if" or "if only" thinking about the past (e.g., "What if I'd done this?" "If only I hadn't said that!"), or even just ruminating about it, often extends from a desire to keep it alive within us. We don't want to move forward, so we come up with painful ways of clinging to a situation through fantasy or curiosity. If we want to be present with our lives today, though, we need to let ourselves truly grieve and release these unhelpful tendencies. When we engage in them perpetually, we may suffer for decades about something that we could've worked through when the situation happened.

As we grieve, it is normal to think sad-feeling thoughts about the past and living in the future without whatever it is we miss, and it is also normal to have a long, deep emotional journey in some cases, sometimes for the rest of our lives following the deaths of loved ones. It is often written in grief counseling literature that "grief is a process, not an event." When sad-feeling thoughts come up following a loss, it's important to do our best to be kind to ourselves while striving to not fall into "what if" or "if only" thinking to whatever degree we can. Some thinking like this is normal, understandable, and perhaps even unavoidable, but it is beneficial to take care that it doesn't become a habit or prominent topic in our thinking. It is also helpful to continue the everyday practice of working to keep our thoughts fact-oriented, accurate, wise, and compassionate. There is an ocean of difference too between "I'm so sad to think of future holidays without my mother" and "I regret not spending more time with her," which can be central in mourning, and thoughts like, "If only she'd gone for a checkup six months earlier," "If only I'd gone home the last couple of Thanksgivings," and so on. At first, some "what if" and "if only" thoughts may be part of processing the pain of the loss, especially as we recognize, honor, and learn from our regrets and other aspects of the situation, but we don't want to feed them beyond that. In grief counseling, we frequently observe people being "stuck" in grief, and in my experience, when that happens, it usually involves loops of "what if" or "if only" thinking.

Grieving can be a highly individual process. There is no one right way to do it, and I have found that one of the best things we can do with grieving is allow ourselves to have whatever process we need to with it and not judge what that is. At the same time, studying different cultural approaches to grief or psychological frameworks of grieving may help with the grieving process, like William Worden's tasks of mourning. These tasks are to accept the reality of the loss, work through the pain of the grief, adjust to an environment without our loved one, and emotionally relocate them in our lives in a new way. These tasks don't have to occur separately or in sequence, and how we perform them can vary significantly. An example of emotional relocation following the death of a loved one is to make a space for honoring them in our lives by keeping their photo on an altar. One activity that can aid with processing grief is to write a letter to the person we lost or severed ties with expressing all the things we want to say that we couldn't, which we then keep in a safe place to reread when we miss them. Many people experiencing grief also find benefit in telling their story to others, learning about others' experiences with grief, or participating in grief support groups. Loss is fundamental to the human experience, and because of this, I believe we have an innate ability to cope with it. We may need to do some digging to access this ability, but it is there, and prioritizing alignment with Spirit will help us get to it.

Sometimes when people cling to the past, they are clinging less to a situation itself and more to aspects of it that they miss in their lives. For example, perhaps they are fixating on their high school friendships less because they miss those individual people (though they probably do to some extent) and more because they miss intimate friendships. By recognizing this, they can then resolve to engage more intimately with the friends in their lives now. This in turn will likely help them find a sense of closure or ability to move forward from the past. Similarly, someone may find themself pining away for a former relationship more because they miss the way they felt supported and nurtured by it than because that person was a good long-term fit for them. Having recognized this, they can seek out ways to feel more supported and nurtured, either in a relationship or in general. In light of this, a simple question to ask ourselves when we longingly look to the past is "How much do I think I miss this particular situation versus an aspect of it I could nurture in my life today?" Sometimes the main reason the grass appears greener in our memory of the past is because we aren't sufficiently watering it where we are.

If we find ourselves fixated on wanting answers to questions about what happened with someone, like after a messy breakup, that can anchor us in suffering and is good to work to release or dial down. The most direct approach to dealing with this would be to reach out to the person, assuming that is appropriate, and have a conversation. If this isn't an option, though, there are others. One technique is to imagine the worst possible answers we could receive from the other person and then recognize that we could live with whatever they are, even if that is painful. I don't believe we need these answers, though. I have studied the works of many spiritual masters over the years, and no one has ever even hinted at a sentiment like "You can't be healthy and whole until you hear back from that ex." It may take some time and doing, but through aligning with Spirit and keeping our thoughts fact-oriented, accurate, wise, and compassionate, we can forge ahead. Whenever we have a thought like "What if I just called them again?" or "If only they had treated me better," we can remind ourselves that's either impossible or not healthy for us to do or think about, explain why, and then honor our pain and comfort ourselves. If we analyze the situation carefully and own the facts of our participation in it, we will find a way to move forward eventually.

I believe that there is no answer that we need in life that Spirit can't provide, and we can always ask Spirit directly for one, as in prayer or ritual. It might take a while to reach us, and we also must be open to receiving it, but any answer we truly need will come in some form. We may not like it, and it might not satisfy us entirely, but if it is needed, we have access to it. In our grief, not wanting to move forward can prevent us from getting closure even if we receive an answer or have a closure conversation, though, which is important to recognize. In that case, it may be beneficial to apply the CBT technique of considering what we might say to a close friend in a similar situation who asked for our counsel.

Romantic relationships in particular can be hard to get closure from and leave behind if our attachment system has its hooks in someone. The attachment system, which is proposed in attachment theory, is said to be the fundamental aspect of our psychobiology that clings to relationships. After a certain point, we essentially bond with a partner to the degree of forming a physiological unit, with them being involved in the regulation of our heart rate, blood pressure, blood hormone levels, and breathing.[29] When our attachment system fixates on someone, we can feel like we're possessed, which is particularly true if we have what's usually called an "anxious" attachment style. Attachment styles, put roughly, are patterns of behavior that typically appear in relationships, rooted in the care we receive in early childhood. We tend to either have comfort connecting, which evidences a secure attachment style; be aloof and struggle to connect, which is an avoidant attachment style; or go into emotional overdrive in relationships, which is the anxious style.

When people appear to lose their minds in relationships, behaving in ways that seem uncharacteristic, that's generally the attachment system at work. Often, when it escalates to that degree, it's because they are in a relationship with someone who isn't meeting their attachment needs, like by sending mixed signals. This causes them to feel insecure and anxious, resulting in a rollercoaster of emotions. For this topic, I can't recommend

29. Amir Levine and Rachel Heller, *Attached: The New Science of Adult Attachment and How it Can Help You Find—and Keep—Love* (New York: TarcherPerigee, 2010), 26.

learning about attachment theory enough. Once we have an understanding of how the attachment system works, and see it in ourselves and others, it can become easier to navigate (even though the ride can still be bumpy). This is similar to the benefits of educating ourselves about depression and anxiety or addiction when those are things we struggle with. The best book I know on this subject is *Attached* by Amir Levine and Rachel Heller, which I frequently recommend to clients. With some understanding about attachment styles, we usually judge ourselves less and gain a bit of space from what's happening when our attachment system is in overdrive, which can help us act on behalf of our well-being in relationships.

Breaking free from someone when our attachment system is locked on them can be a bit like detoxing from a substance. With time away and refusing as best we can to engage in thoughts that cause us to cling to the other person, the attachment will fade and we will move on. We can also appreciate how the thoughts accompanying any unhealthy urges we experience aren't from our authentic voice. For example, it's not our authentic voice or Spirit telling us to binge eat at one a.m., buy a pack of cigarettes after not smoking for a month, or text our ex whom we had a toxic relationship with. Those are systems within our brains hijacking our inner narratives, like what happens with depression and anxiety. With time and distance, we will likely become able to see that it is healthier to let go of our ex, provided we don't keep the torch burning with "what if" and "if only" thinking and other thought processes like them.

If you try the recommendations in this section to help with closure and nothing seems to work, you can also ask Spirit for help, like with seeking answers. I've had wonderful results with this over the years. Spirit has its own timetable, so sometimes responses don't come as quickly as I'd prefer, but when I'm at a loss for what to do, I ask for aid, and then the asking helps me let the issue go for some time. I trust that a response will come, and usually within a few days to a week, one does. This hearkens back to the earlier, central point in the affirmations that begin each "Planting New Beliefs" section in this book: we don't have to know how the responses will come. We just need to be willing to receive them and open to the possibility that they will come. In our willingness, we create a space for the responses to reach us, and then they do.

Affirm — I am a divine being, effortlessly and endlessly worthy. Nothing that has happened to me in the past need hold the strings of my thoughts and emotions forever. I can find whatever peace I need to through aligning with Spirit and thinking compassionately.

And so it is.

Exercises

Journal about the following questions: What messages about closure did you grow up with? How did these messages influence how you felt, thought, and acted? What does closure mean to you? What role do you see closure as having played in your life? What role would you like to see closure play in your life moving forward? If you received beliefs about closure that you want to shift, what are they and how would you shift them? How do you think your life could change by believing these new thoughts (i.e., what might their impact be on your feelings, thoughts, actions, etc.)?

Are there any experiences in your life that you feel like you don't have closure around? If so, how might you apply a technique from this section to it?

These are the questions I ask clients when they go through a breakup (or leave a job):

* What did you like about the relationship?
* What did you dislike about it?
* What did you learn from it, about yourself and in general?
* What do you want to experience again in a future relationship?
* What do you never want to experience again?
* How do you want to behave differently in a future relationship?
* Are there any red flags or yellow lights that you want to mind in future relationships because of this one?

Aging

How we feel about aging usually reflects the influences we grew up around to a significant degree. For example, many cultures foster fears of aging and encourage taking great steps to pretend like it doesn't exist or to delay it, and if that is true of our culture, we likely share in that outlook to some extent, which may occur consciously or subconsciously. If elders are venerated and treated with the utmost respect in our culture, the importance of that is probably within the plot of our inner garden about older adulthood.

Aging is a reality of life, and there is value and beauty in it. Though there are some difficulties that accompany aging, like a reduction in physical and mental agility, there is also often wisdom, insight, and perspective. We are meant to age, and anything we are meant to do is sacred.

This is another opportunity for us to eject unhealthy beliefs from our minds that humans have imposed on the natural world. What these are will depend on our particular backgrounds. They may be beliefs like "Aging means I'm not sexy anymore" or "Aging means I can't have new adventures." Most of these kinds of limiting beliefs are clearly ill-founded when we examine them. When we discover them, it's important to point this out to ourselves and affirm more accurate thoughts in their place. When they aren't, like "as I get older, I will be less able to rock climb," that is a moment to accept the turning wheel of life and look to other opportunities for enjoyment.

Some supportive thoughts to help with aging include that it is natural and holy, it has benefits if we are willing to look for them, and there is no way we can be anything other than exactly the age we are meant to be in each moment. If the earth is sacred and the process of life is sacred, then so is aging. There is enrichment in our living through the grief of change and the deeper embodiment we feel over time within ourselves and in life. Aging is not the end of our fun or the beauty of our lives. It is a natural process of transition, and that is as holy as the birth and death of the universe itself.

Affirm — I am a divine being, effortlessly and endlessly worthy. Aging is a sacred part of the human experience, providing it with depth and breadth. I celebrate the insights and opportunities that come from each new vantage point along my journey. There is so much I can learn, and so much to love, as I embrace the process of aging.

And so it is.

Exercises

Journal about the following questions: What messages about aging did you grow up with? How did these messages influence how you felt, thought, and acted? What does aging mean to you? What role do you see aging as having played in your life? What role would you like to see aging play in your life moving forward? If you received beliefs about aging that you want to shift, what are they and how would you shift them? How do you think your life could change by believing these new thoughts (i.e., what might their impact be on your feelings, thoughts, actions, etc.)?

Write a letter to yourself articulating the benefits of being at your current age, while also acknowledging any difficulties or challenges. What is special about this age in the arc of your life? What is sacred about it? How does the rest of your life look in the context of it? Try to do this every year.

Conclusion
Gardening Together

When we perform the work in this book, a few things usually happen if it is a fit for us. As our inner gardens become weeded and beautifully cultivated, we begin to enjoy a greater sense of serenity, inspiration, and fulfillment in our lives. We come to know, through direct experience, some of the power of thought to shape our perception of reality, emotions, and well-being. We realize that we have far more freedom than we thought, a freedom we can offer our children and respectfully model for other adults in how we live.

In reaching the point where our inner gardens become wonderful places to live in most of the time, it's critical to recognize that we aren't here to garden alone. We are part of a bigger picture, the human ecosystem, which itself is a facet of the earth's, and tending to our individual plot is not enough when there is so much suffering in the world. We can't ignore the pain of our fellow humans or the destructive effects humanity has wrought in the plant and animal kingdoms. We must do more.

Some people's inner work leads them to withdraw from loved ones when those loved ones are in pain, often because of spiritual teachers who say or suggest that being with others who are suffering can cause us some kind of spiritual harm, that it can "lower our vibration." I feel grateful that one of the primary spiritual teachers in my life taught the opposite and emphasized service—not only because it benefits others, but also because service is a means of connecting with Spirit and purifying the heart. She taught that as we give, we receive too, and that divine love is infinite. Rather than lower our vibration, being present to people in need from a foundation of spiritual alignment raises it, and for many, serving others, whether it's family, friends, community members, or even total strangers, is one of the primary sources of fulfillment in life.

It can be true that we need to cocoon ourselves some as we heal and learn how to have healthy boundaries, but this shouldn't become our norm or lifestyle. When it does, that's another instance of spiritual bypassing, of hiding from something that's difficult that can be faced in an aligned way and integrated into our spiritual path. How could the point of spirituality be to only be around people when they're in a good-feeling state of mind? There is little freedom and depth in that.

When it comes time to care for a loved one, we can apply what we've learned about connecting with Spirit and tune in to the Spirit within them. This will hold us in a spiritual mindset and help us provide comfort without feeling overburdened. If we are highly empathic, we can also learn psychic tools to provide us with boundaries to keep us from absorbing too much emotional energy, and there are plenty of practices for clearing what energy we do absorb. I'm sure most of us know people who would unload their problems on us every moment of the day if they could, and those are people to draw firm time boundaries with, which is something we can also learn how to do. For instance, when we begin a phone call, we might say, "I have about thirty minutes for this conversation" to set a clear boundary. We may grow apart from these people altogether and feel it is warranted to end these relationships, which can happen on a path of personal transformation, but that is different from generally avoiding suffering to not negatively impact our mental state. It's one thing to develop healthy boundaries in our lives, which is an important part of establishing well-being, and another to neglect a loved one in pain so as not to bum ourselves out. Or to have our ability to care for people who are suffering erode away because of the judgment we have about suffering, seeing it as some kind of spiritual failing or immaturity. With the lens of compassion in our minds, we can be a comforting witness to the pain and suffering of others, and most people aren't looking for more than that. Our task becomes far easier when we understand that we aren't usually being asked to problem-solve, give advice, or make everything okay.

The state we can aim for when comforting others is similar to meditation and something we can learn from practicing it: quiet the mind, connect with Spirit, and then simply be with what is, offering words of care and validation. If they ask for advice, we can give it as humbly as possible (while recognizing and respecting that adults are the sovereigns of their lives), but otherwise, we can just be there for them with love. Then when we leave the conversation, we can release it fully, aside from perhaps following up later if that's called for while honoring whatever boundaries we need for self-care. Meditation teaches us how to do this too because we do the same thing with extraneous thoughts while meditating. In each session, we practice letting go of our thoughts about what's happening in our lives or otherwise and focusing on something else. All of this is how I'm able, as a highly sensitive person, to be a therapist. I have tight boundaries around my professional role, as well as firm psychic boundaries, and I provide my expertise and knowledge and then let the rest go, knowing it is not my work or burden to bear. I am not here to force my clients to engage in therapeutic practices or learn their lessons for them, which I can't do anyway. I do my best to be fully present with them and when a session ends, I release it.

Living in today's world can be paradoxical and challenging when it comes to how we address suffering in larger domains than the interpersonal. Centuries ago, none of us would've known there was a crisis on one part of the earth if we lived on the other side of it. We wouldn't even have known what was happening a few cities over. Today, the news delivers us a platter of suffering in each moment if we choose to look at it, and that can come with heaping portions of guilt that didn't exist for people before. It can create a sense of turmoil within us around what we could or should do, raising questions like "To what degree should I allow myself a comfortable and satisfying life while others suffer in such terrible, preventable ways?" "If we can do something, shouldn't we?" "What is realistic and fair, and what isn't?"

I suspect some of you are hoping I'm going to provide you with a clear answer to these questions that feels comfortable to digest. I can't. Only you can decide within your heart and mind what is enough for you. The way I made peace with this in my life is two-fold. First, I accept my humanness. We can each only do so much, and we aren't individually responsible for all the ills of the world. The psychic weight of shouldering that burden would pulverize anyone in an instant. We can't do it. What we can do, though, is try to figure out what our part is and do that, which usually includes being helpful where we are and looking at other places where we have concrete power to make a difference. Also, I think it is important to recognize that even having the space, capacity, and resources to consider this matter is a privilege, and accordingly, I believe that the more we have, the more responsibility we have to give. I think the converse of this is also true, so if all we have the capacity to do is pay our bills, support our family, and get by, there is no failure in that.

The next thing I did, which an old boss of mine facilitated as an exercise in our office, was create a personal mission statement for my life and career. In drafting the mission statement, I identified specific areas in which I wanted to use my abilities to serve others. These included promoting holistic wellness, experiential spirituality, and social equity. The mission statement became like a magic spell about my life and career, and over the years, as I worked in alignment with it, my life and career moved in the direction of it until both greatly embodied it.

You can create a personal mission statement by asking yourself what you want your life to be about and brainstorming around that, and then synthesizing what comes up into one or two sentences. Your personal mission can also change over time if you want, but having an articulated mission statement helps give our service efforts and lives focus. We are more effective when we devote ourselves to a few things rather than being spread thin trying to address all the world's problems. It is important to be aware of what the diverse issues in the world are and to offer support to others engaged in a variety of initiatives, but we don't have the capacity to effectively tackle all of them ourselves. Being strategic about efficacy will yield a greater impact. I think many people feel so overwhelmed by the sheer mass of problems in the world and unsure of how to best be helpful that they do little beyond argue about politics and occasionally donate money. Imagine instead if everyone who could afford to devoted even one strategic hour a week to a just cause and what a difference that could make.

That said, I don't rest on my laurels with what I do now. I feel that I should be doing more, and I allow myself to have this nagging guilt because I think it's true. I don't believe we shouldn't enjoy our lives because there is profound suffering in the world, but I also think it is critical to stay mindful that we have more work to do, and when we see opportunities to help and can, to participate in them. We can do this while holding the truths we have learned and experienced: that we can experience a source of well-being that is beyond the reach of thought-dependent reality, and that so much of our suffering is because of our thoughts and the oppressive systems that impact us. These thoughts and systems don't need to be there.

When we offer aid to others and are in a position of societal privilege, another critical dimension is to center the people we are working on behalf of. To listen to them, to not speak over them, and to include them in all levels of decision-making. When we don't center the voices of the communities we're trying to serve, we can be paternalistic and impose ourselves on others, which isn't helpful. They know what's best for them better than we do. We just happen to be the ones with more power to level the playing field, and not because we earned it or are superior, which is crucial to understand. We must recognize that not only do we not know what's best for others, but we may also have much to learn from them. We only see things to the degree that we humble ourselves before them. What wisdom might others carry from their constellation of experiences that is disparate from ours? If they come from another culture, what can we learn from their different worldview? The playing field can't become level unless we do this work together, striving to honor each other as fully as we can. I also believe it is critical, more than ever, that we approach the earth and all its creatures with enough humility to find a way to live in harmony with this planet.

So this is a tension I say we honor. A healthy guilt that we hold space for that calls us to do better for the world. If enough of us can live in the tension of this guilt and act on it for the betterment of all while simultaneously healing and aligning with Spirit, we will revolutionize life as we know it. Then one day, most of us will enjoy it, freely. That day may seem far away and indistinct, and this might sound extremely naïve, but we can get there if we work together. If we want a world like that to come though, we must envision it, believe in it, and act to make it real. Each of us has to find something to champion to help us get there, large or small. For me, that is the divine power of the human heart, which is why I know there is cause to hope. Always.

Affirm — We are all divine beings, effortlessly and endlessly worthy. We deserve unconditional love and acceptance, which is ever available within us, and the freedom of self-discovery. Together, we have the power to create a world where every child is afforded this and flourishes like a wildflower in the sun. When the time is right, in accord with our aligned action and commitment to service, that world will come about.

And so it is.

Bibliography

Amritanandamayi, Mata, and Amritaswarupananda Puri. *The Eternal Truth.* Kerala, India: Mata Amritanandamayi Center, 2007.

Beck, Judith. *Cognitive Behavior Therapy: Basics and Beyond.* 2nd ed. New York: Guilford Press, 2011.

Bourne, Edmund J. *The Anxiety and Phobia Workbook.* 5th ed. Oakland, CA: New Harbinger Publications, 2010.

Branch, Rhena, and Rob Wilson. *Cognitive Behavioural Therapy Workbook for Dummies.* 2nd ed. West Sussex, England: John Wiley & Sons, 2012.

Brown, Brené. "Listening to Shame." Filmed March 2012 in Long Beach, CA. TED video, 20:22. https://www.ted.com/talks/brene_brown_listening_to_shame/.

———. "The Power of Vulnerability." Filmed June 2010 in Houston, TX. TED video, 20:03. https://www.ted.com/talks/brene_brown_on_vulnerability/.

Byrom, Thomas. *Dhammapada: The Sayings of the Buddha.* Boston, MA: Shambhala Publications, 1976.

Campbell, Joseph, with Bill Moyers. *The Power of Myth.* New York: Anchor Books, 1991.

Carson, Rick. *Taming Your Gremlin: A Surprisingly Simple Method for Getting Out of Your Own Way.* Rev. ed. New York: Quill, 2003.

Crane, Rebecca. *Mindfulness-Based Cognitive Therapy.* New York: Routledge, 2009.

Crowley, Aleister. *Magick: Liber ABA, Book 4.* York Beach, ME: Samuel Weiser, 1994.

Dass, Ram. *Be Love Now: The Path of the Heart.* New York: HarperCollins, 2010.

Doidge, Norman. *The Brain That Changes Itself.* New York: Penguin Books, 2007.

Editors of *Hinduism Today* Magazine. *What Is Hinduism?: Modern Adventures Into a Profound Global Faith.* Kapaa, HI: Himalayan Academy, 2007.

Ekers, David, Lisa Webster, Annemieke Van Straten, Pim Cuijpers, David Richards, and Simon Gilbody. "Behavioural Activation for Depression; An Update of Meta-Analysis of Effectiveness and Sub Group Analysis." *PLoS One* 9, no. 6 (June 2014): e100100. doi:10.1371/journal.pone .0100100.

Fossella, Tina, and John Welwood. "Human Nature, Buddha Nature: An Interview with John Welwood." *Tricycle: The Buddhist Review* 20, no. 3 (Spring 2011): 1–18. https://www.johnwelwood.com/articles /TRIC_interview_uncut.pdf.

Hansen, Katherine. *The Brain Over Binge Recovery Guide.* Columbus, GA: Camellia Publishing, 2016.

Hay, Louise L. *You Can Heal Your Life.* Carlsbad, CA: Hay House, 1984.

———. *The Power Is Within You.* Carlsbad, CA: Hay House, 1991.

Hayes, Steven C., and Spencer Smith. *Get Out of Your Mind and Into Your Life: The New Acceptance and Commitment Therapy.* Oakland, CA: New Harbinger Publications, 2005.

Hays, Pamela A., and Gayle Y. Iwamasa. *Culturally Responsive Cognitive-Behavioral Therapy: Assessment, Practice, and Supervision.* Washington, DC: American Psychological Association, 2006.

Henry, P. L. "The Caldron of Poesy." *Studia Celtica* 14–15 (1979/1980): 114–28.

Hepworth, Dean, Ronald Rooney, Glenda Dewberry Rooney, Kimberly Strom-Gottfried, and JoAnn Larsen. *Direct Social Work Practice: Theory and Skills*. 8th ed. Belmont, CA: Brooks/Cole, 2010.

Herbert, James D., and Evan M. Forman. *Acceptance and Mindfulness in Cognitive Behavior Therapy: Understanding and Applying the New Therapies*. Hoboken, NJ: John Wiley & Sons, 2011.

Holman, Dawn M., Katie A. Ports, Natasha D. Buchanan, Nikki A. Hawkins, Melissa T. Merrick, Marilyn Metzler, and Katrina F. Trivers. "The Association Between Adverse Childhood Experiences and Risk of Cancer in Adulthood: A Systematic Review of the Literature." *Pediatrics* 138, supplement 1 (November 2016): S81–S91. doi:10.1542/peds .2015-4268L.

Holmes, Ernest. *The Science of Mind: The Complete Edition*. New York: TarcherPerigree, 2010.

Hruby, Adela, and Frank B. Hu. "The Epidemiology of Obesity: A Big Picture." *Pharmacoeconomics* 33, no. 7 (2015): 673–89. doi:10.1007 /s40273-014-0243-x.

Jebb, Andrew T., Louis Tay, Ed Diener, and Shigehiro Oishi. "Happiness, Income Satiation and Turning Points around the World." *Nature Human Behaviour* 2, no. 1 (January 2018): 33–38. doi:10.1038 /s41562-017-0277-0.

Johnson, Sharon. *Therapist's Guide to Clinical Intervention: The 1-2-3's of Treatment Planning*. 2nd ed. San Diego, CA: Elsevier, 2004.

Jongsma, Arthur E., Jr., and Mark Peterson. *The Complete Adult Psychotherapy Treatment Planner*. 5th ed. Hoboken, NJ: John Wiley & Sons, 2014.

Kimsey-House, Henry, Karen Kimsey-House, Phillip Sandahl, and Laura Whitworth. *Co-Active Coaching: Changing Business, Transforming Lives*. Boston, MA: Nicholas Brealey Publishing, 2011.

Koenig, Karen. *The Food and Feelings Workbook: A Full Course Meal on Emotional Health*. Carlsbad, CA: Gürze Books, 2007.

Kondo, Marie. *The Life-Changing Magic of Tidying Up: The Japanese Art of Decluttering and Organizing*. Translated by Cathy Hirano. Berkeley, CA: Ten Speed Press, 2014.

La Cour, Peter, and Marian Petersen. "Effects of Mindfulness Meditation on Chronic Pain: A Randomized Controlled Trial." *Pain Medicine* 16, no. 4 (2015): 641–52. doi:10.1111/pme.12605.

Levine, Amir, and Rachel Heller. *Attached: The New Science of Adult Attachment and How It Can Help You Find—and Keep—Love.* New York: Tarcher-Perigee, 2010.

McKay, Matthew, Jeffrey Wood, and Jeffrey Brantley. *The Dialectical Behavior Therapy Skills Workbook: Practical DBT Exercises for Learning Mindfulness, Interpersonal Effectiveness, Emotion Regulation, and Distress Tolerance.* Oakland, CA: New Harbinger Publications, 2007.

Mitchell, Stephen. *Tao Te Ching.* New York: Harper & Row, 1988.

Myss, Caroline. *Anatomy of the Spirit: The Seven Stages of Power and Healing.* New York: Penguin Random House, 1996.

Pilgrim, Peace. *Her Life and Work in Her Own Words.* Sante Fe, NM: Ocean Tree Books, 1982.

Rao, Pingfan, Raymond L. Rodriguez, and Sharon P. Shoemaker. "Addressing the Sugar, Salt, and Fat Issue the Science of Food Way." *npj Science of Food* 2, no. 12 (July 2018): n.p. doi:10.1038/s41538-018-0020-x.

Ronen, Tammie, and Arthur Freeman, eds. *Cognitive Behavior Therapy in Clinical Social Work Practice.* New York: Springer, 2007.

Taylor, Jill Bolte. *My Stroke of Insight.* New York: Plume, 2009.

Tolle, Eckhart. *The Power of Now: A Guide to Spiritual Enlightenment.* Novato, CA: New World Library, 1999.

Trungpa, Chögyam. *Meditation in Action.* Boston, MA: Shambhala Publications, 1991.

Vonnegut, Mark. *The Eden Express.* New York: Laurel, 1975.